The Criminalization of Immigration

The Criminalization of Immigration

Truth, Lies, Tragedy, and Consequences

Robert Hartmann McNamara

An Imprint of ABC-CLIO, LLC
Santa Barbara, California • Denver, Colorado

Library of Congress Cataloging-in-Publication Data

Names: McNamara, Robert Hartmann, author.
Title: The criminalization of immigration : truth, lies, tragedy, and
    consequences / Robert Hartmann McNamara.
Description: First edition. | Santa Barbara, California : ABC-CLIO, LLC
    [2020] | Includes bibliographical references and index.
Identifiers: LCCN 2019044909 (print) | LCCN 2019044910 (ebook) | ISBN
    9781440873706 (hardcover) | ISBN 9781440873713 (ebook)
Subjects: LCSH: United States—Emigration and immigration—Government
    policy. | United States—Emigration and immigration—Economic aspects. |
    United States—Emigration and immigration—Social aspects.
Classification: LCC JV6038 .M36 2020 (print) | LCC JV6038 (ebook) | DDC
    325.73—dc23
LC record available at https://lccn.loc.gov/2019044909
LC ebook record available at https://lccn.loc.gov/2019044910

ISBN: 978-1-4408-7370-6 (print)
        978-1-4408-7371-3 (ebook)

24 23 22 21 20   1 2 3 4 5

This book is also available as an eBook.

Praeger
An Imprint of ABC-CLIO, LLC

ABC-CLIO, LLC
147 Castilian Drive
Santa Barbara, California 93117
www.abc-clio.com

This book is printed on acid-free paper ∞

Manufactured in the United States of America

To Caroline Bradley: for whom I have so much respect.

Contents

List of Figures and Tables

Preface

As a sociologist, I am accustomed to examining data, reviewing what is known about a topic, and offering an assessment of the various explanations for social phenomenon. A review of my research also shows a wide range of interests, including issues relating to race, crime, poverty, health care, and other topics in criminal justice. In all of these projects, I make every effort to offer a balanced and unbiased assessment of the topic and let the data and the people involved tell the story. When I became interested in studying immigration, I took a similar approach.

As I started reading about immigration and the issues surrounding it, I found myself fascinated and confused at the same time. I read many research studies, including ethnographic accounts and books on the problems related to immigration in the United States and learned a great deal about the issues and challenges immigrants and their families experienced. I also read government reports, monographs by various immigrant advocacy groups, and many more articles. As I learned more, I realized how little I understood the immigration process, and it occurred to me that most people likely had no idea how it all works either. What most people are left with are media accounts and commentary by politicians about immigration—all of which can easily be colored by agendas, biases, and misinformation.

This project evolved into a book that offers an objective assessment of immigration so that the average person can learn and understand what is really going on, particularly since much of the information provided to the public is often in contrast to what is actually occurring. As I hope to show, this system is, by any meaningful criteria, broken and plagued by political agendas and uncompromising narratives. I also made an effort to separate fact from fiction, which was a difficult task because many of the inaccuracies about immigration are consistently repeated in the media. I have tried my best to avoid creating the impression of a political agenda or a bias. I honestly make every effort to simply let the data and people's comments tell the story. Still, we live in an era in which disagreements are often met with claims of "fake news" or attacks on the credibility of the author. It is also the case that a discussion of almost any issue often requires a person to take a position or side, with clear lines of "for and against" as part of the dialogue. Regrettably, in the United States today, there appears to be more division than unity, and attacks on other points of view and the people who present them are seen as fair game. Also regrettable is the fact that the president of this country seems to have put his stamp of approval on such a strategy, with frequent verbal attacks on those who disagree with him.

This is also a topic that continually develops. It seems like every day there is a news story or event that relates to immigration—so this could be a book that has no ending. Even now, almost daily, I discover new articles and developments about immigration. For example, as of this writing, President Trump has publicly stated that he intends to detain families and children indefinitely, despite rules that regulate how long immigrants can be detained. This comes on the heels of claims of abuse, overcrowding, and the inability of immigration officials to provide adequate housing for detained immigrants.

An important challenge for readers is to recognize that a discussion of immigration in the United States cannot exist in a vacuum. Our history shows a consistent pattern of mistreatment of minorities, and U.S. policy has routinely overreacted to a perceived threat of some kind. In addition to the "invasion" of undocumented immigrants from Central America and Mexico, a recent example of this is seen in the recent mass shootings that have occurred around the country. While mass shootings are a relatively rare event in general, the timing of these episodes is being framed as a consequence of immigration. They are also being presented from a political dimension, where white nationalism has been said to escalate people's willingness to engage in extreme violence in response to the threats presented by immigrants from Central America. In truth, even President Trump himself has attempted to link the shootings to immigration issues, although this has gotten far less attention than the dangers of white nationalism. The result of these shootings and the fears of white nationalism has generated yet another national conversation about gun control.

While this is not a new topic, it relates to some of the discussion in this book, particularly moral panics and the fear-based decision making that such events evoke. So many politicians, eager to capitalize on the moment, are calling for all manner of gun control legislation, using the shootings as the basis for such legislation. What immigration and mass shootings have in common is not the link to white nationalism, although that connection is readily evident by the evidence left by the suspects in the killings. Rather, the connection between immigration and mass shootings is the tendency to allow fear to drive so many poor and dangerous decisions related to social policy.

In the end, as I began writing this book, I realized we all have a part to play in the brokenness of immigration policy in this country. I also wanted to help the average person understand how and why we have criminalized an entire group of people based on inaccurate information, irrational fears, distorted media accounts, and political messaging. While politicians, policy makers, and the media have a responsibility to bear for distorting much of what the public understands about immigration, we all ultimately have a duty and obligation to respond to the problem in a moral, ethical, and compassionate way. It is unrealistic to think that we can deport our way out of the problems of immigration, but it is also unreasonable to think we can have open borders. The focus of our efforts should be in finding a fair and thoughtful solution without the distractions and jabs offered by politicians and policy makers who have their own reasons for convincing the public about the nature, extent, and solutions to the problem.

Acknowledgments

While there are always many people to thank in any book project, I owe a special thanks to my editor at ABC-CLIO, Debbie Carvalko. The idea for this book emerged as part of a larger discussion about working with Praeger, a publisher with whom I have a long-standing relationship. Debbie's ideas and editorial skills were integral to what comes in the following pages. Her enthusiasm for the project and hard work greatly improved this manuscript, but any errors, omissions, or oversights are mine to bear. Thank you, Debbie, for your friendship and for the opportunity to bring issues, problems, and insight to the people who matter.

CHAPTER ONE

Introduction

- At a rally in Houston, Texas, in 2018, President Trump stated, "You know what a globalist is? A globalist is a person that wants the globe to do well, frankly, not caring about our country so much. And you know what, we can't have that. You know, they have a word. It sort of became old-fashioned. It's called a nationalist. And I say, 'Really, we're not supposed to use that word?' You know what I am? I'm a nationalist. . . . Use that word."[1]

- In Charlottesville, Virginia, what began as a protest by white nationalists of the removal of a Confederate statue resulted in riots and the death of a young woman. Two days later, Trump stated, "I think there is blame on both sides. You had some very bad people in that group. But you also had people that were very fine people, on both sides." A year later, Trump attempted to walk back his controversial comments by tweeting: "The riots in Charlottesville a year ago resulted in senseless death and division. We must come together as a nation. I condemn all types of racism and acts of violence. Peace to ALL Americans!"[2]

- In April 2019, President Trump threatened to close the Mexican border completely, in part because of his lack of funding for the construction of a border wall and because he believes the flow of immigrants into the United States constitutes an "invasion."[3]

The preceding quotes offer important insight into the changes occurring in the United States. President Trump's critics are quick to point out that his comments spur the actions of groups in this country that spawn hatred and violence against others, particularly minorities. While President Trump cannot be held responsible for the actions of others or how his comments are interpreted, such commentary raises a variety of questions about the extent to which some groups feel threatened about the demographic changes occurring in the United States.

This book focuses on the structure of immigration policy in the United States as well as the intended and unintended consequences of those decisions; there is real value in placing those discussions into some type of framework of understanding. Some observers might argue, for example, that the challenges related to immigration in this country are symptomatic of a much larger set of problems that relate to political, social, and economic hegemony; white privilege; the inevitable consequences of capitalism; and the growing inequalities around the world.

Changes to the demographic profile of the United States, in part due to immigration, has caused some people to conclude that diversity, a hallmark of a democratic society, is unpatriotic. The fear generated from the "threat" of diversity is part of the reason for the popularity of the slogan "Make America Great Again." It is also one of the reasons for the rise in popularity of white nationalism. While nationalism is not a new concept, President Trump's commentary and apparent support for it have emboldened some groups to support and encourage the use of violence and hatred of other groups, and it has resulted in the promotion of an extreme form of cultural, political, and economic isolationism in the United States.

White nationalism is not a position held by the majority of the U.S. population, but the tendency toward the use of violence and the general intolerance toward others are considerable sources of concern. White nationalism also represents a challenge to American ideals of diversity and plurality. While many proponents of the latest version of white nationalism argue its ideology focuses more on rejecting political correctness and promoting the preservation of American culture, most experts note the real issue relates to a fear of the decline of white dominance—sometimes referred to as *white genocide*.[4] In other words, white nationalism is based on the belief in white superiority, and the infusion of minorities, particularly large numbers who can leverage political control, is seen as contributing to the decline of mainstream culture and the society as a whole. Because there is no middle ground between the celebration of diversity and the narrowness of white nationalism, tensions are high, and identity issues are intertwined with policy decisions and political platforms.[5]

White Nationalism—A Primer

What exactly is white nationalism? President Trump claims that he rejects racist ideology and is "the least racist person there is,"[6] and he has chosen to use the term *nationalism* to describe an emphasis on promoting American culture. Nationalism is also seen in Trump's efforts to place the United States at the forefront of his domestic and foreign policy decisions.

For Trump and his supporters, making America great again involves having a particular cultural identity rather than a culture based on ideals and values that transcend any particular dominant group.

According to most experts, white nationalism, like white supremacy, places the interests of white people over those of other racial groups. White supremacists and white nationalists both believe that racial discrimination should be incorporated into law and policy because white people are innately superior to people of other races and should maintain political and economic dominance.[7]

The problem with white nationalism, however, is not that it is overtly racist, although some would undoubtedly argue that it is synonymous with white supremacy. As some experts have noted, the real problem is that whiteness has been the default category in terms of political, economic, and cultural power, and the preservation of whiteness inevitably contains elements of racism and discrimination. For many Americans, the culture and nation as a whole are simply extensions of what they have always known—whites are in power, and they determine the course of the country. However, when threats to what people have come to know and understand about what it means to live in the United States emerge, the reaction is generally elevated levels of fear and anxiety about the future.[8]

Such fears are heightened by demographic shifts, such as decreasing birth rates for whites and the increase in minority representation, particularly in positions of power. Such shifts are perceived as reducing the size and scope of white influence. This is why supporters of white nationalism argue that the United States should protect its white majority by limiting immigration as well as prohibiting other strategies that enhance multiculturalism.[9]

As is often the case when fear drives decision making, there is a tendency to romanticize the past as being a happier time, when the country was more unified and stable. As it relates to immigration, the current narrative and policies are described as an effort to return to a time when there was greater unity in this country—meaning less diversity. Trump's comments about what immigration has "done" to Europe reflects such a position.[10]

What makes this fear so dangerous is that as the messaging and rhetoric surrounding the threat grows, so does the level of fear about the problem. This can result in the public becoming susceptible to manipulation of the facts and ignoring effective and reasonable ideas about solutions to the problem. That is, the gloom and doom rhetoric, coupled with outlandish claims, including factually incorrect information, promoted again and again, can easily lead to justifying all manner of decisions that would otherwise be seen as unacceptable and counter to what has "made America great" in the past. In short, what would normally be seen and understood as racist or discriminatory becomes blurred, and the decisions begin to sound reasonable to the public.[11]

White Nationalism, Race, and the Trump Administration

President Trump's political platform capitalized on the fears and anxieties about demographic changes, and efforts to promote minorities, such as affirmative action, have been identified as a threat to the American way of life. His slogan, "Make America Great Again," suggests that America is no longer great. One of the reasons for this, he argues, is based on the country's inability to put "our" needs before others. As a symbolic and literal display of this form of isolationism, Trump has remained committed to building a massive wall along the Mexican border and to make it more difficult for people, particularly from non-European countries, to immigrate to the United States and become citizens.[12]

Another example of Trump's commitment to white nationalism was his appointment of Steve Bannon, a self-proclaimed white nationalist and leader of the alt-right movement, as his senior counselor and chief strategist. This decision brought the topic of white nationalism into the mainstream discussion about American culture, politics, and economic decisions. While Bannon eventually left the White House, the fact that he was given such an important position demonstrated Trump's agenda and what has become known as the *populist movement*.[13]

The intersection between white nationalism, race, and the Trump administration is seen in several policy decisions and commentary. While President Trump has claimed he is not a racist and his proclamations of nationalism focus on the protection of the United States, critics point to a number of examples where his rhetoric and policies raise serious questions about whether there are racist undertones to his agenda.

For instance, Srikantiah and Shirin (2019) contend that President Trump's position on immigration is really designed to preserve the country's predominantly white identity. They argue that evidence of this is seen in Trump's opposition to the removal of Confederate monuments, which he has described as a threat to "our culture." His comments following the death of a protestor in Charlottesville, Virginia, which was the largest gathering of white supremacists in years, when he stated there were some "very fine people on both sides of the debate," raised many questions about his feelings regarding race. In fact, Trump began his presidential campaign by denouncing Mexican immigrants as "rapists" and has described undocumented immigrants as "animals."

Additionally, some experts point out that Trump described the need to prevent immigrants from "shithole countries," a reference to Haiti, El Salvador, Honduras, Guatemala, and some African nations, from coming to the United States. He also suggested that immigration is generally a cultural threat to the United States, not simply one related to economic or national security. As an illustration, in describing the immigration issues in Europe, Trump stated that it had changed the fabric of Europe and that Europeans are "losing their culture." Trump further stated, "We don't want what is happening with immigration in Europe to happen with us!"[14]

While some might claim that these comments may indicate a lack of sensitivity or perhaps a fundamental lack of understanding of the complexity of the issues, questions remain about whether Trump's claims and policies are actually race-neutral.[15] For instance, in 2017, Trump attempted and ultimately succeeded in passing a Muslim travel ban, which prevents certain people from Muslim countries from entering the United States. Additionally, the Trump administration ended the temporary protected status for noncitizens from El Salvador, Haiti, Nicaragua, and Sudan that protected people who were unable to return home because of the civil unrest in those countries.[16]

Trump also attempted to end the Deferred Action for Childhood Arrivals (DACA) program, which allows children who entered the country without documentation to obtain work permits. This has racial undertones, since the vast majority of DACA recipients are Latino and people of color. The administration has also targeted Mexican and Central American asylum seekers who are fleeing their countries due to violence by reducing the overall number of accepted asylum applications and making it more difficult to meet the criteria needed for admission.

The Trump administration also initially implemented policies that separated children from their families. The backlash from this latter decision ultimately led Trump to reverse this policy, but only because of the overwhelmingly negative response by the American public. Since 2018, Trump has reinstituted this policy, albeit in a slightly different form. Finally, the Trump administration has escalated immigration enforcement and detention and taken steps to process deportation cases quickly, without adequate due process or giving noncitizens a chance to prepare an adequate defense.[17]

As Srikantiah and Shirin (2019) point out, while these changes are not specific to particular immigrants, the effects of these decisions fall heavily on noncitizens of color. When they are considered along with his public statements about certain groups, there remain important concerns about whether these policies are part of a comprehensive immigration policy or whether the underlying justification for them involves elements of white nationalism.

One might think that these changes are the work of a particular president. While it is easy to vilify President Trump for many of his comments and policies, it would be misguided to think that one person could have such a dramatic impact on changing the direction of the United States and its treatment of others. In fact, it could be argued that race has played a role in a host of historical decisions regarding minorities and immigrants to the United States. The exclusion of certain groups based almost solely on race were a feature of federal law as far back as the 1800s, with the Chinese Exclusion Act, and this trend can be documented for different groups well into the 1960s.[18]

Moreover, while President Trump brazenly boasts about getting his way on issues related to the constitutionality of his policies and decisions, his belief that his positions are supported by the U.S. Supreme Court is not completely inaccurate. Historically, when challenges were made to laws that clearly targeted particular groups, the Court has generally upheld congressional efforts. For instance, the U.S. Supreme Court upheld the Chinese Exclusion Act, essentially arguing that if the legislative branch of government deemed it important to pass a law restricting certain groups from entry into the United States, or removing those already present, the Court did not want to intervene in such decision making.[19] This is sometimes referred to as the *plenary power doctrine*; the federal courts grant wide latitude to Congress and to the executive branch of government to regulate issues such as immigration.

The plenary power doctrine is a critical feature of the current administration's success in lawsuits brought against it by advocacy groups and individual immigrants. As has been documented, even when lower courts and appellate courts have granted consideration of a particular legal issue regarding immigration, the U.S. Supreme Court has typically overturned lower court rulings. This is true even when lawsuits are filed about certain policies and actions that constitute a violation of the equal protection clause of the U.S. Constitution. This may be why Trump has consistently pointed out that he gets less support from the lower courts, but he contends, "Look, I expect to be sued. And we'll win in the Supreme Court."[20]

In sum, white nationalism and what has been more broadly referred to as the *alt-right movement* suggest that any attempt to dilute the American culture from its natural selection based on racial purity is a threat to national security.[21]

White Nationalism and the Criminalization of Immigration

President Trump's statements along with the policy changes related to immigration have led some experts to argue that we have stigmatized the idea of immigration, suggesting that people who come to the United States, legally or otherwise, are somehow less valuable and worthy of admission. The phrase that describes the process of limiting access for immigrants and the punishments associated with any type of violation of immigration law is known as the *criminalization of immigration.*[22] A more thorough discussion of the criminalization process, the reasons for its development, and the practical consequences of this stigmatization will be the focus of the subsequent chapters of this book.

However, it is important to note that while Trump's immigration policies are perhaps intensive, intrusive, and insensitive, his efforts are similar to what other U.S. presidents have done with regard to immigration. This is not a defense of those efforts or of the language used to describe and promote them, but it would be unfair to only criticize President Trump for the failure to pass a comprehensive immigration policy that reflects a reasonable and responsible effort to address the problem. In fact, as we will see in chapter 7, the current strategy used by the Trump administration is arguably little more than a copy of what President Reagan used in the 1980s.

Moreover, the problems related to immigration in the United States are similar to what is occurring around the world; many countries are embracing populist views and restricting the flow of immigration across their borders. Such a discussion of the global impact of immigration is generally beyond the scope of this book, but a brief overview offers valuable insight, since the issues of nationalism, immigration, and the humanitarian crises experienced by many groups are not unique to the United States.

Trump, Immigration, and National Emergencies

In a speech before the United Nations in 2018, President Trump made his position against globalization quite clear, and he even urged other countries to join him in rejecting it as an economic, political, and social ideology. In doing so, Trump informed world leaders of his commitment to a form of isolationism as part of his domestic and international policies.[23]

As evidence of his commitment to such a position, President Trump has promised to build a massive wall along the Mexican border to stem the flow of illegal immigration. He also promised that the Mexican government would pay to build the wall, which it has consistently refused to do. In 2018, Trump made claims that the construction of the wall had begun, but the funds approved by Congress were for replacing sections of the existing border fence that needed repair, not for the construction of a new state-of-the-art wall with an estimated cost of $25 billion.[24] In fact, the federal government experienced the longest shutdown in its history as a result of a standoff between the president and Congress over the funding.

In early 2019, Trump attempted to circumvent Congress by declaring a national emergency at the border, which would allow him to use funds not approved by Congress to build the wall. This was a widely controversial move, one that even caused some Republicans and Trump supporters to disagree with such a measure. Lawsuits were filed, and legal challenges will likely delay the construction of the wall until after 2020. However, in May 2019, a federal judge rejected a lawsuit filed by Congress that attempted to block Trump's plan to divert funds for the wall. The judge ruled that the House did not have legal standing to sue President Trump for using funds approved by Congress for a different purpose. House Democrats, who had brought the lawsuit, argued that diverting the funds violated the separation of powers doctrine of the U.S. Constitution.[25]

The decision to declare a national emergency came on the heels of a two-month-long effort by Trump to convince Congress of the need to build a wall along the Mexican border. As part of the funding package approved by Congress, which constitutionally determines funding for government projects, about $1.3 billion was allocated for about fifty-five miles of fencing. President Trump signed the package into law to avoid a second government shutdown, the first of which had lasted thirty-five days and left approximately eight hundred thousand workers without pay.[26]

Soon after signing the bill, Trump threatened to declare a national emergency and use his executive powers as president to divert funds from other military projects to build the wall. The emergency declaration, according to White House officials, would enable the president to divert $3.6 billion from military construction projects to the wall. President Trump also proposed to use presidential discretion to tap $2.5 billion from counternarcotics programs and $600 million from a Treasury Department asset forfeiture fund. Combined with the $1.3 billion authorized for fencing in the spending package, Trump would have about $8 billion for barriers, significantly more than the $5.7 billion he unsuccessfully demanded from Congress.[27]

Despite the concerns expressed by members of his own party, Trump followed through on his plan in early 2019. Trump stated, "We're going to confront the national security crisis on our southern border, and we're going to do it one way or the other. It's an invasion. We have an invasion of drugs and criminals coming into our country."[28] Critics question the need for a wall, often referring to it as a vanity project by the president to fulfill a campaign promise. Others claim the crisis is a manufactured effort to gain public approval and to set up Trump's bid for reelection. Critics point out that illegal border crossings dramatically decreased in 2018, from 1.6 million in 2000 to 400,000 in 2018.[29]

Others claim that Trump himself recognized the absence of any real emergency when he stated, "I didn't need to do this, but I'd rather do it much faster. I just want to get it done faster, that's all."[30] Critics have also noted that the general public generally disagrees with such an approach. Most Americans oppose Trump's emergency declaration, according to polls. A Fox News poll in 2019 found 56 percent against it, including 20 percent of Republicans.[31]

Supporters of Trump's decision counter that there has been a dramatic increase in border crossings in recent times. Since October 2018, the Border Patrol has detained 136,150 families traveling with children. This is a significant increase from the previous year, when 107,212 families were detained.[32] Additionally, Trump supporters point out that declarations of a national emergency have been used by presidents in the past. Presidents have declared national emergencies nearly sixty times in the past, but most of them dealt with foreign crises and involved freezing property, blocking trade or exports, or taking other actions against national adversaries.

In fact, there have been only two other instances when a president has acted without legislative approval.[33] George H. W. Bush did so in 1990 in anticipation of the war in the Persian Gulf, and in 2001, George W. Bush spent funds just after the 9/11 terrorist attacks. In those instances, however, the president appropriated military funds for military action against an identified enemy, and those actions had not occurred after Congress had rejected the president's course of action.[34]

Finally, Trump was a vocal critic of President Obama's use of executive authority during his administration. When President Obama failed to gain consensus on an immigration policy, he essentially prevented millions of illegal immigrants from being deported. In 2014, Trump tweeted, "Repubs must not allow Pres Obama to subvert the Constitution of the US for his own benefit & because he is unable to negotiate w/ Congress."[35]

In March 2019, President Trump made another dramatic announcement: he would consider closing the border completely unless Mexico did something to address the growing immigration crisis. While Trump had made similar claims in the past, this latest threat of closing the Mexican border was an extraordinary step in a long line of immigration-related decisions. Most experts pointed out that closing the border could have a significant impact on both countries' economies—an estimated $1.7 billion in goods and services flow back and forth across the border daily[36]—but Trump remained committed to the idea.

In April 2019, President Trump reconsidered his plan, stating that the Mexican government had taken some steps to secure its own border. However, his admonition to the Mexican government was that it had to do more to arrest migrants and address drug trafficking. Trump also threatened to impose tariffs on automobiles produced in Mexico if the country failed to demonstrate significant improvement in these areas.[37]

About a month later, in May 2019, President Trump followed up on his threat by imposing a 5 percent tariff on all Mexican goods, with the promise to increase the tariff to 25 percent until the immigration crisis had been resolved. In response, Mexican president Lopez Obrador stated that he was committed to finding an acceptable solution to the problem, and he sent envoys to Washington to reach an agreement that would avoid tariffs. He also reiterated that Mexico had stepped up its immigration enforcement policies. According to some reports, Mexico is now detaining double the number of migrants per day than a year ago and three times as many as in January, when the Mexican government opted to give visas to Central Americans, hoping they would stay in Mexico.[38]

Similarly, Trump threatened to cut an estimated $500 million in aid to several Central American countries that were said to be the source of the rise in illegal immigrants into the United States. While most experts note that a viable solution to the problem is to address the political and economic crises in those countries that propel people toward the United States in the first place, Trump argued that these countries, primarily Honduras, Guatemala, and El Salvador, had not done enough to warrant continued support. He stated, "We're not paying them anymore because they haven't done anything for us."[39]

The election of a new president in El Salvador occurred in May 2019, and President Nayib Bukele promised to collaborate with the United States to end the problems that had created the humanitarian crisis in the first place. Calling his country a "sick child" that needed to be healed and promising to improve the strained relations with the United States over the violence and oppression of previous regimes, Bukele remarked that there are many reasons to be optimistic about the future in El Salvador.[40]

At the present time, the decision to withhold funding to Central America is still pending. Although Trump cannot eliminate all the aid to those countries because the funds have been appropriated by Congress, he does have the authority to limit it to some degree. Most experts note that reducing the funding would increase the flow of immigrants to the United States rather than decrease it.[41]

Separating Fact from Fiction: Immigration in the United States

Is it really the case that the United States is experiencing an "invasion" by "rapists," "criminals," and "animals," as portrayed by President Trump? Do undocumented immigrants really present such an extreme threat to national security that it warrants the construction of a massive border wall, not to mention the commitment of resources and personnel to prevent immigrants from coming into this country? Can we separate fact from fiction?

More importantly, what do most Americans think about the challenges presented by immigration? Clearly, some groups espouse a white nationalist/white supremacist approach to all manner of social problems, but do they speak for the majority of Americans or are they simply the most vocal group and now have a president who appears to be sympathetic to their cause?

A Brief History of Immigration in the United States

With the exception of the hundreds of thousands of African slaves who were brought to the United States against their will, the United States has a long history of immigrants seeking to come to the country in search of a better life. For example, in the 1600s, some of the first settlers to what became the United States, the Pilgrims, were fleeing religious persecution in Europe. The original Puritans, numbering perhaps one hundred individuals, established a colony in Plymouth, Massachusetts, and many others followed them. Experts estimate that nearly twenty thousand Puritans came to Plymouth in the decade between 1630 and 1640.[42]

As other groups decided to migrate to the New World, the realities of doing so changed the trajectories of their lives. Because the cost of making the trip was beyond their means, it is estimated that at least half of the white Europeans arrived as indentured servants. In addition, thousands of English prisoners were shipped to the colonies as indentured servants.

In the late 1600s, blacks were taken from West Africa and brought to America as slaves. While laws were passed in the early 1800s prohibiting the slave trade, the practice continued, which led to approximately four million slaves being brought into the United States by the time of the U.S. Civil War in 1861.[43]

Another major wave of immigration occurred from around 1815 to 1865. The majority of these newcomers came from Europe. A massive famine in the mid-nineteenth century led many Irish people to migrate to the United States. One estimate was that in the 1840s, almost half of the immigrants were from Ireland, nearly five million between 1820 and 1930. In addition, during the nineteenth century, nearly five million German immigrants came to the United States, many of whom settled in cities such as Milwaukee, St. Louis, and Cincinnati. Additionally, by 1920, nearly four million Italians and over two million Jews from Eastern Europe had migrated to the United States. In total, in forty years of enormous growth, more than twenty million immigrants had come to the United States.[44]

In response to the massive influx of immigrants, many Americans began to resent their presence, seeing them primarily as an economic threat in the job market. Like the Hispanics and Latinos of today, in the 1800s, Chinese immigrants were seen as taking jobs away from U.S.-born citizens, as they were willing to work for less and take on jobs that citizens did not want. In response, Congress passed the Chinese Exclusion Act of 1882, which banned Chinese laborers from coming to the United States. In 1917, in response to the extraordinary growth of the immigrant population, Congress enacted legislation that required immigrants over sixteen years of age to pass a literacy test. The Immigration Act of 1924 created a quota system that restricted entry to 2 percent of the total number of people of each nationality in the United States.[45]

By the early 1960s, calls to reform U.S. immigration policy had mounted, largely due to the momentum generated by the civil rights movement. At the time, immigration was based on the quota system established by the Immigration Act of 1924. Civil rights advocates argued that the quota system was discriminatory against certain European groups, particularly Greeks, Portuguese, and Italians, who argued that Northern Europeans were getting special treatment.[46]

In 1965, Congress passed the Immigration and Nationality Act, sometimes known as the Hart-Cellar Act of 1965, which did away with quotas and allowed Americans to sponsor relatives from their countries of origin. The act provided for preferences to be made according to certain categories, such as relatives of U.S. citizens or permanent residents, those with skills deemed useful to the United States, and refugees of violence or unrest. Though it abolished quotas per se, the system did place caps on per-country and total immigration as well as caps on each of the aforementioned categories. This new immigration policy would increasingly allow entire families to establish their lives in the United States. This change in policy also reconfigured the face of immigration; while more than half of all immigrants in the 1950s came from Europe, the majority of U.S. immigrants today come from Asia and Latin America.[47]

Throughout the 1980s and 1990s, illegal immigration was a constant source of political debate, as immigrants continued to come into the United States. The Immigration Reform and Control Act in 1986 (IRCA) attempted to provide better enforcement of immigration policies and to create more possibilities for migrants to seek legal solutions. For instance, the act collectively granted amnesty to more than three million illegal aliens.[48]

The economic recession that hit the country in the early 1990s was accompanied by a resurgence of anti-immigrant feeling, particularly among lower-income Americans who felt they were competing with immigrants for jobs. The fact that many of the jobs taken by immigrants were those that lower-income Americans would not perform did not distract Congress from passing more restrictive immigration laws. In 1996, Congress passed the Illegal Immigration Reform and Immigrant Responsibility Act (IIRIRA), which addressed border enforcement and the use of social programs by immigrants.[49]

In 2002, the Homeland Security Act created the Department of Homeland Security (DHS), which has taken over the enforcement of immigration policy. Interestingly, the policies used in the 1960s to address immigration are essentially the same ones being used today. That is, immigrants can enter the United States either by receiving temporary or permanent admission. A member of the latter category is classified as a lawful permanent resident and receives a green card granting eligibility to work in the United States and to eventually apply for citizenship.[50]

The DREAM Act and DACA

During his administration, President Obama attempted to provide temporary legal relief to many undocumented immigrants. In 2012, a program known as Deferred Action for Childhood Arrivals (DACA) offered renewable two-year deportation deferrals and work permits to undocumented immigrants who had arrived to the United States as children and had no criminal records. Obama argued that DACA was an intervening solution, and he attempted to influence Congress to pass the DREAM Act, which would have benefited many of the same people.

The first version of the Development, Relief, and Education for Alien Minors (DREAM) Act was introduced in 2001. As a result, young undocumented immigrants have since been called *Dreamers*. Since its creation, there have been multiple versions of the legislation, which outlines a pathway for undocumented youth in the United States. Despite support in Congress from various senators and congress members, none of the versions of the legislation has become law.[51]

In 2012, DACA was created by the then secretary of homeland security Janet Napolitano. DACA provided temporary relief from deportation (deferred action) to certain young undocumented immigrants that had been brought to the United States as children. DACA has enabled almost eight hundred thousand eligible young adults to work lawfully, attend school, and plan their lives without the constant threat of deportation. However, unlike federal legislation, DACA does not provide a permanent legal status to individuals and must be renewed every two years. In 2017, the acting secretary of homeland security Elaine Duke essentially ended the 2012 DACA program. Since then, no new applications for DACA have been accepted, and current DACA beneficiaries whose status was set to expire before March 5, 2018, were permitted to renew their status for an additional two years. Any person for whom DACA expired on March 6, 2018, no longer has deferred action or employment authorization.[52]

For DACA beneficiaries and undocumented youth, there remain significant barriers to completing a college degree to enhance their job opportunities. Colleges and universities each have their own policies about admitting undocumented students; some deny them admission, and others allow them to attend. However, even when undocumented students are allowed to attend college, tuition is often too expensive for them to remain on campus. Given that undocumented students do not qualify for financial aid, it is unlikely students can even afford to attend a public university. To address part of the challenges for undocumented students, some states have created the opportunity for them to receive in-state tuition. However, while this mitigates one dimension of the problem, the absence of financial aid continues to hamper those individuals seeking to complete a degree.

In 2014, Obama attempted to extend DACA benefits to undocumented parents of U.S. citizens and permanent residents. However, nearly half of U.S. states sued his administration, alleging that the program, known as Deferred Action for Parents of Americans (DAPA), violated federal immigration law and the U.S. Constitution. The U.S. Supreme Court ruled in 2016 that the program was unconstitutional.

Despite these efforts, the Obama administration actually deported more than three million people during President Obama's tenure, more than what Presidents George W. Bush and Bill Clinton achieved. In fact, according to one researcher, Obama has been referred to as the "deporter in chief," a disparaging word play on the president's role as commander in chief.[53] However, Obama's advocates claim that his efforts focused on illegal immigrants who had committed serious crimes.[54]

As previously mentioned, since the start of his administration in 2016, President Trump has signed several executive orders that increased enforcement and expansion of detention as part of his immigration strategy. These are controversial because questions remain about the legality and constitutionality of the use of executive orders in such cases without congressional approval. For example, Trump signed an executive order that expanded the deportation of any unauthorized immigrant who could not prove that he or she had been in the United States for two years without a court hearing.[55]

Another executive order focused on preventing terrorists from entering the United States by banning nationals from Iran, Iraq, Libya, Somalia, Sudan, and Yemen from entering the United States and suspending the U.S. refugee program for 120 days. These actions, particularly the ban on travelers from seven Muslim-majority countries, drew widespread protests and legal challenges. The so-called travel ban eventually found its way to the Supreme Court, where a revised version of the order was declared constitutional.[56]

In addition, Trump attempted to limit the flow of legal immigrants into the United States by reducing the number of refugees admitted and making it more difficult for people to obtain political asylum. In early 2018, the Trump administration implemented a zero tolerance policy whereby all illegal immigrants were arrested and criminally prosecuted. As a result, thousands of children were detained separately from their parents or guardians. In response to widespread protests and criticisms, Trump ended the family separation policy.[57]

The federal government is generally responsible for enforcing immigration laws, but it may delegate some immigration control duties to state and local law enforcement. However, the degree to which local officials are obliged to cooperate with federal authorities is a subject of intense debate. Proponents of tougher immigration enforcement have labeled state and local jurisdictions that limit their cooperation with federal authorities as *sanctuary cities*. There is no official definition or count of sanctuary cities, but the Immigrant Legal Resource Center identifies more than six hundred counties with such policies.[58]

President Trump issued an executive order to block federal funding to sanctuary cities and reinstated the Secure Communities program, in which state and local police provide fingerprints of suspects to federal immigration authorities and transfer individuals assumed to be illegal immigrants to federal authorities. He also ordered the expansion of enforcement partnerships among federal, state, and local agencies. Several cities are challenging Trump's order in court. In March 2018, the Justice Department filed a lawsuit against California, alleging that several of the state's laws obstruct federal immigration enforcement. The main issue is whether state and municipal agencies can be controlled by the federal government.[59]

Public Opinion and Immigration

There has been considerable media attention about the construction of the wall along the Mexican border as well as several accounts about caravans of immigrants from Central America headed to the United States. There are also a host of other newsworthy items, such as the federal government's attempt to separate families of illegal immigrants. Given all these extraordinary events, it might seem that the general public considers immigration in general and illegal immigration in particular to be topics of considerable priority. It may even seem, as some politicians have portrayed it, that the general public is worried about the negative impact immigration could have on the economy and American culture. However, the data suggests a different picture.

For example, a 2017 Gallup poll found that 71 percent of Americans considered immigration a "good thing" for the United States. In 2016, about 84 percent supported a path to citizenship for undocumented immigrants if they meet certain requirements. About two-thirds of Americans thought immigration levels were too high in the mid-1990s, a number that has been cut in half in 2016. Similarly, the popular argument against immigration, that they take jobs from hard-working Americans and adversely impact the economy, has found little support in public opinion polls; the percentage of Americans who stated that immigrants actually help the economy is at the highest point since 1993. The share of Americans calling for lower levels of immigration has fallen from a high of 65 percent in the mid-1990s to just 35 percent, near its record low.[60]

Overall, a majority of Americans have positive views about immigrants. Nearly two-thirds of Americans say immigrants strengthen the country "because of their hard work and talents," and just over a quarter say immigrants burden the country by taking jobs, housing, and health care. Roughly half of the U.S. public said immigrants are making things better through food, music, and the arts, and over a third said immigration should be kept at its present levels.[61] The fact that most people think immigrants make an important contribution to the country and its culture, coupled with opinion polls that look favorably upon immigration, raises questions about whether immigration is on the minds of the American people as much as it is for some politicians and pockets of dissatisfied people. We will have more to say about this later in the chapter, but, for now, it makes sense to offer an assessment of how extensive immigration impacts the United States.

The Extent of Immigration in the United States

In 2017, the United States had approximately 44.4 million people living in the United States who had been born in another country, more than any other country in the world. Since 1965, the number of immigrants living in the United States has more than quadrupled. Today, immigrants account for 13.5 percent of the U.S. population, nearly triple the share (4.7%) in 1970 (see figure 1-1).[62]

Over three-quarters of the immigrants in the United States are in the country legally, but a quarter are unauthorized, about 11 million people, according to the Pew Research Center in 2017. From 1990 to 2007, the unauthorized immigrant population tripled in size—from 3.5 million to a record high of 12.2 million. During the economic crisis of 2008, the number declined and has since leveled off.[63]

Not every immigrant living in the United States wants to become a U.S. citizen, a process called *naturalization*, but for those who do, there are certain requirements, such as having to live in the United States for five years. In 2017, there were 986,851 immigrants who applied for naturalization. The number of naturalization applications has climbed in recent years. However, Mexican immigrants have the lowest naturalization rate. According to Mexican-born green card holders, the reasons for this stem in part from language challenges as well as a general lack of interest and financial obstacles.[64]

That said, in 2017, Mexico accounted for approximately 26 percent of all U.S. immigrants, while immigrants from South and East Asia comprised another 27 percent. In fact, Asians are projected to become the

Immigrant share of U.S. population nears historic high

% of U.S. population that is foreign born

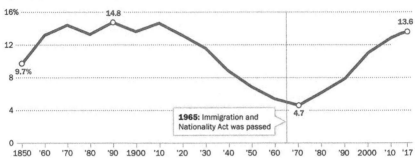

Figure 1-1   Trends in Immigration (U.S. Census Bureau, "Historical Census Statistics on the Foreign-Born Population of the United States: 1850–2000" and Pew Research Center tabulations of 2010 and 2017 American Community Survey (IPUMS). Pew Research Center. Available online at https://www.pewresearch .org/fact-tank/2019/06/17/key-findings-about-u-s-immigrants.)

largest immigrant group in the United States by 2065, surpassing Hispanics. Researchers at the Pew Research Center estimate that, in 2065, Asians will make up some 38 percent of all immigrants; Hispanics, 31 percent; whites, 20 percent; and blacks, 9 percent.[65]

Assuming current immigration trends, immigrants and their descendants are expected to account for nearly 90 percent of the population growth in the United States through 2065 according to the Pew Research Center. This is particularly true given that the percentage of immigrant women who gave birth in the past year was higher (7.4%) than among U.S.-born women (5.9%).[66]

Immigrants—A Profile

According to the U.S. Census Bureau, immigrants comprise about 14 percent of the U.S. population. If we include U.S.-born children of immigrants, they constitute about 27 percent of the U.S. population. The United States granted nearly 1.2 million individuals legal permanent residency in 2017, either due to family reunification; employment opportunities, meaning they are needed in various industries; or for other reasons. Hundreds of thousands of individuals legally work in the United States under various types of nonimmigrant visas. In 2017, the United States granted close to 180,000 visas for high-skilled workers and nearly 250,000 visas for temporary workers in agriculture and other industries.[67]

In fact, immigrants made up roughly 17 percent of the U.S. workforce in 2017 according to the Pew Research Center; of those, around two-thirds were in the country legally. Collectively, immigrants represent almost half of all domestic employees and a third of workers in the manufacturing and agricultural industries. Thus, the U.S. economy needs immigrants, and many of the jobs performed by immigrants are those that many U.S. workers are unwilling to do. In fact, according to another study, if the U.S. policy against immigration continues, the U.S. workforce is expected to decline considerably in the future.[68]

Some of the controversy about immigration relates to those who enter the country illegally. According to the Pew Research Center, illegal immigrants comprise about eleven million people. While it is obviously difficult to accurately count this population, the available data suggests that the rates of illegal immigration have declined, particularly since 2009, when the economic crisis eliminated numerous jobs for all workers in the United States. Many illegal immigrants returned to their home countries in search of job opportunities, and since that time, the rate of illegal immigration has remained low. For instance, in 2017, U.S. Customs and Border Protection reported a 26 percent drop in the number of people apprehended or stopped at the southern border, and arrests of suspected undocumented immigrants jumped by 40 percent.[69]

More Facts versus Fiction on Immigration

Another interesting pattern regarding illegal immigration is that once people cross the border into the United States, they tend to find jobs and build a life for themselves. According to the Pew Research Center, more than half of the undocumented immigrants have lived in the country for more than a decade, and nearly one-third are the parents of U.S.-born children.[70]

What is also noteworthy is that while the controversy surrounding border security continues, with President Trump shutting down the federal government because he did not receive funding for his proposed border wall, most of the undocumented population in this country are what are known as *overstayers*, people who legally obtained visas and simply remained in the United States after they expired.[71]

Separating fact from fiction is also found in President Trump's claims that illegal or undocumented immigrants are responsible for drug trafficking. In fact, the research on this subject consistently shows that the vast majority of illegal drugs that come into this country occur at legal border checkpoints. Thus, the image of illegal immigrants serving as couriers for the drug cartels, who bring drugs into this country when they cross the border, represents very little of the actual drug trafficking problem. The United States might be better suited to address the challenges at legal border checkpoints than to consider stemming the flow of illegal immigrants to resolve the drug problem in this country.[72]

Similarly, the claim made by President Trump and his supporters about the criminal activity of illegal immigrants is questionable. While a proportion of illegal immigrants do commit crimes once they arrive in the United States, as will be demonstrated in the next chapters, the rate of criminal activity committed by undocumented immigrants clearly indicates that the portrayal of immigrants as criminals is an exaggeration.

Perhaps more disturbing is the recent practice of manufacturing immigrants as criminals. While the rhetoric and narrative offered by President Trump and other politicians and policy makers—in which immigrants are characterized as rapists, murderers, and animals[73] who contribute to drug trafficking[74] or are linked to terrorists[75]—attempt to sway public opinion about stemming the "invasion" of immigration into this country, in the majority of cases, what has actually occurred is that certain minor offenses, such as traffic violations or administrative offenses, have been modified to constitute more serious crimes.

By elevating minor offenses to crimes, and by making the offenses retroactive, more immigrants are eligible to be detained, deported, and labeled as criminals. Repeat offenses, known as *aggravated felonies*, regardless of when they occurred, escalate the stigma and justify longer and more severe punishment. They also make offenders immediately eligible for deportation. However, as the data shows, immigrants, even those who are undocumented or who crossed the border illegally, constitute a small percentage of all criminals and far less than U.S.-born offenders.[76] Why? Because immigrants do not come to the United States to commit crimes; rather, they come to this country in search of a better life—and most of them find it. This is underscored by the length of time most immigrants stay in the United States and by the fact that they buy homes, pay taxes, and build a life for themselves that is reflective of the American dream.

This focus on portraying immigrants as criminals overshadows the conforming behavior of the vast majority of immigrants in the United States and serves to justify a punitive narrative that includes putting them in prison, violating due process standards, and enhancing efforts at deportation. While taking a hard-line approach about immigration, with "proof" that the public is safe from criminals, makes for a good campaign speech, it is more of a fabrication of a problem than actually solving one. The tendency to blur the accuracy in the various narratives offered about immigrants and the actual trends in the data is perhaps of greater concern.

Let us also not forget that the "immigration problem" in this country is occurring in large part because of U.S. contributions to many of the economic, political, and social problems in the immigrants' home countries, where thousands of people are fleeing violence, political oppression, and victimization. We will go into more detail about this in another chapter, but President Trump's recent attempt to cut funding to those countries only exacerbates a complex problem and does not reduce the flow of immigrants into the United States.[77]

This is not to suggest our borders should remain open to everyone, but it does mean the public, politicians, policy makers, and even agencies given the task of enforcing current immigration law are all contributors to a complex problem that has no easy solutions and that contains a host of unintended negative consequences for immigrants as well as for the country as a whole. As previously mentioned, we cannot simply blame President Trump for the immigration problem since it was not of his creation. He has to bear some responsibility for the way he has handled it, particularly how he has exacerbated an already sensitive and thorny problem, but he is not the only one responsible.

Members of Congress, policy makers, law enforcement, and court personnel must also accept some of the responsibility for the problem. Their agendas and efforts to justify their existence, along with unreasonable mandates, have resulted in overcrowding, a backlog of cases, violations of rights and due process, and the creation of a public health crisis, and these contribute to the challenge of finding realistic and reasonable solutions as well.

However, the public's responsibility is often overlooked in the discussions of immigration. We have contributed to the problem through our own fears and insecurities of different groups. We have ignored the problems and failed to take a definitive stand on immigration, and we have allowed politicians to enact and implement certain policies that have contributed to the problem. In the process, we have created the criminalization of immigration. It might be easy to minimize or trivialize this dimension of the immigration problem, but we must remember that politicians and policy makers typically respond to the perceived or real fears and concerns of those they represent.

If we were to be honest about our fears and anxieties about immigration—how some of us think immigrants are taking jobs from us (even though many of us do not want those jobs), or feel that our culture is being diluted in some way (even though we have always been a country of immigrants, making diversity a way of life), or ignore the contributions and examples that immigrants make in improving our way of life (many Chinese immigrants built the transcontinental railroad, immigrants built the infrastructure and most of the urban areas around the country, and our homes and yards are built and maintained by immigrants), or disregard how immigrants serve as examples of our most important cultural values (consider the courage, perseverance, commitment to family, discipline, hard work, integrity, and dedication offered by immigrants)—we might see particular groups and immigration in general in a different light.

In the subsequent chapters of this book, I outline the nature of the criminalization of immigration with an eye toward separating "fake news" from empirical evidence and demonstrate the impact such an approach has on the immigrants, their families, and the country as a whole. No one wins or benefits from the policies we currently use, except perhaps those who are in the business of deporting and incarcerating people. More importantly, we cannot simply deport or detain our way out of this problem. Similar to the misguided efforts to address the crime problem in the 1980s, where we could not incarcerate our way out of the War on Drugs, we cannot simply close the border completely or deport every immigrant, legal or undocumented. Instead, there must be a more thoughtful approach to finding a balance between Americans' core values and a reasonable concern about national security.

In chapter 2, a larger discussion of the criminalization of immigration is offered. This chapter includes a more detailed examination of moral panics and how the public's fears are exploited by those who have an economic, social, or political incentive to keep people afraid of immigrants, particularly those from a certain part of the world. This examination involves a discussion of what is known as *neoliberal politics* and how it has shaped current social policy on immigration.

In chapter 3, we begin an examination of the different agencies responsible for implementing U.S. policies on immigration. This chapter begins with the police, who serve as the first point of contact for immigrants. The discussion includes the incentives police departments sometimes use to increase stop-and-frisks and arrests for even minor violations. Within this context, the rationale to justify such an approach will be offered, or what some experts refer to as the *broken windows theory*. As we will see, the problem with using the broken windows approach is that it can easily morph into a form of zero tolerance policing and create conflict instead of solving problems.

Such an effort easily applies to immigration enforcement, especially in those communities that allow officers to work in collaboration with immigration officials to target immigrants for selective enforcement. U.S. Immigration and Customs Enforcement (ICE) has arguably created immigration policy as well as enforced it. In some ways, this is understandable, given that the agency was created and funded with essentially a single directive—and it has responded by creating a climate that justifies its own existence.

Chapter 4 examines the judicial process after an immigrant has been identified as undocumented and detained. Drawing from the literature, efforts are made to understand how the administrative procedures used to process immigrants depart from other forms of criminal prosecution, where due process and other aspects of the system are currently being minimized or ignored. As we will see, the original goal of using prosecutorial discretion was designed to selectively target hardened criminals who also happen to be undocumented immigrants. Unfortunately, discretion has been superseded by a zero tolerance approach that casts a wide net and is focused on the single goal of deportation. Since 2018, when the federal government came to the conclusion that zero tolerance policies do not work, the current approach is to release families upon their apprehension while they await their deportation hearing. However, such a strategy has resulted in many families not showing up for their hearings.[78]

Likely because of the realization that the numbers fitting into the category of violent offenders is small, which is inconsistent with the narrative of immigrants as criminals, the use of discretion and good judgment has been replaced with a more efficient goal of processing large numbers of offenders. The recalibration of what constitutes criminal behavior becomes an important feature of this process. That is, we have redefined some of the behaviors that immigrants can be charged with, and the escalation of their status as felons creates a climate in which they are more likely to be detained and deported. Such a decision did not happen as a by-product of the behavior of offenders but as a result of a more conscious effort to label immigrants as criminals.

In chapter 5, the issue of detention is examined. At a time when criminal justice experts and even some policy makers are reconsidering the value of a "get tough" philosophy of punishment for criminals in general, a different approach is currently being used for immigrants. In fact, as the data shows, we appear to be more than willing to continue the policies of the past, despite the obvious challenges of overcrowding, delays in processing cases, and how such an approach contributes to the mass incarceration of minorities in this country.

Chapter 6 examines the impact of the criminalization of immigration in terms of the consequences that deportation and detention have on families as well as the economic, social, educational, and psychological costs associated with providing assistance to U.S.-born children. Issues related to foster care, adoption, and the lack of resources available to children and young adults who were brought into the United States illegally by their parents are also considered. Also included is a discussion of the problem of unaccompanied children who attempt to cross the border.

Finally, in chapter 7, we examine the broader context of the current immigration problem with an eye toward understanding how the problem has become so desperate for so many immigrants. Here we explore U.S. support of regimes in some of the most violent and unstable countries in Central America, where citizens have little choice but to flee the unrest and dangers associated with the lawlessness in those countries. The United States has supported those currently in power in a misguided attempt to thwart the threat of communism, which has led to unprecedented numbers of people arriving at U.S. borders and created one of the most looming humanitarian crises of our generation. In this context, we will also compare U.S. policies and strategies to what is occurring in other countries in a broader discussion of the global migration problem occurring all over the world.

Additionally, potential solutions to the problem of immigration as well as the role of the United States as a world leader are explored. Despite President Trump and his supporter's rejection of globalism, a pathway of isolationism is unrealistic and dangerous, as all countries are interconnected and must address the mistakes of the past with an emphasis on the greater good.

CHAPTER TWO

The Criminalization of Immigration in the United States

- "It says something about our country that people around the world are willing to leave their homes and leave their families and risk everything to come to America. Their talent and hard work and love of freedom have helped make America the leader of the world. And our generation will ensure that America remains a beacon of liberty and the most [hope-filled] society this world has ever known."[79]

  —George W. Bush

- "We are a nation of immigrants. We are the children and grandchildren and great-grandchildren of the ones who wanted a better life, the driven ones, the ones who woke up at night hearing that voice telling them that life in that place called America could be better."[80]

  —Mitt Romney

- "Everywhere immigrants have enriched and strengthened the fabric of American life."[81]

  —John F. Kennedy

In chapter 1, I offered the idea that the recent immigration policies in the United States were creating a climate of punishment and the criminalization of immigration. Such intensification of border security and the enforcement of many immigration laws have a host of economic, social, and political consequences, and some decisions have resulted in legal challenges.

In April 2019, the director of the Department of Homeland Security (DHS), Kirstjen Nielsen, abruptly resigned after President Trump demanded the agency do more in terms of its ability to address the influx of immigrants to the United States. Those demands included the renewal of the decision to separate children from families of detained immigrants and an extension of how long children could be detained. It also included denying applications for asylum and forcing asylum seekers to wait in Mexico while their cases are reviewed, which is a violation of federal law.[82]

Within hours of Neilson's resignation, the director of the U.S. Secret Service was informed that he would be relieved of his duties (the Secret Service director reports directly to DHS). Additionally, the acting deputy director of the DHS, Claire Grady, also resigned. Such a dramatic shakeup, along with the resignations of other officials across the Trump administration, raises questions about what exactly is being asked of employees and their respective agencies. One explanation is that agencies charged with immigration enforcement were not carrying out Trump's orders quickly enough, so he took steps to replace agency leaders with people more closely aligned with his positions on immigration.

Critics point out that many of Trump's demands and policies were, in fact, illegal, which led those directors to refuse to carry out those orders, to resign, or to attempt to convince the president to modify his stance on particular issues. This was especially true of Trump's decision to revise the family separation policy that drew such heavy criticism from members of Congress and the general public. Similarly, Trump ordered Homeland Security officials to deny applications for asylum, which is in violation of federal law.[83]

In this chapter, the effects of the intense immigration policies issued by the Trump administration are explored. The heavy reliance on deportation and dependence has a series of ripple effects in terms of how all immigrants, both legal and undocumented, are being perceived. We refer to this trend as the *criminalization of immigration*, in which certain acts are recalibrated and defined so that they result in criminal prosecution and the status of being an immigrant makes one eligible and vulnerable to a wide range of sanctions. However, this process, while purportedly applied to all immigrants, appears to impact and target a much greater proportion of immigrants of color, particularly those from Central American countries and Mexico.

Immigrants and the Criminal Justice System

As a result of the stepped-up enforcement of immigration policies by the Trump administration, there has been an increase in the number of apprehensions, deportations, and prosecutions of illegal immigrants. For example, the number of apprehensions at the U.S.-Mexico border has sharply decreased over the past decade or so, from more than one million in 2006 to about three hundred thousand in 2017. In fact, there were actually more apprehensions of non-Mexicans than Mexicans at the border; in 2017, apprehensions of Central Americans at the border exceeded those of Mexicans for the third time since 2014.[84]

In 2018, according to the Migration Policy Institute, the Border Patrol reported a total of 404,142 apprehensions at the southern and northern borders, a significant increase from 310,531 in 2017 and closer to the 415,816 apprehensions in 2016. The majority of apprehensions, 98 percent, occurred along the southwest border. While apprehensions were up in 2018, they remained a small share of the 1.6 million that occurred during the peak year of 2000.[85]

Within the United States, where U.S. Immigration and Customs Enforcement (ICE) is responsible for the internal enforcement of immigration policy, agency officials made 158,581 administrative arrests in 2018, an increase of 11 percent from 2017. It should be noted that an administrative arrest is the arrest of an individual for a civil violation of U.S. immigration law, not a crime, and the offense is adjudicated by an immigration judge or through other administrative processes, not a criminal court judge.[86] This is an important distinction that will be revisited later in the chapter.

Deportations

When examining the data on the deportation of immigrants, two key terms become important, *removals* and *returns*, which involve the movement of immigrants who are deemed to be deportable or inadmissible to the United States for one reason or another. As the names imply, one involves returning an immigrant to his or her country of origin, and the other involves removing the immigrant because of some type of violation of immigration law. Border Patrol and ICE both conduct removals and returns, and in 2018, according to the Migration Policy Institute, there were 256,085 removals and returns carried out by ICE, an increase of 13 percent from 2017 (data on the number of removals or returns by the Border Patrol were not available for 2017 or 2018 at the time of this writing).[87]

In 2016, according to the Pew Research Center, around 340,000 immigrants were deported from the United States. In 2017, about 295,000 were deported (see figure 2-1).[88] Overall, the Obama administration deported about 3 million immigrants between 2009 and 2016, a significantly higher number than the 2 million immigrants deported by the Bush administration between 2001 and 2008.

Immigrants convicted of a crime made up a minority of all deportations in 2017, the most recent year for which statistics by criminal status

U.S. deportations of immigrants slightly down in 2017

In thousands, by fiscal year and criminal status

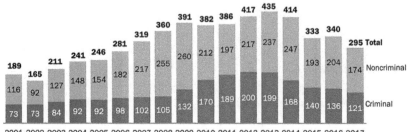

2001 2002 2003 2004 2005 2006 2007 2008 2009 2010 2011 2012 2013 2014 2015 2016 2017

Figure 2-1 U.S. Deportations by Criminal Status (Note: Criminal status is based on prior criminal conviction. Data refer to removals by U.S. Department of Homeland Security. Source: U.S. Department of Homeland Security publications. Data for 2001–2004: "Yearbook of Immigration Statistics: 2010." Data for 2005–2014: "Yearbook of Immigration Statistics: 2014." Data for 2015, 2016, and 2017 from "Yearbook of Immigration Statistics" for each respective year. Pew Research Center. Available online at https://www.pewresearch.org/fact -tank/2019/06/17/key-findings-about-u-s-immigrants.)

are available. Of the 295,000 immigrants deported in 2017, some 41 percent had criminal convictions, meaning 59 percent of those deported had not been convicted of a crime. In fact, since 2001, approximately 60 percent of the immigrants deported had not been convicted of a crime.[89]

Detention of Immigrants

Detaining noncitizens is not a new strategy in the United States. At the turn of the century, about 20 percent of the immigrants examined at Ellis Island were detained due to health concerns or because of legal questions about their status.[90] By the early 1950s, detaining migrants no longer seemed necessary. European and Asian migration had fallen drastically as a result of the Immigration Act of 1924 and the Great Depression of the 1930s. In 1954, government officials felt that most migrants could be released while their cases were being reviewed. Detention was reserved as a tactic for migrants who were deemed likely to flee or who posed some sort of threat to the country. This position changed in the 1980s with the migration of Cubans into the United States.[91]

During the 1980s, Americans came to see Cuban exiles as a dangerous threat and used detention as a primary strategy. During the Mariel boatlift, approximately 125,000 Cubans fled Cuba for the United States; many of the migrants were not criminals but had been labeled "antisocial" by Cuban officials. When the migrants arrived, thousands of them were placed in military bases while they waited to be sponsored by someone who would agree to take care of them until they could become self-sufficient.[92]

As the months went by, most exiles left the military bases, but those who had no family members or acquaintances in the United States often had difficulty finding sponsors, which was the only way they could leave the camps, other than leaving the United States all together. This was not an option for Cuban immigrants since the Castro government refused to take them back.[93]

By 1982, about four hundred unsponsored Mariel Cubans were sent to prisons, primarily to the maximum-security penitentiary in Atlanta. Because the U.S. government had become concerned that another large migrant group would come to the United States from Cuba, U.S. immigration policy was modified from one that had previously allowed immigrants to remain free while their cases were processed to a policy that focused more on detention as a default strategy. This was also an era of "getting tough" on criminals in general, where there was an unprecedented level of incarceration of all types of offenders in the United States.

Building off the Reagan and Clinton administrations' policies on immigration, in 2008, during the first term of the Obama administration, an average of more than 30,000 immigrants were held in detention per day. This was the result of a "detention bed quota" imposed by Congress and the enhanced efforts to target immigrants with criminal convictions, many of whom were subject to mandatory detention. During the Trump administration, the U.S. policy reflects the growth of detention as a strategy and the development of privately run prisons.[94] In 2018, ICE reported the average daily number of the detained immigrant population was 38,106 per day, which increased to 49,447 by March 2019.[95]

How Did We Get Here?

Given the enormous costs and effort involved in implementing the current immigration strategy, it is reasonable to ask how we arrived at the decision to engage in the widespread criminalization of a people and of a process. As mentioned chapter 1, despite his critics, it is too easy to simply blame President Trump as the source of the problem, particularly his tendency to offer "alternative" facts and "fake news" of his own, where the accuracy of his claims about immigrants and immigration in general are often at odds with the data. Instead, we must examine the criminalization of immigration as a phenomenon that has many actors, each with their own set of motives and agendas, who have collectively created a climate in which all immigrants, legal and undocumented, are cast with suspicion and doubt and for whom their standing in and value to this country have been jeopardized.

The Public's Responsibility

In examining the history of U.S. immigration, we see a fairly consistent pattern of policies and the mistreatment of groups, even those who are compliant, who attempt to assimilate into American culture, and who emulate the very traits and behaviors Americans say are most important. Underlying much of this behavior is fear—which is sometimes the basis of poor decision making and discriminatory treatment.

A good illustration of how irrational fears can result in extraordinarily misguided behavior is found in the popular children's movie *Smallfoot* (2018). In the movie, a Yeti named Migo lives in the mountains with his family and a community guided by a sense of order and purpose. The village has existed for hundreds of years, safe in the knowledge that all of their laws and histories are carved into small stones. Those stones are kept and worn as a garment by the Stonekeeper—an elder Yeti who reminds the village residents of their sacred laws and truths. In fact, one of the stone laws is never to question the stones. However, one day, Migo finds himself on a mountainside where he sees the fabled Smallfoot—a human. According to the stones, humans do not really exist.

When Migo goes back to his village and tells everyone what he saw, the Stonekeeper's immediate reaction is to deny that it actually happened and to claim that it was what we would call "fake news" in today's world. When Migo keeps asking questions, the Stonekeeper banishes him from the village until he learns that some questions do not need to be asked. The Stonekeeper later admits that he knew the stones contained a number of purposely crafted lies, but hiding certain truths from the other Yetis kept the village safe from harm.[96]

The sociological message of the movie is that people tend to fear what they do not understand, and they often construct images, attitudes, feelings, and behaviors that may or may not be accurate or true. This fear also justifies all manner of mistreatment of others. Even when people are presented the truth about a group of people or an event, they have trouble believing it because of *confirmation bias*. That is, people search for clues and evidence that confirms what they think they already know and ignore or minimize facts or evidence that run counter to that line of thinking.

In fact, confirmation bias can be so compelling that people sometimes accuse and attack those who are presenting the information, calling it "fake news" or questioning the motives of those presenting it. Again, the problem is that people think they already know what is going on, and additional insight that runs counter to the narrative creates doubt. *Smallfoot* is a great illustration of how policy makers and politicians attempt to act as Stonekeepers to shape the public's perceptions of a problem or issue.

Moral Panics and Immigration

Another way to understand how fear drives people's perceptions of a problem and what to do about it relates to a concept known as *moral panics*. Essentially, a moral panic is defined as an irrational and widespread fear that some condition or population threatens the safety and interests of a community or society.[97]

Moral panics are problematic because the media not only initiate and perpetuate the fear through the presentation of an issue but politicians contribute to the problem by passing laws or enacting policies that are justified because of the urgency to "do something" about it. The research on moral panics suggests that they are often focused on marginalized people based on race, ethnicity, religious beliefs, nationality, or sexual orientation.[98] In many ways, the immigration "invasion" that is being portrayed in the media and promoted by federal officials is a good illustration of a moral panic.

Sociologist Stanley Cohen, in his book *Folk Devils and Moral Panics*, outlines the notion of moral panics and offers insight into how they develop. Essentially, Cohen argues that moral panics occur in a five-stage process:

1. A moral panic begins with some type of threat to the way of life of mainstream society and culture.
2. In crafting a narrative, the media and invested stakeholders portray the threat in a way that is easy to understand to society at large.
3. As a result of the exposure to the threat, widespread fear is generated. Since the threat has been presented in simple and symbolic ways, the public's limited understanding results in simply reacting to the threat instead of a deeper understanding of what is occurring or why.

4. Politicians and policy makers, ever mindful of the need to be seen as quick to address problems and concerns by the public, respond to the threat with new laws, policies, or programs to address the issue.

5. The combination of the public's fear coupled with the actions taken by policy makers and politicians results in certain groups or conditions being seen as a threat to be eliminated. Typically, the way this is done is through an escalation of law enforcement and prosecution of those groups.[99]

Some experts note that moral panics allow the government to exert control over certain individuals and to even take dramatic steps normally considered outside its scope of authority. Because of the "urgency" of a moral panic and the need to "ensure" people's safety, this sometimes includes limiting certain people's rights and privileges, even if they are citizens.[100]

There have been many moral panics throughout U.S. history. For instance, in the 1980s and 1990s, some scholars noted that the famed War on Drugs spurred the get tough approach to crime that led to unprecedented rates of incarceration of drug offenders, primarily minorities. The justification of this approach, underscored by extensive media accounts of the rise in popularity of crack cocaine, ultimately led to a host of policies, laws, sentencing guidelines, and other strategies that resulted in the need to build more prisons, stigmatized a large segment of the African American population, and added a more concentrated police presence in poor and minority neighborhoods. Such actions, arguably, also led to the rise of racial profiling, "driving while black," and other tactics that are discriminatory in nature and continue to create tensions between the police and minorities.[101]

The development of moral panics can easily be applied to the immigration problem in the United States. As long as immigrants are portrayed as a threat (as President Trump has consistently done in his references to them as "animals," "rapists," and "drug traffickers"), social policies that criminalize their behavior are justified. Those who cross the border illegally, for example, are portrayed as a threat to the public since they committed a crime by coming into the country illegally. Such logic makes sense in one respect; they did break the law when they crossed the border illegally. However, we must also consider the circumstances under which crossing the border is a crime.

As shown in the coming chapters, crossing the border illegally has not traditionally been seen as anything more than an administrative or civil matter. However, under a get tough approach to immigration, we have recast this behavior as a serious crime, which subjects offenders to detention and deportation. Other minor violations have also been redefined to identify immigrants as aggravated felons despite the fact that most of these acts are not considered violent or criminal acts if committed by U.S. citizens.

Othering and Immigration

The description of moral panics provides an explanation of why the problem of immigration has been given nationwide attention. To be fair, the problem is a serious one and requires a thoughtful approach to solving it, but questions remain about whether immigration is a criminal problem, a humanitarian one, or a combination of the two. Under the current administration, the criminalization or stigmatization of immigration is the policy response to the growing threat of immigrants underscored by comments in the media and the portrayal of immigrants in general by President Trump. These extraordinarily restrictive policies are designed to keep immigrants from entering the United States at the border and to identify, detain, and deport those who have already entered or remained in the country illegally.[102]

But what is the source of the fear? Why is it that the public is so afraid of immigrants, particularly since the United States has a long history of immigration and is often described as being a country composed of immigrants? It is also the case, as mentioned in chapter 1, that most Americans think immigration is a good thing for the country and its people. The answers to those broader questions can be found in the notion of *othering*. Othering has many definitions and interpretations, but the common denominator is that it provides a mechanism for both unifying a group of people while also creating a category for those who exist outside the boundaries of membership. Stated differently, othering serves to marginalize some individuals and groups and to justify their neglect, exploitation, and mistreatment.[103]

The criteria used to determine when one group or individual is part of the "other" category could be religious beliefs, gender, race, ethnicity, social class, sexual orientation, or skin tone. In this context, being different is a bad thing. Another term used to understand the idea of othering is *tribalism*, where membership in a particular group serves as a protective measure, unless, of course, that particular group has been identified as outside of the larger group. In those instances, the marginalized group can become a target of derision, exclusion, and discrimination.[104]

In sum, when sociologist William Graham Sumner first described the notion of in-groups and out-groups, he argued that there is a natural

tendency for people to have positive reactions toward people like themselves, what he called a *code of amity*, and an equally natural tendency to
exclude others that are dissimilar in characteristics, what he called a *code
of enmity*. In the process of developing in-group solidarity by excluding
others, the inevitable hostility and social tension created toward the out-
group was a natural consequence of human interaction. Parenthetically,
Sumner also described the tendency for people to judge other cultures by
one's own, believing theirs to be superior to out-groups; he called this
ethnocentrism.[105]

The notion of othering often results in the development of stereotypes
and mischaracterization of an out-group's attitudes, values, beliefs, and
behaviors. When such instances occur, dominant groups have a greater
tendency to justify and rationalize a host of discriminatory behaviors and
practices against that group that might never be considered if the same
standards were applied to themselves. In the end, othering is a function of
irrational fears and concerns by groups in power that marginalized out-
groups pose some sort of threat to the mainstream culture and way of life.

It is fair to say that the concept of othering is not part of mainstream
language or everyday conversation. However, examples of othering are
relatively easy to find, particularly in the United States and especially as it
relates to the treatment of immigrants and minority groups. One such
example is the *Southern strategy*, which emerged in the late nineteenth
century in the American South. For decades, the South had been a single-
party political system dominated by the Democratic Party. However, upon
the passage of the Civil Rights Act of 1964, Republicans attempted to take
advantage of the resentment toward the civil rights movement among a
segment of the white population. Republicans criticized the Democratic-
controlled federal government for enabling the poor, forcing the racial
integration of public schools, and attacking states' rights and local control
of government. As a result, by the 1970s, the South had become decidedly
Republican. Evidence of this success was seen in Nixon's landslide presidential election in 1972, where he won every Southern state by wide margins over Democratic candidate George McGovern.[106]

Efforts to generate, perpetuate, and escalate fears of certain groups,
particularly whites, as part of the political process is not new. This
approach has been used to justify all manner of policy decisions, such as
the stigmatization of Asian immigrants, starting with the Chinese Exclusion Act and including the internment of hundreds of thousands of American citizens of Japanese descent during World War II. In virtually all
instances in which fears resulted in changes in policy, legislation, and
successful political campaigns, politicians and policy makers used a

particular narrative to incite fear and resentment toward a minority group that posed the most serious threat.

Some versions of these narratives were outright hostile toward the targeted groups, while more nuanced approaches were designed to promote a form of nationalism, which was a polite way of arguing people had to choose a side in the debate—they were either for the country or against it.[107] The real danger in such an approach is that the justification for mistreatment is normalized and considered acceptable. There is also a tendency over time for people to simply respond to the categories without much thought to how or in what way they were created. This is not because people are lazy, ignorant, or vindictive; rather, it is simply a way for them to gain some understanding of the world around them.

These narratives and understanding of targeted groups can be used to justify all manner of decisions, including marital partners, employment decisions, and whether certain individuals who belong to particular groups are trustworthy, more or less likely to engage in criminal behavior, or have the capacity or talent for success. When we are simply reacting to a socially created classification, there is a tendency to think those discriminatory or prejudicial actions are normal, acceptable, and justified. It also explains how institutional discrimination can emerge, even among people who would normally think of themselves as fair-minded.

As it relates to the current U.S. immigration policy, the narrative that characterizes immigrants from Mexico and parts of Central America as "animals," "rapists," "drug traffickers," and the like is designed to capitalize on the fears of victimization of the American public. However, it would be shortsighted to think that a majority of the American people believe what is being presented about immigrants. As the public opinion polls show, there is not nearly as much support for Trump's policies as he would like us to believe. The danger lies in the constant barrage of misinformation about immigrants, as it can lead those who are less informed about the issue to draw erroneous conclusions about the problem and its solutions.

What is missing from the political rhetoric and narratives about immigrants from Mexico and Central America in particular but is consistently offered in the empirical research is the value that immigrants bring to the countries they wish to enter. As Monterroso (2019) explains, immigrants solve several problems for countries, particularly the United States, which will experience a shortage of workers in the future. Additionally, most experts point out that while immigrants may initially make use of social services when they arrive in the United States, over time, their efforts more than cover those expenses and make significant contributions to the country's economy. In other words, even if one were only viewing immigrants as an economic investment, they are a bargain, particularly since the United States is destined to need their labor in the future.[108]

While the public may not believe the narrative being offered by policy makers and politicians about immigrants, they continue to allow the current policies of mistreatment to continue. It is our responsibility as citizens to recognize these manufactured fears for what they are and to respond by seeing the immigration problem for what it is rather than what we have been led to believe about it.[109]

Politicians' Responsibility

As previously mentioned, the politics of immigration reform in this country has a long history of identifying groups as a threat and of politicians being afraid to educate the public on the problems and promise of immigrants. Congress has not been successful in passing a comprehensive immigration reform law, in part because the issues are complex and consensus is difficult to achieve. However, as Gonzalez O'Brien (2018) discusses in his book *Handcuffs and Chain Link: Criminalizing the Undocumented in America*, politicians often seem more motivated by appearances than actually doing the hard work of finding a reasonable and morally defendable compromise. As he points out, politicians have made efforts over the years to pass immigration legislation based on how immigrants, particularly from Mexico, were perceived.

President Trump's public statements about the urgency of a need for a massive wall along the Mexican border is underscored by his attacks on those who disagree with the accuracy of his statements or the facts that support his position. Parenthetically, it is a bit ironic that President Trump is frequently critical of the news media for distorting the facts on certain topics, which he calls "fake news," as much of his portrayal of immigrants in the United States flies in the face of the actual data about them.

At a more macrolevel of analysis, the longstanding policies made by previous administrations to support dictators in such countries as Nicaragua, Haiti, Honduras, Guatemala, and El Salvador have contributed to the decline of the rule of law in those countries and allowed drug cartels, street gangs, and organized crime, along with corrupt political leaders, to rule with impunity. The violence and unrest created in those countries have subjected many of their citizens to extreme forms of poverty, exposure to violence, and threats by gangs, leaving families little choice but to flee their homes. Thus, an understanding of the scope of the problem of immigration currently seen at the U.S.-Mexico border stems from many of the decisions made by U.S. officials to support, encourage, and train the military leaders of those countries.

Latinos and Hispanics Are the Most Recent Targets

Additionally, the current climate that focuses on Mexican and Central American immigration is the latest in a long line of concerns about immigrants coming to the United States. Gonzalez O'Brien (2018) points to three main themes that have shaped social policies regarding Latino and Mexican immigration. First, while early efforts to curtail immigrants into the United States focused on European immigrants, who were also seen as a potential economic, criminal, and cultural threats, Mexican immigrants were largely exempt from these policy changes. Part of the reason for that was due to the need for cheap Mexican labor. However, as the policies that focused on European immigration began to have their intended effect, attention was turned toward the potential "problems" Mexican immigrants posed to the country.[110] Second, the end of World War I called attention to the lack of security at the Mexican border by U.S. officials. Third, and perhaps most significantly, the start of the Great Depression at the end of the 1920s caused much greater concern about nativism and the need to protect American jobs from outsiders.

These three factors were said to be critical to understanding how social policy changed and led to the development of the criminalization of Mexican and Latino immigration.[111] For instance, after the Mexican-American War in 1848, Mexico gave land to the United States that is now the Southwestern states, and former Mexican nationals who did not want to relocate to Mexican territory were allowed to naturalize as U.S. citizens. No restrictions were placed on Mexican immigration, and Mexican labor played a large role in the economic development of the Southwest. In fact, by the 1920s, the Southwest had become one of the nation's most valuable agricultural areas, with Mexican workers accounting for a significant part of the labor force. While Mexican laborers regularly crossed back and forth over the border to work, immigration issues focused on restrictions for European immigrants, particularly from Southern and Eastern European countries, who were seen as potential political dissidents and troublemakers.

In fact, Mexican immigration was not really a focus of attention at all in Congress, and unrestricted crossing was not seen as a criminal act, even after the Immigration Act of 1917 was passed. This legislation technically made crossing the border at nondesignated locations an administrative violation. The law also required all immigrants to pay a head tax and submit to a literacy test. However, Mexican laborers were exempt from these requirements. Why? It is likely because Mexican laborers were seen as a valuable resource to the economy, and they were also perceived as less threatening than other types of immigrants.[112]

Legislative Efforts

The Johnson Reed Act of 1924 increased efforts to control immigration by setting quotas for immigration at 2 percent of the total number of individuals of a given nationality living in the United States. This significantly reduced immigration from Southern and Eastern European countries and favored those from Northern and Western Europe. However, Mexican immigration avoided the quotas, likely because of the perceived value of Mexican labor and because the border was perceived as too vast to effectively control. While the act also created the U.S. Border Patrol, it was a small agency with limited resources.[113]

The restrictions on immigration from the Johnson Reed Act of 1924 was one of the most important pieces of immigration legislation in U.S. history and lasted until the 1950s. It restricted cultural changes in the content and characteristics of immigrants coming into the United States while also reducing immigration flow in general. However, it was during the Great Depression of the 1930s that the general public and members of Congress began to see Mexican immigration as more of a threat.[114] This was particularly true in the latter part of the 1920s and led to the passage of Senate Bill 5094 in 1929. Also known as the Undesirable Aliens Act, the bill focused on illegal border crossings and made the act a misdemeanor punishable by up to a year in prison and fines up to $1,000. Moreover, for those who had already been deported, the offender could not return to the United States. If the individual did so, the act constituted a felony with a two-year prison sentence and a fine of $1,000.[115]

Thus, S.5094 made undocumented reentry into the United States a felony and specifically targeted Mexican immigrants. While some European immigrants had been the focus of immigration laws in the past, Congress had never assigned a criminal label to their actions—the laws simply restricted their ability to come into the country. In contrast, Latino and Mexican immigrants were considered felons if they attempted to return to the United States and were eligible for detention as well as deportation.

In the decades following the passage of S.5094, millions of Mexican immigrants were labeled "illegal," and there was a more concerted effort to apprehend them. This included the infamous Mexican Repatriation as well as Operation Wetback, which involved large-scale efforts to send Mexicans back to Mexico. Operation Wetback is still used by many experts to describe large-scale raids conducted by immigration officials to deport Mexicans. Still, the government acknowledged the need for Mexican labor, which is what led to the creation of the famous Bracero program, which was designed to foster Mexican labor without violating immigration law.[116] As Calavita (2010) describes, the Bracero program, which ran from 1942 to 1965, allowed Mexicans to come to the United States as guest workers. The problem, however, was that the number of laborers brought into the United States under this program was too small to meet labor demands, which led employers to rely on undocumented workers, for which there were no penalties at the time.[117]

In 1965, Congress attempted to resolve the immigration issue through the passage of the Hart-Cellar Act, which eliminated the quota system that had been part of the Johnson-Reed Act of 1924 and improved upon the Immigration and Nationality Act of 1952. Instead of quotas from certain regions of Europe, the Hart-Cellar Act used regions of the hemisphere—170,000 immigrants from the Eastern Hemisphere and 120,000 from the Western Hemisphere. Additionally, countries in the Eastern Hemisphere had an annual cap of 20,000 people, but those in the Western Hemisphere did not. This strategy was designed to create some balance with previous legislation, which gave greater opportunities for immigrants from Northern and Western European countries. While the Hart-Cellar Act helped to boost legal Mexican immigration, it did little to address the problem of undocumented immigration.[118]

The 1980s was a period of change in the country's stance on Mexican immigration, as evidenced by the passing of Immigration Reform and Control Act of 1986 (IRCA). The rationale behind the passage of this law was the general failure of penalties to stop the flow of illegal immigration from Mexico coupled with the recognition that U.S. companies needed Mexican labor. IRCA granted amnesty to millions of undocumented immigrants who had been working in the United States and established a guest worker program to meet the needs of U.S. companies. The focus of IRCA was on holding employers responsible for hiring illegal immigrants, not the criminalization of immigration.[119] There was still funding for enforcement efforts through the Border Patrol, but the goal was to remove the incentive for employers to hire illegal Mexican immigrants.

There was also a more concerted effort to enhance border security, which was designed to make it harder for illegal immigrants to cross over into the United States. As it became more difficult to cross the border, largely due to increased numbers of Border Patrol agents and other efforts,

undocumented workers were less likely to try to return to Mexico voluntarily once they made it across. Evidence of this trend is seen in the dramatic increase in the number of undocumented immigrants between
1986 and 1996.[120]

The main reason for the failure of IRCA was that the only dimension of
the plan that was effective was the amnesty program. Loopholes were created in the legislation that allowed employers to continue to hire illegal
immigrants through the use of private contractors, who typically used
forged documents to show immigrants were legally authorized to work in
the United States. Similarly, the guest worker program was difficult to
manage and did not provide enough legitimate workers to meet employer
demands. Thus, none of the elements of this legislation reduced the flow
of illegal immigration to the United States, and as a result, new legislation
was passed that had a more punitive element to it. In fact, the amnesty
program, which was designed to be the foundation of a more humanitarian and responsible immigration policy, was seen as simply rewarding
people for their bad behavior. Thus, while IRCA was seen as a failure to
address the immigration threat to this country, the idea was sound but
the execution fell short of expectations.[121]

As Gonzalez O'Brien (2018) points out, such a critical policy failure led
to a return to a previous perception and solution to the problem. In fact,
Gonzalez O'Brien offers the idea that this is a common reaction to a significant change in strategy. That is, when an untested and unproven strategy fails, there is a strong inclination to return to a previous approach,
even if that particular effort had also been shown to be ineffective. Such is
the case with U.S. immigration policy in the 1990s.

As President Clinton took office, crime and immigration became primary issues of concern for Congress. In fact, the heated debate about
immigration began with California's Proposition 187 in 1994, which
involved the legality of allowing children of undocumented immigrants
the right to obtain an education in California public schools and none-
mergency health care. The rationale behind Proposition 187 was largely
based on the perception that undocumented workers represented a criminal threat to the public and should therefore be limited in terms of access
to social services.

Additionally, in that same year, discussions about the North American
Free Trade Agreement (NAFTA) also brought focus on immigration and
the economy, as critics pointed out that NAFTA would result in the loss of
jobs for American workers. An added factor in the discussion and perceptions about Mexican immigration was the initial attack on the World
Trade Center in 1993 by someone who was identified as an immigrant.

According to some experts, these three events strongly influenced an increase in nativism against immigrants in general and Mexicans in particular.[122]

What makes the immigrant-as-criminal narrative so compelling during this period was that there were already heightened concerns about crime, something Clinton capitalized on during his first years in office. Thus, the immigration issue was increasingly seen and understood in Congress as a law enforcement issue. This is supported by the movement away from IRCA as policy regarding immigration to one that focused more on punishment. This was particularly true given that many undocumented immigrants had technically engaged in criminal behavior by illegally coming into the country.

In 1996, Congress passed the Illegal Immigration Reform and Immigrant Responsibility Act (IIRIRA). This legislation represented a shift back to criminal penalties and the criminalization of immigrants from Mexico and was seen as the solution to undocumented immigration into the United States. The importance of IIRIRA as a driving force behind the criminalization of immigration was seen in two primary ways. First, the act allowed undocumented immigrants to be held in jail or prison while they waited for their deportation hearing. This meant that those apprehended essentially served prison time for a civil violation. More importantly, while waiting for the deportation hearing, the undocumented immigrants had no right to indigent status, which would have made them eligible for legal representation at the hearing. If they wanted legal counsel, they had to pay for it or represent themselves in immigration court.[123]

Second, the federal government often entered into agreements with local law enforcement, who essentially had the authority of a federal immigration officer. This was significant because it blurred the role of local law enforcement, particularly since it made reporting of crimes by undocumented workers much less likely.

Finally, IIRIRA carried with it severe penalties for undocumented immigrants who were apprehended. According to the act, whether due to illegally crossing the border or simply overstaying a legal visa, if they remained in the United States for more than 180 days and were caught, they would not be eligible to reenter the country for three years. If they had been in the United States for more than a year, they could not legally return for a decade. In these instances, there was no right to an appeal. In an effort to ramp up the enforcement arm of the legislation, Congress authorized the hiring of thousands of Border Patrol and U.S. Immigration and Naturalization Service (INS) agents along with significant funding for extensive fencing along the U.S.-Mexico border near San Diego.[124]

Interestingly, as Gonzalez O'Brien (2018) offers in his analysis of congressional debate about the IIRIRA, in virtually all of the debates and discussions in Congress, the evidence presented to support the position of immigrants as criminals often consisted of existing congressional committee reports to document the problem. By all accounts, this evidence was usually inaccurate and contained subjective commentary that was not supported by the actual data. Still, such tainted testimony resulted in supporting the rhetoric that immigrants were a threat to the U.S. economy and national security.

In fact, an empirical review of the literature has consistently shown that there is generally no relationship between immigration and criminal behavior, and in those cases where some evidence does exist, the trend is in the opposite direction of what members of Congress proclaimed.[125] As Gonzalez O'Brien (2018) points out, politicians were more concerned about giving the appearance of a get tough approach to crime, welfare, and immigration and simply reverted back to the standard used in the past when considering the country's immigration policy.

To be fair, the public needs to accept some of the responsibility here, for politicians were doing what they thought was in the country's interest as well as engaging in a bit of self-serving behavior—getting reelected sometimes matters more than doing what is right. Given that the public has not planted a flag on this issue and indicated their desires to their representatives, the actions by members of Congress are understandable if not misguided.

The Media's Responsibility

As previously mentioned, part of the problem with the issue of immigration relates to how it is being presented to the public. While some politicians are using an inaccurate narrative to portray immigrants as criminals or to incite people's fear about their role in this country, the vehicle by which that message is being sent, the media, also has its own agenda.

Some people like to think that the news media is in the business of providing people with accurate information about events and situations that occur around the world, and while there is some truth to this point of view, one has to also recognize that the news media is a for-profit business. The more sensational or dramatic the story, the more likely people are paying attention to it. This means there is a built-in incentive for all media to promote the dramatic, even if it is not completely accurate.

As most fiction writers will point out, every good story needs a villain, and the plot needs to generate some type of emotion for the reader. In the case of immigration, the more rhetoric offered by politicians about the threat to national security posed by immigrants, the more dramatic the story. Similarly, the more immigrants can be portrayed as villains, even if it is based on false narratives or fabricated facts, the more likely the public is paying attention to the issue.

Thus, the media plays a role in the social construction of the criminalization of immigration by the language used about immigrants in the stories offered; by how the issues are being presented, particularly if they omit important facts that present a different perspective on the subject; and by increased coverage of those who offer the rhetoric in the first place. The lack of objectivity, then, becomes a critical aspect of the framing of the issue of immigration. Regrettably, as less trust is placed in the media to provide the objective facts, a gap is created; the public still needs a source of reliable information to understand the issues. This is particularly important as irrational fears influence people's thinking about the problem.

The Economics of Immigration: Neoliberalism

While it is important to recognize the sociological factors that shape immigration policy in the United States, there is also something to learn by examining the economic developments that have essentially created the global migration problem. In other words, as we consider how the criminalization of immigration has occurred in this country, we need to better understand the impact of what are known as neoliberal policies and reforms that have occurred around the world.

As Golash-Boza (2015) points out, neoliberalism has three important elements. First, it is an ideology that argues the government's role is to protect property rights and to promote free markets and trade. Second, the way this is accomplished is through promoting competition, individuality, and a sense of entrepreneurship. And, third, neoliberalism asserts that funding for programs such as welfare and government assistance are a drain on the system and should be reduced. Given that all countries are integrated into a global economy, it is best for all countries to limit all forms of government assistance.[126]

As it relates to its ideology, there is a clearly defined attempt to limit the role of the government in terms of helping the poor. Similar to the ideas found in the works of Adam Smith, neoliberalism argues that the free market will offer solutions to the problems the poor experience. As the federal government embarks upon implementing neoliberal policies, the policies are designed to improve the overall competitiveness of the United

States in a global economy as well as to protect the interests of those who benefit most from the existing system.

Neoliberalism—A Primer

How does neoliberalism work? Neoliberalism was seen in practice during the 1960s and 1970s when several developing countries borrowed money from the World Bank in an effort to build a solid infrastructure and jump-start their respective economies. The money was used for large-scale projects, such as the building of dams for electricity, improvements to agricultural production, and the construction of trade ports, all of which allowed these countries to engage in the global economy by having the capacity to ship and receive products and services around the world.[127]

However, as interest rates and oil prices climbed in the 1980s, many of these countries had difficulty paying back their loans, and they then turned to International Monetary Fund (IMF) to pay their debts and stabilize their economies. While the IMF agreed to loan money to these countries, one of the stipulations was that the countries adopt a series of neoliberal reforms. This included the privatization of certain industries, tax reductions, various forms of deregulation, promotion of foreign investment, trade liberalization, and reductions in social services and public assistance to the poor. All of these reforms were seen as the primary method by which the countries could repay their debts.[128]

For instance, deregulation incentivizes investment in part by removing protections for workers and the environment. The privatization of public enterprises typically results in an infusion of foreign investments, which spurs economic growth. Trade liberalization often encourages international trade as the rate and extent of tariffs is dramatically decreased. Tax cuts also create a favorable climate for foreign investment. And reductions in social service programs provide countries with the resources that allow them to pay off their debts.[129]

In sum, the spread of neoliberalism around the world has allowed many countries to participate in the global economy in a way that would not have been possible otherwise. Neoliberalism in those developing countries also resulted in higher levels of emigration, as workers were theoretically provided the freedom to move to countries where work was more plentiful and offered higher wages. This had two main effects: the excess number of unemployed persons in those countries was reduced, and the workers who left were able to send money home, thereby sustaining the economy for those who were unable to work.

Neoliberalism, Immigration, and the United States

The effects of neoliberal reforms in developing countries significantly impacted the United States and its economy during the 1980s. First, many U.S. manufacturing jobs were sent to other countries where the standards of living (and wages) were lower.[130] While this trend began forty or fifty years ago, the impact of these changes is still being felt today. That is, instead of expanding the manufacturing sector in the United States, many U.S. corporations moved production overseas. For this to occur, of course, international agreements had to exist between these corporation and foreign governments, which is a primary feature of neoliberal reforms. An example in the United States is the North American Free Trade Agreement (NAFTA).

These reforms, and others like it, essentially reconfigured the U.S. economy from a manufacturing to a service economy. This was a significant departure from an economy that had, since the end of World War II, been based on the production of commodities, particularly steel-based industries and the automobile industry. These jobs offered middle-class wages for earners who had limited skills and educational backgrounds and allowed them to support a family. During the 1950s and into the 1960s, the average incomes of these workers steadily grew. However, by the 1970s, incomes had leveled off, and by the 1980s, many of these well-paying manufacturing jobs had begun to disappear, primarily due to outsourcing and global competition from other countries that could produce products of equal or higher quality at a far lower price.[131]

As the U.S. economy shifted from manufacturing to a service sector economy, a segregated workforce was created, with high-skill positions such as bankers and attorneys on one end and low-skill jobs that further the economic inequality in the workforce on the other. Many of the service sector jobs were unavailable to those who had once worked in the factories since they could not develop the skills needed to perform them. At the same time, immigrants filled many of these low-paying service sector jobs that did not require particular skill sets. As Singer (2012) points out, in 2010, immigrants made up nearly 20 percent of the workforce and were overrepresented in specific industries, such as construction, agriculture, and food services.[132] In short, the economic restructuring that was prompted by deindustrialization and globalization, designed to keep the United States with a competitive economic advantage, has led to a large segment of the workforce impoverished in low-wage jobs.[133]

Early signs of neoliberalism in the United States were also seen in how the federal government allocated funds to cities and states. As Harvey

(2005) explains, it was during the end of the 1970s that the federal government's approach to funding for cities and states for social programs began to reflect elements of neoliberalism. During this time, President Nixon began to withdraw funding to cities and states for social programs, such as education, transportation, and public health initiatives, which were all part of the "urban crisis" of that era, and directed funds toward public safety and tax benefits for the wealthy. This early version of "trickle-down economics" that became so popular in the 1980s dramatically increased the existing inequalities between the wealthy and the poor.[134]

According to Golash-Boza (2015), the extent of neoliberalism in developing countries resulted in many migrants coming into cities and urban areas from rural ones because that is where the jobs were located. These dramatic economic changes resulted in the expansion of the workforce in those countries, which allowed the economic transition in places such as Mexico to experience such growth. However, at the same time, this expansion resulted in other problems, including social and economic inequality, which spurred immigration to other countries.

As previously mentioned, neoliberalism theoretically opens up a host of opportunities for labor migration across the globe, but not all of those opportunities are equally distributed. While countries tend to benefit from immigrant labor, including the United States, it is important to exert social, political, and economic control over these workers, including limiting the size of the population. Because neoliberalism functions when there is a contingent of compliant workers who are willing to work for low wages, there cannot be too many workers, since this will affect employment opportunities and the need to provide social services for those who are unemployed—which affects revenue and profits. In other words, while countries may need migrant workers for the economy to grow, there is also an effort to constrain immigration by curtailing the number of workers and ensuring that the jobs they take are in the lowest sectors of the market.[135]

However, as inequality increases and real wages drop, the result is higher levels of unemployment. In response, the state must exert control over this population to ensure discontent is effectively managed. In fact, some experts argue that as the state reduces funding for social services for the poor, it can lead to dissent and increases in crime by frustrated workers. Instead of increasing funding for the poor and unemployed, the government response is greater enforcement by the police and the criminal justice system.[136]

As Harvey (2005) explains, incarceration and deportation become essential strategies to not only address the problems of workers who may not want to participate in low-wage work but also to protect corporate interests. In 2011, for example, the construction industry lost more than a quarter of its jobs, many of which had been filled by immigrants. In that same time period, millions of immigrant men were deported. As many scholars point out, this was not a coincidence but rather a response to keep the size of the labor pool in that industry stable.

It is also true that incarceration and deportation as strategies are expensive and are not considered in the neoliberalist approach, but as neoliberalism creates economic insecurity for those at the bottom of society, the state must have some type of mechanism to respond. That mechanism is enhanced crime control strategies. These are particularly important as an economic crisis begins to impact the middle class. This is when fear and insecurity about the future can reach a critical level, and the criminal justice system can be seen as a way for politicians to show they are responsive to people's concerns by attempting to deport all immigrants and enhance national and local security through greater enforcement, apprehension, and punishment.[137]

The Criminalization of Immigration

Gonzalez O'Brien (2018) explains that there are three threat frames that drive the efforts to criminalize immigration. First, despite the need for and reliance on Mexican labor, immigrants from this country have often been painted as an economic threat because they are willing to perform tasks at wages below that of U.S.-born workers. Second, immigrants from Mexico are also seen as a potential threat based on the misguided belief that Latinos in the United States are not as interested in assimilating into mainstream U.S. culture nor willing or able to do so as quickly as other immigrant groups. And, third, immigrants from Mexico and other Central American countries are framed and stigmatized as criminals based on the fact that they entered the United States illegally. While this is technically true for those who entered the country without the proper documentation, one has to consider the context in which this act has been interpreted and understood, both in the past and in light of recent conceptualizations of immigrants.[138]

A Perfect Storm of a Complex Problem

The discussion of immigration in general and the criminalization of immigration in particular is a complex and multilayered phenomenon. It is important to note four critical factors that frame the problem, the discussion, and the possible solutions to it. First, the problem begins with a mass migration of refugees, primarily from Central America and Mexico, who are fleeing civil conflict, poverty, and a humanitarian crisis not seen before.

Second, the sitting U.S. president arguably espouses white nationalist/supremacy discourse and has consistently and very publicly disparaged certain immigrant groups, resulting in a form of negative labeling of all immigrants. Such rhetoric fuels the behavior of hate groups, who espouse racist ideology in the name of patriotism and self-protection.

Third, there is a battle between fact and fiction from the White House and the president in regard to immigrants that involves false narratives, fake news, and extensive misinformation, including the actual threat immigrants to the United States pose and whether a border wall is a legitimate and viable strategy as part of the immigration strategy.

Fourth, as many social scientists and immigration experts have noted, there is a heavy reliance on punitive measures as a solution to social problems. In fact, some argue that the "get tough" approach and a "law and order" campaign about a problem like immigration reflects an inability to find effective solutions and demonstrates a remarkable lack of understanding of the issues.

In sum, we are all to blame for the immigration problem in this country, and the current solution creates an entire class of criminals who are not really criminals at all. Such efforts also result in a form of mass incarceration that is not only misguided but takes resources away from other more pressing problems. As we continue to embrace the criminalization of immigration as a part of U.S. social policy, it makes sense to describe and assess the different issues surrounding the various agencies within the criminal justice system. It also makes sense to offer insight into whether such an enforcement-heavy strategy is sustainable or achievable. As I discuss in chapter 1, it is unrealistic to think that the United States can deport its way out of the immigration problems facing the country

In the next chapter, we will examine the issues surrounding the enforcement of Trump's immigration strategy. As the police are on the front lines of identifying, arresting, and detaining undocumented immigrants, what challenges do police departments face in executing such strategies? How do municipal agencies and their federal counterparts, such as ICE, interact and collaborate? How are existing crime control strategies, such as the broken windows theory, a cornerstone of policing in the twentieth and twenty-first centuries, being used to eradicate immigrants from the United States?

CHAPTER THREE

The Police and Immigration

- In April 2019, President Donald Trump threatened to release detained migrants apprehended at the U.S. border into sanctuary cities. Trump stated, "We'll bring them to the sanctuary city areas and let that particular area take care of it. We can give them an unlimited supply. Let's see how happy they are."[139] Most commentators concluded that this was a measured political ploy designed to punish those cities for refusing to cooperate on the strict enforcement policies enacted by the Trump administration.

- "We believe local law enforcement should be working with federal law enforcement authorities, but we don't believe we should be doing their job for them. We have enough to do, responding to tens of thousands of 911 calls, and we're not looking to take on an unfunded mandate of taking on immigration. Immigration enforcement always has been and should be a federal responsibility. We are not trying to turn our backs on our federal law enforcement partners. We can work with them and assist them as they do their jobs. We cannot do their jobs for them."[140]

  —Police Chief Tom Manger, Montgomery County, Maryland

- "This is the sheriff you're talking about, with a gun and badge that enforces the law. Nothing is going to stop me from cracking down on illegal immigration as long as the laws are there."[141]

  —Joe Arpaio, former sheriff in Arizona

In the last two chapters, the emphasis was on explaining the issues and complexity of immigration, with a particular focus on the *what* of the current immigration situation in the United States. The next three chapters will describe the *how* of U.S. immigration policy, meaning the actual processes used to identify, arrest, and detain immigrants in the United States.

In this chapter, we examine what is perhaps the most visible aspect of U.S. immigration policy: the police. For most people, an encounter with a police officer is the first interaction they have with the criminal justice system. As it relates to immigration enforcement, there is generally a two-dimensional approach: federal law enforcement and state and local law enforcement. At the federal level, the U.S. Border Patrol primarily focuses on restricting the flow of immigrants at the U.S. border. As part of the interior enforcement strategy, which is designed to target undocumented immigrants who are already residing in the United States, Immigration and Customs Enforcement (ICE) is the agency that identifies, locates, and detains those individuals pending their deportation. While ICE is involved in more than immigration enforcement, these two agencies represent the thrust of the efforts by the federal government to address undocumented immigration in the United States.[142]

The second dimension of enforcing immigration policy in the United States involves participation by state and local law enforcement agencies. Some of these agencies have become involved in interior immigration enforcement by collaborating with ICE and federal officials in their particular efforts. However, this is a controversial issue, as court cases, legislation, and policy decisions have designated the federal government as the entity responsible for immigration enforcement. The issue is also controversial because not all cities, states, and municipal departments agree that immigration enforcement is or should be part of their particular mandate.[143]

While some cities are willing to cooperate with federal officials on immigration matters, others have refused, citing jurisdictional issues, ideological concerns, and the incompatibility of goals for local police departments to engage in immigration enforcement. These cities are known by the unofficial moniker *sanctuary cities*, and their politicians, policy makers, and police chiefs around the country have been subjected to considerable criticism by President Trump for their stances on immigration. In fact, at one point, President Trump threatened to withhold federal funding from cities if they did not cooperate with ICE officials. More recently, as the opening quote demonstrates, President Trump has threatened to actually send detained undocumented immigrants to sanctuary cities as a political ploy to gain local cooperation.[144]

While the ideological issues of whether local law enforcement should be involved in immigration enforcement are significant, and while there may be legal questions that need to be answered by the courts about whether the president can order local agencies to cooperate with federal officials, including the withholding of federal funding as leverage, there are a host of practical issues that relate to immigration enforcement for local law enforcement.

Of paramount importance to local law enforcement officials is how participation in immigration enforcement interferes with improving community relations and trust with residents. This is particularly true for people of color, who are the primary targets of immigration enforcement and who have already expressed concerns about the trustworthiness of the police. In short, as many police chiefs and others have noted, local law enforcement cannot claim to protect and serve everyone equally if they are involved in immigration enforcement.[145]

The rationale behind the current federal immigration enforcement strategy largely stems from the assertion that the presence of undocumented immigrants in the United States contributes to increased crime rates and higher levels of victimization of citizens. That is, because immigrants represent such a significant threat to the public by their involvement in crime, a more intensive and intrusive form of enforcement is warranted. However, the evidence simply does not show such a trend. The crime rates for immigrants, even undocumented ones, is vastly lower than it is for U.S.-born citizens.

Additionally, the vast majority of immigrants are contributing members of society, having lived in the United States for about a decade and raised families, purchased homes, and paid taxes.[146] Yet, their presence has been a source of tension, fear, and concern by politicians and policy makers, who attempt to enhance the public's fears through the creation of a moral panic about immigration in general and immigrants in particular. In fact, what has occurred is a redefinition of minor offenses, such as traffic violations, along with a concerted targeting of Latinos and Mexican residents to elevate their eligibility for criminal prosecution. In the case of undocumented workers caught up in this political ploy, the result is detention and deportation.[147]

This manufactured fear of immigrants as criminals is not a recent development. Immigration and criminal justice experts have noted that the narrative about immigrants as criminals, as burdens to the economy by taking jobs away from Americans and overtaxing public assistance, has been a consistent feature of U.S. policy since the 1800s, all in contrast to the available facts and data trends. The only difference seems to be which particular group represents the most recent "threat." In this latest round of stigmatization, there has been a considerable dedication of resources for the arrest, prosecution, detention, and deportation of thousands of Latino and Hispanic immigrants.[148]

Federal Law Enforcement and Immigration

The relationship between the federal government and state and local law enforcement is a complicated one that dates back to the early years of the United States. As Armenta (2017) points out, during the first one hundred years of this country, the federal government passed a variety of immigration laws, but it lacked the capacity to implement them since there was no agency tasked with their enforcement. Similarly, the federal government passed naturalization laws detailing how immigrants could become citizens, but it did not really become involved in the admission or expulsion of immigrants. Instead, these tasks were left to each state, which established their own criteria and mechanisms to determine how immigrants came into the country.[149]

However, in the late 1800s, a series of Supreme Court decisions outlined the federal government's authority to regulate and enforce immigration laws. For example, the 1849 *Passenger* cases struck down mandatory head taxes on all incoming passengers, and the 1875 *Chy Lung v. Freeman* case struck down a California law that allowed states to deny entry into the state based on immigrants' moral background.[150] These cases also resulted in the creation of a clearly defined enforcement arm to implement U.S. policy on immigration. The two main agencies currently responsible for immigration enforcement are the U.S. Border Patrol and the U.S. Immigration and Customs Enforcement agency (ICE).

The History of the U.S. Border Patrol

As mentioned in chapter 2, the creation of the U.S. Border Patrol was part of the Immigration Act of 1924. While a small agency in the beginning, with little in the way of resources, the Border Patrol's mandate was more symbolic than as an actual instrument to interdict illegal immigrants into the United States. Given the vastness of the southern border, few people expected the Border Patrol to consistently patrol the thousands of miles between the United States and Mexico and stop the flow of illegal immigrants.[151] In fact, as previously mentioned, given the frequency with which Mexican workers crossed the border to participate in the U.S. economy, there was little reason to make strict enforcement a priority. Rather, the federal government welcomed Mexican labor and focused more attention on Chinese and European immigrants, who were seen as a much greater threat to the country.[152]

Although the Border Patrol was technically responsible for apprehending all illegal immigrants, the primary threat, particularly during the nineteenth and twentieth centuries, was the Chinese immigrants who attempted to enter the United States in violation of the Chinese Exclusion Act of 1882. With the passage of the Immigration Acts of 1921 and 1924, which placed limits on the number of immigrants legally authorized to enter the United States, the role of the Border Patrol significantly changed.[153]

In 1933, as concerns about immigrants from Mexico increased, President Franklin D. Roosevelt combined the Bureau of Immigration and the Bureau of Naturalization into the Immigration and Naturalization Service (INS). The Border Patrol also stepped up enforcement of illegal border crossings from Mexico. After World War II, with concerns about border threats, the Border Patrol continued to grow in the number of agents and in the scope of their responsibilities. In response to increases in the number of undocumented workers, the Border Patrol began a series of programs designed to repatriate illegal immigrants to Mexico. However, the costs of operating these programs was significant, and coupled with the fact that they accomplished little to stem the flow of illegal immigration into the United States, the programs were ultimately eliminated.[154]

The challenges created by large numbers of immigrants continually crossing the border illegally resulted in the passage of new laws in the 1950s. Part of the problem was that when Border Patrol agents apprehended offenders and returned them to Mexico, they would simply turn around and make another attempt to cross the border. In response, new laws allowed agents to arrest immigrants who attempted to cross the border illegally. However, Mexican labor was still needed for the local U.S. economy, so while punitive measures such as arrest and repatriation may have made some sense at the time, the need for Mexican labor trumped concerns about border security.

Thus, while the Border Patrol was given the ability to enforce immigration laws through the use of arrest and deportation, the government sent a mixed message about what to do about undocumented workers. The result was a general ambivalence about the immigration problem. That approach changed as the economy fluctuated and the perceived threat of immigrants taking jobs away from U.S. workers became part of the narrative.

This concern about border security became even more apparent during the 1980s and 1990s, but especially after the terrorist attacks on September 11, 2001, when politicians and policy makers began to more carefully examine the protection of U.S. borders. The emphasis on national security was highlighted by the creation of the Department of Homeland Security (DHS) in 2003. During the reconfiguration of agencies, the U.S.

Border Patrol became a part of the U.S. Customs and Border Protection division, under the authority of DHS.[155]

The Border Patrol Today—Current Challenges

As figure 3-1 shows, the number of Border Patrol agents has significantly increased since 2000, when there were 8,580 agents at the border. In 2018, there were over 16,000 agents, which was a decrease from the high of 18,611 in 2013. In 2018, President Trump called for the hiring of an additional 5,000 Border Patrol agents as part of his border security strategy. The problem, however, was that the agency had, and continues to have, great difficulty in filling those positions. Instead of the proposed 5,000 agents, in 2018, the Border Patrol only added 118 Border Patrol agents, with only 3 stationed along the southern border. In part due to an inability to hire more agents, President Trump has ordered thousands of military troops to the border.[156]

Such a trend is unusual for the Border Patrol, which had seen steady increases in staffing since 2011. Part of the reason is the nature of the job itself, where changes in work schedules are frequent, mandatory overtime is often assigned, and agents are sometimes transferred to remote locations, which can create hardships on their families.[157]

To address these challenges, the Border Patrol has tried to target veterans on military bases, conducted fairs on college campuses, been active on social media, and even targeted rural areas in the hopes of recruiting new members. The selection process has also been revised to attract recruits. In the past, the process was so rigorous that the Office of Inspector General estimated that the Border Patrol would have to screen upward of 750,000 applicants to hire 5,000 new agents.[158]

However, there may be good reasons for such a careful screening process. A recent report by the inspector general's office found that about 40 percent of applicants failed the polygraph exam, and another 25 percent failed due to criminal conduct—including charges of domestic violence, illegal drug use, and other criminal behavior. Thus, two-thirds of the candidate pool cannot even meet the broadest requirements for the job.[159]

Training Border Patrol agents is also an issue. According to a recent audit of federal law enforcement training facilities, even if the agency were able to hire all the agents it needs, the current training facilities are unable to adequately train them all in a timely manner. The report also outlines that leadership within the Border Patrol has difficulty in managing the agency, specifically in allocating its personnel and determining an efficient use of staff.

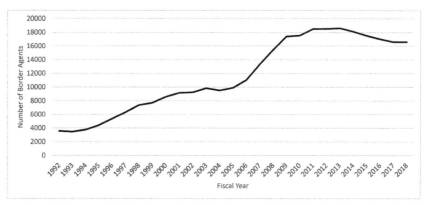

Figure 3-1   Border Patrol Agents along the Southern U.S. Border (U.S. Border Patrol Fiscal Year Staffing Statistics (FY 1992–FY 2018). Available online at https://www.cbp.gov/sites/default/files/assets/documents/2019-Mar/Staffing %20FY1992-FY2018.pdf.)

While the intended goal is to hire agents to patrol the border, in most cases, Border Patrol agents are engaged in a variety of support functions. For instance, according to the inspector general's report, of the 16,717 agents assigned to the southern border in 2017, only 61 percent were actually patrolling the border.[160] Thus, while border security is purported to be a top priority of the Trump administration, with the Border Patrol playing a crucial role in protecting the nation's security, there remain a number of fundamental problems with the agency's ability to meet its mandate.

U.S. Immigration and Customs Enforcement Agency (ICE)

While the U.S. Border Patrol's primary responsibility relates to containing the flow of immigration at the border, the U.S. Immigration and Customs Enforcement (ICE) is designed to enforce immigration laws within the United States. In addition, ICE is charged with identifying and eliminating a wide variety of security issues for the United States. This includes investigating criminal and terrorist activity, human trafficking, computer crime, transnational gang activity, money laundering, and even art theft. The agency has about twenty thousand employees and approximately four hundred offices within the United States and in nearly fifty countries around the world, along with more than two hundred detention centers, and it had an annual budget of $7.8 billion in 2018.[161]

While most people only think of ICE as it relates to immigration enforcement, in fact, ICE has two main divisions: Homeland Security

Investigations (HSI) and Enforcement and Removal Operations (ERO). The latter is the function that most people associate with ICE, as it involves the operation and oversight of detention facilities for illegal immigrants as well as its Removal Division, which handles deportations and other related matters.[162]

HSI includes the investigation and prosecution of a wide range of activities. Within this division are international and domestic operational units, an intelligence-gathering unit, intellectual property units, and other support units, including a SWAT team, an intelligence group, tactical research and a rescue units, designed to assist others in the event of natural disasters.[163]

The ERO is dedicated to the task of enforcing immigration laws and prosecuting and removing immigrants who are identified as illegally living in the United States. ERO officers are also charged with the transportation, detention, and deportation of immigrants. They also supervise released immigrants and the actual prosecution of immigrants who violate either immigration or U.S. criminal laws. ERO manages the Secure Communities program, which identifies removable immigrants located in jails and prisons. This is primarily done through the analysis of fingerprints that are taken when an immigrant has been arrested and booked by a federal, state, or local police department. Once a suspect has been identified as being illegal, ICE officials are notified, and the individual is turned over to them for processing.[164]

ICE's Purpose, Value, and Authority

The creation of ICE was part of a much larger consolidation of agencies under DHS. Prior to the creation of DHS, The INS was responsible for the enforcement of immigration laws. Under the current organizational structure, U.S. Customs and Border Protection monitors ports of entry, U.S. Citizenship and Immigration Services handles visas, and ICE manages detentions and the removal of people who have already been arrested for immigration violations.

In justifying the creation of DHS, President Bush argued that ICE was originally designed to target terrorist activity, but as some experts point out, its creation really represented a shift in how the United States understood the role and value of immigrants. While immigration was once handled by the Department of Commerce and the Department of Labor to reflect the economic opportunities they represented and to address problems as administrative matters, by reassigning that function to DHS, there is a symbolic perception that immigrants, refugees, and asylum seekers are seen as a threat.[165]

As discussed in chapter 2, the current narrative connecting immigration to national security was reflected in the passing of legislation such as the Illegal Immigration Reform and Immigration Responsibility Act (IIRIRA), which was clearly designed to curtail immigration from Central America and Mexico. While this particular law, and others like it, was not initially used to its full effect, today, it allows ICE to pursue, arrest, and detain or deport long-term residents who have committed some type of crime as part of the interior enforcement of immigration policy.[166]

While the establishment of ICE is consistent with the narrative of immigrants as criminals or as a national security threat, some experts have noted that the protection of national security narrative has created problems with clearly identifying ICE's role. The issue is a complicated one, but critics essentially point out that ICE has conflicting responsibilities.

That is, on one hand, DHS is targeted with preventing terrorist attacks, which requires a more forceful, punitive, and quasi-military approach to the problem. At the same time, however, DHS is also responsible for oversight of agencies such as ICE, which are charged with dealing with refugees and asylum seekers and trying to come to grips with a large-scale humanitarian crisis that requires a gentle and supportive approach. As a result, critics ask, how can the country see refugees and immigrants as potential terrorists or threats to national security and also recognize the sensitivity needed to deal with refugees and asylum seekers?[167]

Perhaps even more troubling is the fact that ICE has essentially created its own role in immigration enforcement. This occurred because immigration legislation in the 1990s did not clearly define the role of the federal agencies charged with immigration enforcement. Additionally, given the complexity of the challenges facing these agencies, policy makers offered ICE and the U.S. Border Patrol wide latitude in executing immigration policy. The end result was that ICE in particular was given a significant amount of freedom without a great deal of administrative oversight. This essentially means that ICE not only enforces policy but also makes it.[168]

Such unfettered discretion is a recipe for abuse, and this has generated anti-ICE backlash, with some politicians, advocates, and others calling for the elimination of the agency all together. Abolishing ICE is a consistent strategy offered by Congresswoman Alexandria Ocasio-Cortez and even by some agents within the agency itself, who cite the conflicting problems. Others, such as Senator Kirsten Gillibrand, argue that perhaps the time has come to reassess the purpose and goals of ICE and craft a mission that carefully outlines its purpose.[169]

This lack of clarity in defining an agency's role, coupled with unchecked accountability, leads to abuses. Such a situation is analogous to what happens in prisons, where abuses of inmates often go unaddressed because of inmates' marginalized status. In a similar manner, abuses of immigrants and their due process rights are sometimes ignored because of their status as noncitizens.[170]

The general unwillingness of Congress and policy makers to address the problems of abuses of authority are likely a result of a perception that what ICE agents are doing is protecting national security. In the dirty business of keeping the country safe, the perception may be that certain irregularities or questionable practices must be overlooked since agents need a lot of latitude in carrying out their mission.[171]

Evidence of the dangers of such an approach are seen in numerous reports of abuse violations committed by ICE and Border Patrol agents. For example, in April 2019, *The Intercept* published a report on ICE's treatment of children, and the American Civil Liberties Union (ACLU) of San Diego published a similar report on Border Patrol abuses of children in May 2018. What these investigations reveal is a consistent pattern of physical, verbal, and even sexual abuse—in some cases involving children.

As the reports show, even when cases are brought to prosecutors to hold offenders accountable, only a small percentage of individuals are found guilty, and even then, offenders often go unpunished.[172] This lack of accountability for agent behavior is a consistent theme within the Border Patrol. Between 2013 and 2016, five independent investigations were conducted of the Border Patrol, and each report consistently noted that the agency is in need of greater accountability and training in its approach to immigrant law enforcement.[173]

As Golash-Boza (2015) points out in her study of the detention and deportation process, despite a series of memos from the director, ICE agents routinely disregard stated agency policy goals under the assumption that they could delay compliance or they could simply wait for new leadership to assume control.[174] This will be further discussed in chapter 4, but such practices reflect a lack of sufficient administrative oversight.

The Basis of Federal Enforcement—The 287(g) Program

As part of the Immigration and Nationality Act of 1996, which contains the previously mentioned IIRIRA, section 287(g) was added to the bill, which authorizes ICE to engage in collaborative efforts in the form of written agreements with state, county, and local law enforcement agencies to perform federal immigration enforcement duties.[175]

These agreements, sometimes known as *task force agreements*, typically relate to law enforcement activities, but they also involve what are known as *jail enforcement agreements*, which allow officers to question detained suspects about their immigration status. In some cases, the collaborations between ICE and local law enforcement contain features of both types of agreements, sometimes known as *hybrid agreements*.[176]

In 2010, the Office of Inspector General identified a lack of training by ICE officials and local law enforcement that raised serious questions about the possibility of civil rights violations. As a result, along with other developments occurring at ICE at the time, the Obama administration phased out the use of task force and hybrid agreements at the end of 2012.[177] That same year, ICE began phasing out its 287(g) agreements in favor of other programs that could remove immigrants more efficiently. The Secure Communities program, which began in 2008, was a key component of the ICE strategy. This program automated immigration checks in jails and prisons by linking the fingerprint data that local police used during arrest and booking, thus allowing federal officials to identify a suspect's immigration status.[178]

ICE officials initially argued that participation in the program was voluntary, but it later became mandatory. After criticisms that the majority of people removed through Secure Communities were not criminals, and after a number of lawsuits targeted the mandatory nature of participation in the program, ICE phased out Secure Communities in favor of the new Priority Enforcement Program (PEP). While similar to Secure Communities, PEP contained stricter guidelines as to when ICE officials could issue what are known as *immigration detainers*, which request that suspects be detained until they can take custody of them, even if they had legally been released for the original crime. In early 2017, however, with the start of the Trump administration, PEP was eliminated, and the criteria used in the original Secure Communities program were reinstated.[179]

Sanctuary Cities and Policies

As was mentioned in chapter 2, sanctuary cities and policies are those that prohibit or curtail the role of local law enforcement in immigration enforcement. The rationale behind them is that one's immigration status should not factor into whether a witness or victim of a crime reports it to the police. Currently, there are more than six hundred cities and counties and eight states that have adopted sanctuary policies.[180]

As previously mentioned, as part of the Secure Communities program, ICE has increased the number of detainer requests to local law enforcement agencies.[181] However, detainer requests are controversial, particularly since they deprive people of their constitutional rights to due process and unlawful seizure protections. As a result of a series of court rulings, some cities adopted sanctuary policies not on the basis of ideology but as a way of limiting their legal liability from suspects who pursue legal action.[182]

Local Law Enforcement and Immigration

Despite the controversy surrounding sanctuary cities and the role of local law enforcement in the immigration debate, it is worth noting that over the sweep of U.S. history, local law enforcement has routinely been involved in immigration enforcement, even in instances where departmental policy explicitly prohibited it. As far back as 1919, when the main perceived threat to the country was communists, local law enforcement officials, working with the U.S. Attorney's office and federal law enforcement officials, raided homes, bookstores, union halls, and other locations and detained immigrants with the goal of identifying, arresting, and deporting communists who posed a threat to national security. Once the "threat" of communism ended, local police were routinely involved with immigration officials in making arrests and conducting sweeps.[183]

From the 1920s to the 1950s, local police officers worked with public welfare officials and federal immigration officers to deport immigrants who received public assistance. Similarly, during Operation Wetback, the Border Patrol actually created an economic incentive plan in their collaboration with the local police department in El Paso, Texas, where they paid officers a stipend for every undocumented person arrested and turned over to them.[184]

In the 1970s, as a result of court cases and legislation, the authority of local law enforcement in immigration matters was carefully defined, particularly as it related to the ability of officers to stop, detain, or arrest people on the basis of their immigration status. However, this did not prevent officers from making arrests without the legal authority to do so. For instance, in the late 1970s, the Los Angeles Police Department issued a policy, known as Special Order 40, which prohibited officers from inquiring about a person's immigration status or from making immigration arrests. However, a report by the U.S. Commission on Civil Rights found that some officers made arrests despite specific policies prohibiting this practice. The report also found that other departments took a more permissive attitude toward detaining and arresting immigrants, often arguing it was an acceptable strategy given that they believed immigrants were responsible for the crime problem in the United States.[185]

In the 1980s, a more refined distinction was made with regard to civil and criminal immigration violations; state and local police could enforce criminal violations committed by immigrants, but not because of their immigration status. Such restrictions were difficult to determine, of course, given the extent and complexity of such problems as human trafficking, the War on Drugs, and other international crimes that resulted in the arrest of immigrants.

In the early 2000s, many states began enacting laws designed to address the challenges immigrants faced, such as providing opportunities to obtain driver's licenses or access to health care or educational benefits to residents regardless of their immigration status. Many other laws, however, were anti-immigration in nature. For example, some states attempted to require immigrants to maintain possession of proof of legal status at all times as a condition for obtaining social services, and some mandated documentation for employment or declared English as the official language of a given community. In 2007, for instance, Oklahoma passed HB 1804, which required the police to check the immigration status of any person suspected of being an undocumented immigrant and required proof of legal presence as a condition for accessing social services. The bill also made it a felony to offer undocumented workers transportation, a job, or shelter.

In 2010, Arizona passed SB 1070, better known as the "show me your papers" law, which required police officers to investigate a person's immigration status during any interaction and mandated that noncitizens carry proof of their legal presence.[186] Several other states passed similar legislation that was designed to deter prospective immigrants from moving into those states and to make it difficult for residing immigrants to remain, something advocates of these laws called a form of self-deportation.[187]

Many of these laws were challenged because they violated the federal government's authority over immigration laws. In 2012, the Supreme Court ruled that most of Arizona's SB 1070 was unconstitutional, stating that the state could not require local police to verify people's citizenship and officers could not make warrantless arrests on the suspicion that a person might be undocumented. However, the court approved the provision that allowed officers to ask about an individual's legal status during an encounter with that person.[188]

The passing of laws such as those in Oklahoma and Arizona was part of the larger process of criminalizing immigrants and their status in the United States. While discussions of citizenship, belongingness, and how one becomes a naturalized citizen are subject to debate and discussion, these types of laws speak more broadly to the idea that residents often do not perceive of immigrants as having a legitimate place (or space) in this country. Most citizens would never consider it an acceptable strategy to be required to carry papers to prove they are legal residents of the country or a state, and they would likely not consider it appropriate for police officers to routinely stop and search citizens based on the fact that they have the appearance of being an outsider. Yet, in some jurisdictions, this was the approach for Latino and Mexican immigrants.

While such policies are not the norm and do not reflect the majority of communities around the country, they nevertheless have an impact on how the police see their relationship and interactions with immigrants. Similarly, it also shapes how immigrants, whether they are documented or not, view the police. At the practical level, many police chiefs express concerns about local involvement in immigration enforcement, both from the vantage point of the officers on the street as well as at the organizational level in a particular police department. Additionally, the uneven level of participation in the 287(g) program creates disparity problems for immigrants and community residents regarding the expectations for living in a given area.[189]

For those police chiefs who are supportive of collaborations with federal immigration officials, there are a series of strategies and tactics that they argue are consistent with their mission to actively identify, detain, and deport those who are in this country illegally. In fact, some police chiefs have created incentives for officers to achieve certain benchmarks for the number of traffic stops, citations, and arrests of immigrants. While this may sound like racial profiling and discriminatory policing, others argue that it is simply an internal strategy to motivate employees to follow a particular policy.

Additionally, as many scholars point out, the use of driver's licenses and proof of legal residency requirements and valid IDs make immigrants more likely to be arrested but not less employable. Deporting all immigrants, even all undocumented ones, is not possible or even practical since their labor is needed to sustain the national and local economies. However, keeping immigrants as outsiders in terms of their social status serves to keep them compliant and as an exploitable workforce. That is, immigration enforcement is not just about removing people from the country; it is also about controlling the ones that remain so they never really demand equal treatment.[190]

Finally, some police officials are more likely to support collaborations with immigration enforcement for political reasons. As Armenta (2017) points out, while municipal police chiefs generally oppose involvement in immigration enforcement, for the reasons outlined below, local sheriffs, who are elected officials, are often more likely to support collaborations with ICE officials given the perceived popularity of such efforts and the need to appear responsive to the voting public.[191]

Challenges for Local Police in Immigration Enforcement

While the issues surrounding federal enforcement of immigration laws have created a host of issues for the public, policy makers, politicians, and the immigrants themselves, efforts to encourage state and local police to participate in the 287(g) program, or some version of it, result in significant problems for law enforcement.[192] This is true despite President Trump's consistent effort to leverage state and local police agencies in immigration enforcement. In fact, in 2017, Trump called for the creation of a "deportation force" to facilitate the removal of immigrants from the United States.[193] This would be accomplished by empowering state and local law enforcement to expand their roles in immigration enforcement and by threatening to withhold federal funds from any city that failed to cooperate.

To be fair, very little empirical research has been done on the relationship between the police and immigrants. There are more studies on the use of police discretion and on police-community relations, but these typically focus on the interactions between the police and African Americans and other U.S. citizens. However, there are few studies that examine the relationship between the police and immigrants. What is known will be used to shape the discussion in this chapter.

For example, according to a study by the Major Cities Chiefs Association (MCCA), which is a collection of police chiefs who operate in large cities around the country, there are several issues that impact local law enforcement's ability to participate in immigration enforcement. The main areas cited by the MCCA study include the erosion of trust between police and local residents and minority groups, inadequate resource allocation for immigration enforcement, issues relating to training that is both expensive and time-consuming, and concerns about the autonomy and decentralization of local law enforcement.[194]

Trust and Federal Immigration Enforcement

According to the MCCA, entangling local law enforcement with federal immigration enforcement "would result in increased crime against immigrants and in the broader community, create a class of silent victims, and eliminate the potential for assistance from immigrants in solving crimes or preventing future terroristic acts."[195]

Part of the challenge is that residents, particularly immigrants, who already have concerns about the trustworthiness of the police, would be less likely to report crime out of a fear that they might be deported. Given the pivotal role the community plays in the success of any law enforcement effort, the erosion of trust and the escalation of tensions between the police and resident groups will likely result in decreased collaboration. This has a significant impact on crime rates since the police cannot be successful in preventing crime without the buy-in of community residents. In short, if state and local law enforcement is involved in immigration enforcement, the efforts to build relationships with community residents will be negatively impacted.[196]

Inadequate Resources for Federal Immigration Enforcement

Another criticism of participation in the 287(g) program is that local law enforcement agencies are engaging in federal immigration enforcement without adequate reimbursement of expenses. While ICE may provide some reimbursement for detention costs in some cases, it provides minimal funding for training, equipment, and services. State and local police agencies assume all costs for salaries and benefits and those expenses related to travel costs, housing, and training.[197]

Lack of Adequate Training for Officers for Federal Immigration Enforcement

In addition to the lack of funds available for state and local agencies to engage in federal immigration enforcement, there is generally a lack of adequate training for those officers who wish to participate in the process. While some training is provided, the real challenge is how to prevent racial profiling and discriminatory behavior by officers, who may conclude that anyone appearing to be Latino is a suspected undocumented immigrant. It may appear that racial profiling of African Americans is, arguably, on the decline, but such does not appear to be the case for Latinos, particularly in those jurisdictions with large immigrant populations.[198]

Legal Liability and Federal Immigration Enforcement

In addition to the challenges created by discriminatory practices by local police officers, there is the concern about legal liability when officers stop, search, and detain Latinos or those who appear to be immigrants. There is a growing number of lawsuits for warrantless searches of immigrants or instances where ICE detainer requests were inappropriately honored because of illegal detention. For instance, the city of Allentown, Pennsylvania, and Lehigh County, Pennsylvania, settled with a U.S. citizen who was detained for three days pursuant to a detainer request that ICE mistakenly issued. Similarly, Salt Lake County, Utah, paid $75,000 to settle a case brought by an individual held on an ICE detainer for forty-six days after he had posted bail. Still another case occurred in Clackamas County, Oregon, where a woman sued because she had been detained for two weeks based solely on an ICE detainer request.[199]

Organizational Issues and Immigration Enforcement

There are also organizational challenges in immigration enforcement, as some police chiefs who have decided to work with ICE have created a series of incentives for their officers to engage in selective enforcement of immigrants. Such practices have resulted in creating a climate of fear and tension within communities for all minorities, not just Latinos and Mexicans.

As Armenta (2017) points out in her study of policing and immigration in Nashville, Tennessee, there is real value in examining the role of local law enforcement from what has been described as "bottom-up" policing. In other words, while it may make sense at one level to promote the idea that state and local law enforcement can play a significant role in immigration enforcement, such practices interfere with the mission and goals of local police to protect and serve. Perhaps more importantly, however, some police chiefs create and implement misguided policies that may seem at first glance to provide clear guidelines about officers' workload and accountability but actually create the much larger problem of zero tolerance policing.[200]

Broken Windows and Criminalizing Immigrants

The broken windows theory was first described in an article in *The Atlantic* by James Q. Wilson and George Kelling. The basic premise of the model is that disorder is a key element in understanding and preventing crime. Disorder, in the form of graffiti, trash, abandoned cars, furniture, poor lighting, and broken windows in abandoned buildings, creates a climate of fear that causes residents to avoid those areas.[201] Without a surveillance network of residents to report crimes when they occur, the areas become ripe for all manner of criminal activity. The goal, then, is to prevent residents from becoming afraid of an area in the first place, and the primary way to do that is to give the impression that the area is cared for and valued and by addressing minor forms of disorder.[202]

The police play a critical role in preventing disorder by enforcing laws that contribute to the perception that the area is not safe. Despite its popularity with policy makers, police officials, and even the general public, the research on the effectiveness of the broken windows theory is mixed. For example, Braga, Welsh, and Schnell (2015) found that aggressive order maintenance efforts had no significant impact on reducing crime. However, other efforts can have modest reductions in crime, depending on the type of strategy used. Another problem related to the research on broken windows theory is that police departments often use strategies under the umbrella of broken windows theory that are not accurate definitions of the theory, thereby creating problems in assessing their effects.[203]

Perhaps the best example of the challenges in using broken windows occurred in New York City during the 1990s, when broken windows policing essentially morphed into zero tolerance policing. Under this strategy, disorder was targeted by arresting or issuing citations to anyone who violated any law. Zero tolerance policing not only eliminates the use of judgment and discretion by officers, a key component of effective law enforcement, but using the number of arrests and citations as benchmarks for assessing the effectiveness of the reduction of disorder is misguided—not all interactions with citizens end in an arrest or citation. Yet, these informal interactions are important factors in reducing crime and disorder issues in a community.[204]

What appears to matter a great deal in reducing crime, fear, and disorder in a community is resident involvement in the process as well as the development of informal social control strategies.[205] These strategies engender trust between local residents and the police department and create a climate of respect for the civil liberties of everyone, including offenders. Thus, while some may argue that zero tolerance policing works in terms of reducing crime, there are a host of factors that must be considered in assessing the effectiveness of such an approach. More importantly, zero tolerance policing is not the same thing as the broken windows theory.[206]

Broken Windows, Zero Tolerance Policing, and Immigration Enforcement

The use of zero tolerance policing as a justification for reducing crime and disorder in a community is easily applied to immigration enforcement. As Armenta (2017) found, the growth of the Latino and Mexican populations in the Nashville area created a climate of fear among citizens similar to what has been seen in many cities around the country. In response, there was considerable controversy about attempts to pass laws designed to severely restrict and control the lives of immigrants in Nashville.[207]

For example, a concerted effort was made by city officials to declare English as the official language of Nashville. Additionally, a new police chief in Nashville agreed to participate in the 287(g) program, which required officers to work with immigration officials to identify and detain undocumented immigrants. Perhaps the most significant change that occurred in Nashville was related to the ability of immigrants to obtain a driver's license.

When large numbers of Latino immigrants began arriving in Tennessee, they were eligible for driver's licenses and identification cards if they could prove they were state residents. In 1997, the law was changed in response to the Personal Responsibility and Work Reconciliation Act, or what is more commonly known as welfare reform.[208] This new federal law decentralized welfare so that states could customize the funds based on the particular needs of its population. It also required states to collect Social Security numbers on driver's license applications so that states could identify parents who were noncompliant in making child support payments. One unintended consequence of this strategy was that it effectively excluded all foreign-born residents without a Social Security number from obtaining a valid driver's license or an identity card.[209]

In 2004, after much discussion and debate, Tennessee passed a law that restricted driver's licenses to U.S. citizens and legal permanent residents; all others were to receive a new document called the Certificate for Driving (CFD). There were many problems with the CFD. Three years later, the CFD program was eliminated, and new legislation was passed that allowed citizens and legal permanent residents to obtain a standard Tennessee driver's license, with temporary ones issued for legal immigrants who could prove they were authorized to be in the United States for a year. The problem was that this latter consideration excluded thousands of Tennessee residents who were foreign-born who could not prove their legal status because of the way visas were issued.[210]

As Armenta (2017) points out, the debate about driver's license eligibility, the attempts to pass an English First policy, and the willingness of sheriff's offices to participate in the 287(g) program served to marginalize Latino residents. More directly to the use of zero tolerance policing, the challenges related to obtaining a valid driver's license or adequate proof of legal residency provided the police department with the ability to issue citations or to arrest immigrants who did not have the proper documentation when stopped by officers.

The problems became particularly acute for immigrants when a new police chief was hired in Nashville who stressed what he called *accountability-driven policing*, an order-maintenance approach to crime and disorder. As the chief publicly proclaimed, he expected officers to be "proactive," meaning he wanted them to target misdemeanor and non-criminal offenses under the rationale that this leads to a greater ability to identify and intervene in more serious forms of crime. In other words, the chief embraced the idea of the broken windows theory but implemented it as a form of zero tolerance policing. This disproportionately impacted Latino and Mexican immigrants. They were most affected by this strategy largely because the primary approach was to increase the number of vehicle stops.[211]

Aside from the problem of essentially focusing on people of color, the manner in which this approach was implemented was problematic as well. For example, if a police department provides incentives for officers to aggressively target traffic stops and rewards officers who generate large numbers of arrests and citations, it is only reasonable to believe that officers will respond to such benchmarks. This is a common strategy in policing, as arrests and tickets are a quantifiable way of determining the workload and effectiveness of patrol officers. However, the difference is that under normal circumstances, officers do not target particular types of offenders to meet these objectives.

However, in Nashville, and likely in other departments that used this approach, the easiest way to meet those benchmarks was to target Latino and Mexican drivers because the laws surrounding obtaining legal driver's licenses, CFDs, or other documentation, which remained controversial and difficult to navigate, created a climate in which officers could generate stops, citations and arrests with minimal effort. Thus, as a reward to officers who engaged in "proactive policing," those who had high arrest and citation rates were given special consideration in terms of their choice of assignment, scheduling, promotions, and favorable evaluations. In sum, the cultural climate in the department was one in which officers attempted to make as many stops as possible. Latinos and Mexican drivers were the easiest way to meet department benchmarks since they were more likely to have committed some type of violation given the way the laws were written at the time.[212]

In fact, officers were so focused on engaging in traffic stops that they would often attempt to avoid or delay answering actual calls for service since more credit was given to issuing citations and making arrests. Additionally, given the amount of time it takes to process suspects after arresting them, officers routinely issued citations, thereby giving themselves more time during their shifts to increase the number of stops they made.[213]

Officers also often took a legalistic approach, particularly when vehicle stops involved Latinos, meaning they were more likely to issue a citation even when the situation could have been resolved with a different approach. Additionally, given the potential "yield" as a result of an encounter with a Latino, meaning a higher chance that the suspect might be an undocumented immigrant or someone who did not have a valid driver's license, officers sought out Latinos and tended to focus their patrol activities in areas with higher concentrations of Latinos.[214]

In the larger sense, while police discretion is an important part of the role of the police in their ability to enforce the law, misguided incentives, such as quotas or benchmarks for stops, arrests, and citations, create a climate where officers are actually more interested in those types of interactions with citizens than in patrolling neighborhoods, developing relationships with residents, and engendering trust within the community. These are enduring issues in policing, but current immigration efforts and tactics only exacerbate a thorny relationship between the police and minorities.

For the immigrants themselves, the challenges are considerable, particularly since some of the offenses they commit would not be handled the same way if they were U.S. citizens. While one could argue that undocumented immigrants made that choice when they chose to enter or remain in the country illegally, the method of handling these infractions in the past did not strain the criminal justice system nor did it invalidate the contributions immigrants make to the culture, the country, and the economy.

As previously mentioned, in the past, these acts were often considered minor infractions or even administrative matters, but with the change in policy, they became felonies, making immigrants eligible for more serious punishments. Adding to the difficulty, the complaints and concerns of noncitizens are unlikely to gain any degree of consideration by the system, its agents, or even the general public.

In chapter 4, we explore what occurs once officers identify and arrest an immigrant suspected of residing in the United States illegally. As we will see, while the original goal of a stepped-up immigration enforcement policy was designed to target the most serious and violent offenders, the difficulty in doing so resulted in a more holistic approach, where all immigrants are given the same type of treatment in the courts, without much consideration of their circumstances. This approach is not typically used in the normal processing of court cases, but given the number of immigrants entering the system, it has become overburdened with a backlog of cases. The result is a blunted sensitivity to the people involved and their circumstances and the elimination of the use of discretion to effectively resolve a case.

CHAPTER FOUR

Immigration and the Courts

- "The immigration courts are facing an existential crisis. The current system is irredeemably dysfunctional and on the brink of collapse."[215]
  —American Bar Association Report on Immigration Courts

- "We have a generous asylum policy that is meant to protect those who, through no fault of their own, cannot coexist in their home country no matter where they go because of persecution based on fundamental things like their religion or nationality. Unfortunately, this system is currently subject to rampant abuse and fraud. And as this system becomes overloaded with fake claims, it cannot deal effectively with just claims. The surge in trials, hearings, appeals, bond proceedings has been overwhelming."[216]
  —Attorney General Jeff Sessions

- "[Trump's quota plan for immigration judges] is an unprecedented act which compromises the integrity of the court and pressures judges to quickly complete cases, possibly pitting their job security against the interests of immigrants."[217]
  —Ashley Tabaddor, president of the National Association of Immigration Judges

In chapter 3, we explored the role of the police in enforcing current immigration policy in the United States. As previously mentioned, there are two primary paths to immigration enforcement: federal and state/local. The federal agencies responsible for immigration are primarily the U.S. Border Patrol and ICE. While each has a particular role to play, with the Border Patrol primarily responsible for preventing illegal immigrants from entering the United States, ICE's immigration function relates to interior enforcement, meaning those undocumented workers who already live in the United States.

At the state and local levels, there are a host of issues and challenges presented by law enforcement agencies becoming involved in federal immigration enforcement. These include philosophical, legal, and practical issues that explain why local police departments are often reluctant to collaborate with federal immigration agencies. In addition, for those departments that support their involvement in immigration enforcement, the incentives used to encourage officers to be proactive in identifying, arresting, and detaining undocumented immigrants creates a number of questions about the equal treatment of immigrants. Moreover, policies that redefine certain acts as crimes, or elevates their seriousness to felonies, enables officials to detain and deport Latino and Mexican immigrants in a way not experience by other minority groups.

In this chapter, we examine what happens after an arrest. While the vast majority of cases are handled through the issuing of a citation, largely the product of the incentive programs where police officers are rewarded for large numbers of traffic stops, searches, and interactions with immigrants, when arrests are made, the cases are typically processed through immigration courts. As we will see, immigration courts are not like their criminal counterparts, and the rules used to determine guilt or innocence are different for immigrants than for criminal suspects. Additionally, because of the heavy emphasis on the enforcement of immigration policy, with billions of dollars dedicated to Border Patrol and ICE, far less funding has been allocated for immigration courts. The end result is a significant backlog of cases.

While this is problematic for many reasons, given that many immigrants awaiting trial are detained in jails and prisons, there does not seem to be much of an intended effort to address this deficiency. Part of the reason may stem from the fact that many of these immigrants are incarcerated, meaning that, for all intents and purposes, they have been removed from society, regardless of the issue of due process or the actual outcome of the case. Of course, there are implications for this strategy as well, primarily as it relates to the denial of rights to noncitizens and the impact incarceration has on their families. The impact of detention and deportation will be discussed in another chapter. First, it is important to describe the process by which immigrants' arrests are handled.

U.S. Immigration Courts

There are many reasons why people end up in immigration court. Some people are refugees who are fleeing their native countries and seeking asylum in the United States. Other people may end up in immigration court because they face deportation and want to request what is known as a *cancellation of removal*, which would allow them to remain in the United States. A person may also end up in immigration court during the process of becoming a legal permanent resident of the United States.

The agency primarily responsible for immigration enforcement is the Executive Office for Immigration Review (EOIR). After DHS charges an individual with violating immigration laws, EOIR decides whether that individual is removable from the country. If so, a determination must be made about whether the person qualifies for protection or relief from removal.[218] To make these determinations, EOIR's Office of the Chief Immigration Judge (OCIJ) has approximately 414 immigration judges who conduct removal hearings and other administrative court proceedings in approximately sixty immigration courts nationwide.[219]

The federal circuit courts may also issue precedent decisions on immigration issues that are then controlling in that particular federal circuit. The Office of the Chief Administrative Hearing Officer (OCAHO) also resides within EOIR and hears cases involving employer sanctions for illegal hiring of unauthorized workers, employment eligibility verification violations, unfair immigration-related employment practices, and some forms of document fraud.[220] Unlike federal district court judges, who preside over criminal and civil cases involving the federal government, immigration courts have twice the caseload, far less administrative support, and a much smaller budget.

Differences between Immigration Court and Criminal Court

What has to be remembered is that immigration court is a different experience than a criminal court; the latter focuses on due process, the right to counsel, and constitutional protections, and the burden of proof must be beyond a reasonable doubt. In fact, even the agency responsible for governing immigration courts is different: the Department of Homeland Security operates immigration courts. This may not seem like an important distinction, but consider the fact that the Department of Justice (which normally handles criminal cases) is deeply concerned with issues relating to due process and the protection of rights, while DHS is an enforcement agency that is dedicated to the arrest, detention, and deportation of suspects who have been incarcerated without the same protections as a U.S. citizen.[221] Not only is DHS responsible for immigration courts, but people coming before these courts do not have the same constitutional safeguards afforded criminal defendants.

Immigrants, even those who are undocumented, are entitled to some level of protection through the equal protection clause of the Fourteenth

Amendment to the U.S. Constitution. This clause guarantees due process and equal protection for all persons. This means that immigrants have a right to have their cases heard by an impartial judge, the right to present evidence, and the right to retain counsel (but it is not provided free of charge, as in the case of indigent defendants in criminal court). The reason for these distinctions is that immigration violations are considered a civil matter, not a criminal one. Moreover, due process is often compromised in immigration court in favor of efforts to quickly dispense of cases. In fact, as we shall see, a growing number of immigrants are never given the opportunity to attend a hearing because their cases were decided based on expedited reviews.[222]

Another distinction is the role and status of the judge in immigration court. Unlike criminal cases, where the judge is an impartial participant who is an independent member of the judiciary, the judge in immigration court is an employee of the Department of Justice whose duties and responsibilities are determined by the U.S. attorney general, who serves at the pleasure of the president. The role of the immigration court judge is to advise immigrants of their legal rights, to evaluate and assess the evidence, to hear testimony, to adjudicate waivers and applications for relief, and to issue final orders of removal.

Unlike federal district court judges, questions arise about a conflict of interest concerning immigration judges because they lack the autonomy to make rulings independent of outside influences. Given that they work for the U.S. attorney general, itself a highly political role, some critics point out that immigration court essentially becomes a rubber stamp for whatever the president and U.S. attorney general want to happen. Failure to comply with decisions that may run counter to the law, ethics, or political affiliation can result in termination for those judges. Federal judges have none of those concerns since they are free to make decisions based on the law and are shielded from political scrutiny.[223]

The prosecutor in immigration court is an employee of ICE, which is a division of DHS, whose mission is to protect the country from terrorists and other threats. It is worth noting that DHS operates under the authority of the executive branch of government, which raises questions about equity and fairness for immigrants who come to the court for a hearing.

Notice to Appear

When DHS initiates removal proceedings against an individual, a Notice to Appear (NTA) is issued. This is the formal charging document that is filed with EOIR, which then takes charge of the proceedings and issues a decision on whether the individual may be deported.

There are essentially three reasons why someone would receive an NTA: (1) the person is an "arriving alien" who has been stopped at a port of entry prior to admittance; (2) the person is already in the United States but has not yet been formally admitted; or (3) a person has been admitted into the United States but is not eligible for deportation, the reasons for which are described in the NTA document.[224]

A recent change in policy shows that the U.S. Citizenship and Immigration Services (USCIS) typically issued an NTA if the person had a criminal conviction. Today, an immigrant will receive an NTA and be placed into removal proceedings if his or her application for a visa, green card, or naturalization application is denied. An NTA may also be issued if DHS deems that the person has committed an act deemed criminal in nature. This is true whether or not the person has been arrested or charged with the activity.[225] The latter is an area of concern since it gives DHS wide latitude in the arrest and potential deportation of noncitizens.

After the NTA is issued, DHS files the charges with one of the EOIR's immigration courts, which then notifies the person charged with the alleged violation of the protocol for the removal proceedings, the right to seek counsel at his or her own expense, and what happens if the person fails to appear at the scheduled hearing.[226]

During the hearing, a DHS attorney, who represents the government, presents evidence and makes a case as to why the individual should be removed. The person charged, known as the *respondent*, can present his or her own evidence, with or without an attorney, or apply for protection in what is known as *relief from removal*. The immigration judge initially explains the respondent's rights and which laws have been violated. The judge also hears the testimony and renders a decision based on applicable laws and federal regulations.[227]

If the judge determines the respondent is eligible for removal, and if the respondent wants to apply for protection or relief from removal, an individual merits hearing is scheduled, where both sides present arguments and evidence related to the application for relief. Should the immigration judge determine that protection or relief from removal is warranted, the judge then "grants" the application, meaning he or she approves the request.[228]

Asylum Cases

Generally speaking, asylum relief may be granted to people who are unable or unwilling to return to their country of nationality because of

Table 4-1   Affirmative Asylum Cases Filed with USCIS by Country of Origin, FY 2015–2017

	2017		2016		2015	
	Number	Percentage	Number	Percentage	Number	Percentage
Totals	139,801	100%	115,433	100%	83,032	100%
Venezuela	27,579	19.7	14,792	12.8	5,664	6.8
China	16,792	12.0	16,508	14.3	13,877	16.7
Guatemala	12,175	8.7	10,720	9.3	8,277	10.0
Mexico	11,941	8.5	14,660	12.7	8,820	10.6
El Salvador	11,913	8.5	9,414	8.2	7,133	8.6
Honduras	6,978	5.0	5,698	4.9	5,147	6.2
India	4,057	2.9	3,230	2.8	2,276	2.7
Haiti	3,860	2.8	3,004	2.6	1,918	2.3
Columbia	2,650	1.9	1,395	1.2	820	1.0
Russia	2,649	1.9	1,909	1.7	1,447	1.7
All Other	39,207	28.0	34,073	29.5	27,653	33.3

Source: Mossaad, Nadwa. (2019). *Annual Flow Report: Refugees and Asylees 2017.* Department of Homeland Security. Available at https://www.dhs.gov/sites/default/files /publications/Refugees_Asylees_2017.pdf.

past persecution or a fear of being persecuted because of their race, religion, nationality, or membership in a particular group.[229]

An asylum application generally must be filed within one year of the applicant's arrival in the United States, and if the applicant is granted relief, he or she is are allowed to stay as a resident of the United States. Asylum relief may also be granted to an applicant's spouse and children who are in the United States and were included in the approved application. In time, applicants may apply for jobs, permanent residence, and citizenship. Individuals may also apply for what is known as *defensive asylum applications*, such as when they are in removal proceedings.[230]

According to DHS data, in 2019, an estimated 139,801 affirmative asylum applications were received by USCIS in 2017. After eight years of steady increases, this represents the first year of a decline. Venezuela had the most affirmative asylum applications (27,579) followed by China (16,792), Guatemala (12,175), Mexico (11,941), and El Salvador (11,913). The number of defensive asylum applications filed with EOIR also reflected a decrease from the previous year, with 111,887 applications compared to 121,418 in 2017 (See table 4-1).[231]

Along with a decrease in applications, there were lower numbers of approvals of those petitions. In 2018, USCIS approved 30 percent of affirmative asylum applications, a significant decline from the 37 percent from 2017 and 43 percent in 2016. Approval of applications by EOIR also declined from 43 percent in 2016 to 33 percent in 2018.[232]

Due to the large application volume and limited resources, both the affirmative and defensive asylum systems have a significant backlog of pending cases. At the end of January 2019, according to USCIS, there were 352,277 affirmative cases pending, and EOIR reported 821,726 total immigration cases pending, about 30 percent of which were defensive asylum cases.[233]

Appeals in Immigration Court

Immigrants may appeal an immigration judge's ruling or deportation order to the Board of Immigration Appeals (BIA), an agency within the Department of Justice. Less than 10 percent of all cases are appealed, however. The BIA consists of approximately twenty members and hears approximately thirty thousand cases per year. As it is with other appeals bodies, the BIA often issues "affirm without opinion" decisions, where it confirms a deportation order without an explanation or rationale. Typical of most appeals courts, the BIA reviews cases in an effort to discover whether procedural or other errors were made during the removal hearings. In most cases, the BIA decides cases through a review of court transcripts and other documents, although, in some instances, it does hear oral arguments from both parties. BIA decisions are binding, unless they are overruled by the attorney general or an appeal is granted through the federal courts.

As previously mentioned, the U.S. attorney general plays a key role in immigration courts. Federal regulations allow the attorney general to overrule the BIA, to determine the types of appeals it will review, and even to remove BIA members at his or her discretion. In the case of appeals, the attorney general can intervene at any point in the appeals process, take over a case, or inform the BIA to turn the case over to the Office of the Attorney General. This is unusual, however, and typically occurs only once or twice a year.

In the event an immigrant wants to appeal his or her case beyond the BIA, he or she may appeal to a U.S. court of appeals. However, only about 2 percent of all cases heard each year make it this far; in 2016, only 5,240 immigration appeals were filed with federal appellate courts around the country. Part of the reason for this is the lack of success; only about 8 percent of cases filed to appellate courts are granted.

The outcomes of appeals are typically twofold: the immigrant is allowed to remain in the United States or, in the case of an error made by the BIA, the case is referred back to the BIA for correction. However, although an immigrant may not be deported while the case is working its way through immigration court, no such protection is provided when the case is appealed to the federal courts. According to one estimate, roughly half of all immigrants who will have their appeal granted at the federal level risk being deported while the appeal is pending.[234]

As previously mentioned, the attorney general has a great deal of discretion in immigration cases and can overrule a decision by an immigration judge or the BIA. However, such is not a common practice. In 2018, there were three such instances, and the attorney general made modifications to existing policy, such as deciding that victims of domestic abuse and gang violence were not eligible for asylum, as these situations did not meet the criteria. Additionally, the attorney general has ruled that immigration judges are not required to give asylum seekers a full hearing, nor can judges use the practice of administrative closure to remove cases from their dockets. The latter is a discretionary act used by immigration judges in the past to ease the backlog of cases.[235]

Right to Counsel and Legal Representation in Immigration Cases

Immigrants typically appear before the immigration court without the benefit of an attorney. A recent report from the American Immigration Council (AIC) found that only about a third of all immigrants (37%) are represented by an attorney, and a far lower percentage of those who are in jail awaiting their hearings are represented (see figure 4-1).

The reasons for this are related to the expense of hiring an attorney as well as the location where the trial is held. In smaller towns and rural locations, there may not be an attorney skilled in immigration law available. So if an attorney is hired, he or she must travel a considerable distance to meet with the client and appear before the immigration court.[236]

Additionally, immigrants do not necessarily have their immigration hearings in the district in which the offense occurred, as is the case in a criminal trial. Instead, immigrants can be transferred to detention facilities virtually anywhere, often a considerable distance from family, attorneys, and access to the evidence they need to obtain for their cases. Complicating matters further is the fact that the person is in jail, which means he or she cannot visit an attorney at his or her office. Instead, the person has to rely on the telephones in the detention facility, which are sometimes not available.

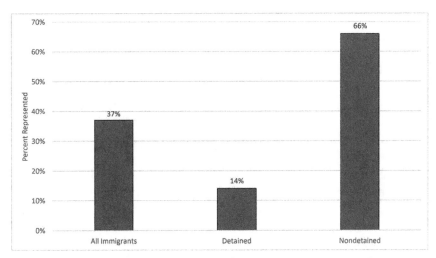

Figure 4-1   Rates of Representation of Immigrants at Removal Hearings, 2007–2012

Another complication relates to the rules governing attorney visits, which are strict and limit the ability of attorneys to communicate with their clients.[237] It is also worth mentioning that immigration enforcement is reliant upon detention. Under current benchmarks, federal funding allows for approximately thirty-four thousand noncitizens to be held in federal detention centers, jails, and prisons each day, which will be discussed more in chapter 5. Such a stipulation raises questions about whether the goal is to detain in the first place, since an emphasis on detention as part of the overall immigration strategy presents challenges for those who need legal representation to obtain it.[238]

However, the research suggests that the impact of having legal representation in immigration cases is critical to their outcome. Drawing on data from over 1.2 million deportation cases between 2007 and 2012, one of the main findings of the AIC study is that access to attorneys is difficult and varies based on a number of factors, including where the case is heard as well as whether the immigrant is detained prior to the hearing. Part of the reason for this, as has been mentioned, was that, unlike a criminal trial, immigrant cases do not provide an attorney if the immigrant cannot afford one. This means the process of obtaining representation is expensive, unless the case is taken by an attorney on a pro bono basis. Immigrants in detention are the least likely to obtain an attorney; as seen in figure 4-1, only 14 percent have an attorney compared to nearly 66 percent of nondetained immigrants.[239]

Additionally, there are more attorneys who are skilled in immigration law in large cities compared to smaller ones, thereby providing greater opportunities for immigrants to obtain counsel. For instance, in New York City, approximately 87 percent of immigrants are able to retain an attorney if they are not detained; in contrast, Atlanta's representation rate was about half that. More importantly, immigrants whose hearings are in smaller cities were more than four times less likely to have an attorney to represent them than those with hearings in large cities (11% vs. 47%, respectively).[240]

Additionally, the rates of representation vary according to the nationality of immigrants, with Mexican immigrants having the lowest representation rate (21%) and Chinese immigrants having the highest (92%). Similarly, the rates of detention also vary considerably by immigrant group. Mexicans had the highest detention rates (78%) compared to Chinese immigrants (4%).[241]

Why do these figures matter? As shown in figure 4-2, immigrants who have an attorney present during their hearing have dramatically different outcomes to their cases at every stage of the court process.

For instance, in about half of the cases where detained immigrants obtained counsel, they were more than twice as likely to have their cases terminated or granted some type of consideration (49% vs. 23%, respectively). Similarly, those who were released and those who were detained were more likely to have their cases resolved in their favor if they had legal representation at the hearing.[242]

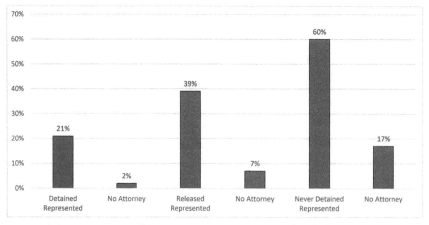

Figure 4-2 Percentage of Immigration Cases Granted Relief or Terminated by Representation, 2007–2012

As figure 4-3 shows, once immigrants were able to submit an application for relief, those with attorneys representing them were more likely to have it granted by immigration judges than those who did not. For instance, those who were detained were about twice as likely to be granted relief with counsel compared to those who did not have an attorney. A similar trend was also found with those who had been released; they were more than three times more likely to win relief (48% vs. 14%, respectively), and those who were never detained were almost five times more likely to win relief compared to those without representation (63% vs. 13%, respectively).[243]

One of the main conclusions of this report and other studies is that having an attorney to represent an immigrant dramatically improves his or her chances of being released from detention, not to mention receiving the overall relief being sought. Given the enormous expense of using detention as part of the enforcement strategy, where in 2016 Congress allocated more than $2 billion for detention of immigrants, perhaps one way to remedy the inequities within the process is through the creation of a publicly funded public defender system for immigrants. Such a strategy could result in an enormous cost savings for the government and ensure that the merits of the case justify the outcome rather than whether the person involved had legal representation.[244]

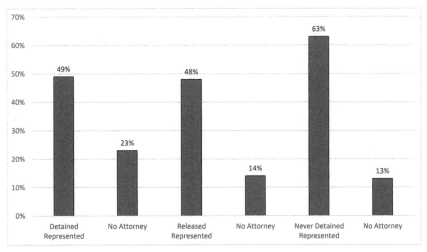

Figure 4-3   Percentage of Application for Relief Cases Granted by Representation, 2007–2012

However, such a proposal is predicated on the idea that detention is a by-product of the process, not the goal itself. In some instances, some scholars have stated that detaining immigrants for the purposes of deportation is the goal, thereby justifying the expense. More importantly, some critics of the process contend that the federal government is counting on the fact that most immigrants will not obtain counsel, which fast-tracks their cases and makes them eligible for deportation.[245]

Thus, while it may seem that the right to counsel is a mere formality, the data suggests that this is a critical factor in determining the outcome of a given immigration case. More importantly, while the study used data from 2016, more recent efforts indicate the problem has not decreased. According to one report, between October 2000 and November 2018, about 82 percent of the people in immigration court without attorneys were either deported or gave up on their cases and left the country voluntarily, but only 31 percent of those with lawyers were deported or left.[246]

Backlog of Cases in U.S. Immigration Courts

The intensity of the immigration enforcement effort has resulted in a significant increase in the volume of cases brought before immigration courts. According to the Transactional Records Access Clearinghouse (TRAC) data from Syracuse University, which tracks data from immigration courts, the number of pending cases on the immigration court's active docket is quickly approaching one million (869,013 as of March 2019). This is nearly double the number of cases that were on the docket in January 2017, when President Trump took office.

As seen in table 4-2, while the problem of delays are seen in virtually every state, ten states make up the majority of the backlog, with Maryland leading the way, where pending cases have more than doubled since 2017. California has the largest number of pending cases in terms of absolute numbers, which is a 54 percent increase since 2017. In fact, the problem has become so severe that members of the American Bar Association are calling it a crisis and have promoted the idea of creating a specialized court, similar to tax court, to address the administrative challenges and delays in processing cases.

Reasons for the Backlog

For the most part, the Trump administration has blamed the backlog on the policies and practices of the Obama administration, claiming that the previous strategies created an incentive for more people to illegally

Table 4-2 2019 TRAC Data on Growth in the Immigration Court Backlog by State

Rank	State*	Beginning of FY 2017	End of November 2018	Percent Increase
1	Maryland	17,074	35,300	107%
2	Georgia	13,955	26,447	90%
3	Florida	32,233	60,793	89%
4	Massachusetts	15,208	28,490	87%
5	New Jersey	27,457	44,096	61%
6	New York	70,303	108,458	54%
6	California	95,252	146,826	54%
8	Virginia	29,467	44,154	50%
9	Texas	91,865	119,401	30%
10	Illinois	23,242	29,922	29%

Source: Transactional Records Access Clearinghouse (TRAC). (2018). "Growth in the Immigration Court Backlog Continues in FY 2019." Syracuse, NY: Syracuse University. Available at https://trac.syr.edu/immigration/reports/542/.

cross the border. Specifically, the Trump administration criticized the Obama administration for its attempt to focus on deporting immigrants with criminal records along with Obama's desire to protect Dreamers, young immigrants who were illegally brought to the U.S. as children. While Trump's criticisms may be seen as a political ploy to explain the problem, the proposed strategies offered by the Trump administration create a host of issues and concerns for several reasons.

For example, the intensification of immigration enforcement has led to the need for more immigration judges. While the federal government did in fact hire more judges, increasing the number to over four hundred, and although these judges are in fact processing cases, the problem is one of scope, volume, and equity. That is, the federal government has dedicated a considerable amount of resources at the enforcement end of the immigration policy, but it has not supported the other components of the process, such as what happens after the immigrants are apprehended. As a result, most cases have at least a two-year waiting period, (approximately 746 days) with some locations taking twice as long to be heard.[247]

Adding to the burden of cases was the impact of the thirty-five-day government shutdown that occurred in early 2019, in which more than four hundred immigration judges were furloughed and nearly sixty thousand hearings were cancelled. The rescheduling of these cases only adds to the backlog effect. Another problem has been the decision by the Trump administration to reopen cases that had been deemed a low priority and closed through the use of administrative closure by immigration judges. This led ICE to reschedule nearly 8,000 cases and could add nearly 350,000 cases back onto the court dockets.[248]

The Trump administration has also changed the way immigration judges are evaluated to include a benchmark on the number of cases they complete. In other words, the judges will be assessed on speed and efficiency rather than on a thoughtful and contemplative review of the evidence in a given case.[249] Recall, these judges are not independent members of the judiciary; they are Justice Department employees who work for the agency. Such a format raises questions about a potential conflict of interest for the oversight and operation of the immigration court system and the need for a separate system.

Finally, the Trump administration has proposed a significant decrease in the use of prosecutorial discretion for immigration cases. This is an important consideration and will be discussed at length in another section of this chapter.[250]

The backlog of cases is creating extraordinary problems in the processing of cases in immigration court, and there are real concerns about the Trump administration's plan on how to address it. The main issue stems from the ability of judges to decide cases on the facts and evidence as opposed to simply expediting the cases and deporting immigrants regardless of their circumstances.

In 2019, the American Bar Association (ABA) proposed a major overhaul of the U.S. immigration system, calling the courts that decide whether to deport immigrants "irredeemably dysfunctional." The ABA has argued that the only way to fix the problem, including the potential conflict of interest of having immigration judges working for the Department of Justice, thereby making objectivity questionable, is to create an Article I court. This court would be similar to tax courts or bankruptcy courts, which are independent of the Justice Department. White House officials scoff at the idea of creating an Article I court, claiming it would be too time-consuming and costly. Instead, the attorney general argued that changes made to the existing system, including the hiring of more immigration judges along with a more efficient processing of cases, will solve the backlog of cases.[251]

However, many experts and commentators note that the focus on speed in resolving cases cannot come at the expense of due process or handling cases based on their complexity. In fact, the ABA, in its latest report, outlines over one hundred recommendations to improve the process, including the rejection of the quota system and the benchmarks of efficiency for immigration judges.

Further, the ABA, along with some members of Congress, have argued that the hiring process for these judges raises questions about their objectivity and whether their political views on immigration are considered in the hiring decision. Interestingly, the ABA produced a similar report nearly ten years earlier with similar findings and recommendations. Such a pattern suggests that little has changed in the processing of immigrants or in the immigration court system in general. The only differences seem to be the increased volume, the decreased attention to due process, and an indifference to delays in processing cases, even in those instances where the defendant remains incarcerated while awaiting a hearing.[252]

Prosecutorial Discretion and Immigration Policy

Because immigration courts are different in both scope and procedural elements from criminal ones, prosecutorial discretion in immigration cases is a bit different as well. As outlined by Zatz and Rodriguez (2015), prosecutorial discretion became a defining feature of immigration policy, if not in actual practice, under the Obama administration.[253] Because it plays such a central role in all other aspects of immigration policy, including the backlog of cases and right to counsel issues, and is consistent with the concerns about zero tolerance enforcement, which has become a common feature of the process, a full discussion of the ideas and realities of prosecutorial discretion is warranted.

There can be little question of the need for discretion in the criminal justice system. In fact, case law has consistently supported the idea that police officers, judges, and prosecutors need the latitude to enforce policy and laws in the execution of justice. A significant amount of research has focused on the use of discretion by police officers as well as the creation of sentencing guidelines for judges, but far less attention has been paid to prosecutors and their authority. In fact, as pointed out by other research, much of the effort to control the discretion of judges and police officers typically affords more flexibility and informal authority to prosecutors.[254]

As is the case with the relationship between policing and immigration, the study of prosecutorial discretion in immigration enforcement is an understudied area of research. Because of the nature of immigration law, which is different than traditional criminal law, a somewhat different perspective is needed in the use of the term *prosecutorial discretion*. For example, in criminal court, prosecutors have the authority to dismiss cases, but their primary function focuses on the decision to charge, especially under federal sentencing guidelines, where the charge largely determines the sentence. In immigration law, prosecutorial discretion occurs at the end of the process, in the decision about who should be deported.[255]

Theoretically, multiple factors shape the use of prosecutorial discretion in immigration cases, such as the available resources designated for deportation and detaining individuals along with the humanitarian impact of removing persons with family and community ties, particularly when spouses and children are U.S. citizens. What is a reasonable and appropriate response to immigration, particularly for those who are undocumented, was a driving feature of immigration policy until more punitive and restrictive legislation was passed in 1996.[256]

Pragmatically, as a result of the restructuring of ICE and its law enforcement function, along with the aforementioned modifications to the function and authority of immigration judges, coupled with the zero tolerance strategies at every level of immigration enforcement, prosecutorial discretion has been severely curtailed in favor of a one-dimensional approach to handling immigration cases.

How Did We Get Here? Internal Policy Development

The recent effort to limit the exercise of discretion by enforcement agents, including judges, was not always the standard operating procedure for handling immigration cases. In fact, the actual use of discretion has been a key component of immigration policy and practice as far back as the late 1700s. For instance, the Alien and Sedition Acts of 1798 gave the president wide discretionary authority to deport any alien he deemed dangerous to the United States. Similarly, the 1918 Alien Law was used to deport anarchists and dissidents. In the 1800s, Chinese men and women were excluded from coming to the United States under the Chinese Exclusion Act.[257]

However, discretion was also used in meeting the country's agricultural needs and those of other sectors of the economy that needed cheap labor. As a result, the Immigration and Naturalization Service (INS) engaged in not only selective enforcement of immigration laws but sometimes also *underenforcement* of the law. This was evident during the famous Bracero period of 1942–1964, when undocumented workers were generally ignored unless they were seen as troublemakers. The general feeling then was that deportation should only be used when it was a reasonable and proportional response to a criminal act.[258]

The rationale for the use of prosecutorial discretion in immigration cases was outlined in a series of internal agency memos that provided guidance for prosecutors. In 1976, the general counsel to the commissioner for INS defined prosecutorial discretion as the ability of a law enforcement official to decide *to* bring a case against an individual for violation of immigration law. In that memo, he also outlined a range of situations in which deportation proceedings should be cancelled, including deferring action based on humanitarian reasons.[259]

This memo significantly influenced Congress when it adopted a series of restrictive laws regarding immigration, especially the IIRIRA in 1996. This law was critically important as it expanded the number and types of offenses immigrants could be charged with and deported for. Under the IIRIRA and the Antiterrorism and Effective Death Penalty Act (AEDPA), both passed in 1996, immigrants—even lawful permanent residents (LPRs)—may be subject to mandatory detention and deportation for an offense that Congress defines as an "aggravated felony" for immigration purposes. An aggravated felony can encompass offenses that range from shoplifting to murder and, for noncitizens, is applied retroactively, even in cases where the offense in question was committed long before it was added to the list of aggravated felonies.[260]

It also essentially eliminated judicial discretion. Additionally, as some experts have noted, the final version of the 1996 laws made the expansion of these offense categories retroactive and precluded most relief options, even for legal permanent residents. The legislation, for example, stripped away the discretion of ICE agents to decide whether to release someone, and it similarly took away discretion from immigration judges in making determinations about particular cases.[261]

The latter was significant since even if an immigration judge wanted to take family ties into account, if an immigrant had an aggravated felony conviction, regardless of how long ago it occurred, whether it was a deportable offense at the time, or whether the offense at that time was a felony, the judge could not consider it. The implication of these changes was that while there was once a smaller class of deportable offenses and judges once had wide latitude in the decision to deport, the 1996 law dramatically reshaped the process of what it means to be an immigrant and an immigrant's status in society.

Given the severity of the 1996 law, some members of Congress and the Clinton administration were concerned about the harshness of the laws and eliminating all forms of discretion in immigration enforcement. In response, the commissioner of the INS, Doris Meissner, outlined an agency directive memo describing the legal basis for prosecutorial discretion and its limits, and she even provided examples of its use. Known as the Meissner memo, the document has become the standard upon which later memos on prosecutorial discretion were based.[262]

The Meissner memo asserted that there were two primary reasons that INS agents were authorized and, more importantly, required to exercise discretion in all phases of immigration enforcement. One reason was that INS could not, and should not, attempt to enforce all laws or to deport everyone. Rather, a judicious use of resources was needed to identify those individuals who present the greatest threat or danger to the country as a whole. Additionally, because the nature of deportation carries with it severe consequences for those involved, attention must be given to family issues and other matters that might broadly be termed "humanitarian concerns." These include family ties in the United States, a history of U.S. military service, and whether the person would be likely to become a citizen at some point in the future. Thus, while earlier immigration laws argued that each case should be assessed on a variety of criteria, and while the IIRIRA created a blanket approach of zero tolerance, the Meissner memo argued that such an approach was not the standard policy of the INS. The exercise of discretion was validated by the U.S. Supreme Court in *INS v. St. Cyr* (2001), which outlined the use of discretionary waivers of deportation cases.[263]

In terms of context, it must be remembered that ICE was created and funded with the goal of identifying, arresting, detaining, and deporting illegal immigrants—their mission and mandate means aggressive enforcement of immigration laws. The Meissner memo, along with the others that came from the director of ICE during the Obama administration, attempted to outline the parameters of the scope of practice for ICE officials. However, internally, such a position was opposed by many ICE agents and its union.

These memos also came at a time when a comprehensive immigration policy was unlikely to occur since the Obama administration was at odds with Congress, which was controlled by Republicans. Instead of achieving the goal of passing a comprehensive immigration law, the Obama administration, in part to appease Congress, opted for a more aggressive enforcement policy. However, an effort was consistently made to define the parameters of ICE's authority and the use of thoughtful strategies to deal with the problem.[264]

A series of additional memos, often referred to as the Morton memos, named after ICE director John Morton, reinforced previous memos that clearly established the value, purpose, and support of prosecutorial discretion in immigration enforcement within the agency. The first Morton memo outlined the priorities of enforcement for ICE officials, and the highest priority was identifying those immigrants who presented a threat to national security and those who had been convicted of a serious crime. The next highest priority was assigned to immigrants who recently illegally crossed the border. A third priority involved those immigrants who attempted to skirt immigration controls already in place and did not comply with an order of removal or who reentered the country illegally after being deported. With regard to the use of resources for detention, an emphasis was made on not detaining disabled individuals, those suffering from a mental illness, nursing mothers, the elderly, or primary caregivers for children.[265]

The biggest problem with the Morton memos was that an immigrant could be charged with the highest priority by either being a terrorist or by committing an aggravated felony, which could be a minor offense such as shoplifting. Equally important was that offenders could be targeted for prosecution even though they were unaware they had violated immigration laws.[266]

In a second and third memo, Director Morton outlined the procedures and protocols to be used in removal cases involving domestic violence and other crimes as well as how removal procedures should be applied to immigrants and the protection of their civil rights. As it was with the Meissner memos, the goal of these documents was to underscore the need for ICE to appropriately use its resources in a selective manner to maximize the priorities outlined for the agency as it related to immigration enforcement.[267]

However, the Morton memos did not cover how ICE was to address the issues of the needs of immigrant teenagers and young adults. To address this, DHS secretary Janet Napolitano created the Deferred Action for Childhood Arrivals (DACA) program in 2012, which outlined the use of prosecutorial discretion in how to handle the deferred action for this segment of the immigrant population. These individuals were seen as different from other groups of undocumented immigrants since they lacked the intent to commit a crime (crossing the border illegally) and had no control over how they ended up in the United States.[268]

The response to these memos by ICE officials, particularly those written by Director Morton, was almost immediate. The most vocal criticism came from members of Congress, but it also came from the ICE agents' union, which represents about a third of all ICE employees. Critics pointed out that the Obama policy articulated in those memos and especially the DACA program amounted to amnesty for millions of illegal immigrants. In fact, these policy directives were so strongly opposed that ICE agents in regional and local offices simply ignored them and continued to enforce immigration regulations with the same zero tolerance approach they had been using in the past.

This is consistent with the historical autonomy afforded ICE and the Border Patrol, where little in the way of oversight was offered from the beginning. This historical context is important since it helps to explain how and in what way ICE agents essentially disregarded policy directives from agency leaders with the hope that not only would there be a change in leadership at the agency level but, prior to 2012, a change in the presidency as well.[269]

Still, after Obama was reelected and supporters and immigration advocates became more optimistic about the passing of comprehensive immigration legislation, ICE and Border Patrol agents continued to operate as they had in the past. Under such conditions, it should not be surprising to learn that this lack of accountability resulted in neglect, abuse, corruption, and excessive violence on the part of law enforcement officials.[270]

In November 2014, a memo from DHS secretary Jeh Johnson rescinded the Morton memos and articulated enforcement priorities applicable to the entire department rather than ICE alone. This memo identified three civil immigration enforcement priorities:

1. threats to national security, border security (specifically those apprehended while attempting to unlawfully enter the United States), and public safety;
2. misdemeanants and new immigration violators (including anyone apprehended after unlawfully entering the United States and who had not been present in the United States since January 1, 2014); and
3. "other immigration" violators, namely those who had been issued a final order of removal on or after January 1, 2014.[271]

The Johnson memo also spelled out when and where discretion could be exercised in the immigration enforcement process. According to the memo, prosecutorial discretion in the immigration context

> should apply not only to the decision to issue, serve, file, or cancel a Notice to Appear, but also to a broad range of other discretionary enforcement decisions, including deciding: whom to stop, question, and arrest; whom to detain or release; whether to settle, dismiss, appeal, or join in a motion on a case; and whether to grant deferred action, parole, or a stay of removal instead of pursuing removal in a case.[272]

In sum, prosecutorial discretion as a practice is an important strategy in immigration enforcement largely because complete enforcement is neither pragmatic nor possible. Consistent with the notion of the use of discretion, it makes sense to prioritize which types of immigration violations should receive the most attention and resources. As outlined in a series of memos by ICE and DHS directors about its value and prescribed use, these policies and strategies have not filtered down to the local level as it relates to immigration enforcement.

This is a theme found in many aspects of the operation of the criminal justice system, where *street bureaucracy* is the term used to describe how and in what ways the philosophical underpinnings of policy are translated into actual behavior by those who are charged with its enforcement.[273] In the case of ICE and immigration enforcement, there appears to have been and continues to be a resistance to any type of oversight as well as the justification of full enforcement of all laws without regard for nuances or degrees of difference.

After all, ICE was created as an enforcement agency, with a narrow purpose, so it makes sense that the agency and its personnel would attempt to justify their existence by demonstrating they are embracing their mandate with data in the form of arrests, detention, and deportation. However, having said all that, during the Obama administration, it appeared that the use of discretion was part of the White House immigration policy, and these directives were essentially ignored.

The current administration appears to have embraced a zero tolerance policy of enforcement, and its priorities are more in alignment with what ICE supports, where all immigrants are subject to scrutiny and potential removal. In fact, in a memo issued by DHS director John Kelly in 2017, shortly after Trump issued an executive order outlining a more intensive approach to immigration enforcement, the use of prosecutorial discretion has all but been disbanded. Part of this memo reads, "Prosecutorial discretion shall not be exercised in a manner that exempts or excludes a specified class or category of aliens from enforcement of the immigration laws." In other words, virtually everyone who is classified as a Latino or Mexican immigrant is subject to scrutiny, and agency personnel have wide authority and little oversight in how they identify, arrest, and prosecute immigrant offenders.[274]

The Kelly memo also stated that "the exercise of prosecutorial discretion with regard to any alien who is subject to arrest, criminal prosecution, or removal in accordance with law shall be made on a case-by-case basis in consultation with the head of the field office component, where appropriate, of CBP, ICE, or USCIS that initiated or will initiate the enforcement action."[275]

Trump's order of priorities for removal people includes those who have been "convicted, charged, or even committed acts constituting any criminal offense; who have engaged in fraud or willful misrepresentation in connection with any official or government matter; who have abused any public benefits program; or who otherwise, in the judgment of an immigration officer, pose a risk to public safety or national security." Although the focus is on "crimes," notice that, instead of actual convictions, mere criminal charges or suspicions by immigration officers will be sufficient for officers to aggressively pursue a course of action.[276]

Moreover, there does not appear to be much interest in following due process protocol or in providing immigration judges with the authority they need to resolve cases that require a humanitarian sensitivity, and delays in the backlog of cases are seen with indifference. After all, immigrants who wait years to have their cases heard are more likely to be in jail or prison during that time anyway—a form of deportation. So perhaps the delays in processing cases are intentional, and perhaps hamstringing immigration judges, particularly since they are already employees of the massive immigration enforcement machine, is appropriate since the goal is to remove as many immigrants, for any reason, as possible.

This is particularly true given that recent policy changes have resulted in mandatory detention for immigrants while they await the outcome of their respective cases. That is, immigrants who have been convicted of certain crimes, including minor offenses, are mandated to detention during their immigration hearings. They often appear in prison uniforms, complete with handcuffs and shackles.[277] While this makes sense for violent offenders who present a risk to the community and public at large, the redefinition of certain acts as crimes results in more immigrants being eligible to be understood and treated like criminals. This is a critical feature of the criminalization of immigration, and it also supports the contention, made by the White House and immigration officials, that many immigrants are criminals who present a risk to national security or contribute to the crime problem.

However, as previously discussed, the actual evidence of the relationship between criminal behavior and immigration is very weak. Crime rates for crimes committed by immigrants are far lower than for those committed by nonimmigrants.

In chapter 5, we explore the issue of detention and the implications of such tactics on the families of those involved. What we see there is a rather disturbing trend that significantly affects the children of the detained or deported parent. What we also see in the literature is an increase in the number of children who attempt to illegally cross the border alone or with siblings. The risks of exploitation and victimization of these children is significant and influences the rise in human trafficking.

We will also examine the consequences of the shift in enforcement and prosecution priorities with an eye toward examining the value, purpose, and advantages to the extensive use of detention as a strategy for immigration. Given the long backlog of cases, often with immigrants remaining in prison while they await a decision about their case or asylum application, what are the consequences for those individuals and their families? Moreover, after decades of a get tough approach to crime in general, with long sentences given to U.S. offenders that has shown little in the way of success, what rationale is being offered to use a similar strategy to increase the number of immigrants sent to detention facilities and deported?

CHAPTER FIVE

The Detention and Deportation of Immigrants

- "I have been inside federal prisons. I have been inside county jails. I've been inside detention centers of all kinds and that's effectively what this is. These kids are incarcerated. They're in custody."[278]
  —Jacob Soboroff, MSNBC reporter, on visiting detention centers

- "Call Immigrant Detention Centers what they are: concentration camps."[279]
  —Jonathan Katz, *Los Angeles Times* reporter

- "The United States will not be a migrant camp, and it will not be a refugee holding facility. . . . A country without borders is not a country at all. We need borders. We need security. . . . We have to take care of our people."[280]
  —President Trump

In chapter 4, we examined the system by which immigrants who have been arrested are processed through the immigration court system, which can result in a variety of outcomes. As was mentioned, there are several issues relating to the immigration court system, including the challenges of managing an enormous backlog of cases, which is largely the result of an intensified enforcement strategy designed to detain and deport undocumented immigrants. This strategy, coupled with the lack of adequate funding for immigration courts, has overburdened the court system to the extent that delays of up to two years or more are commonplace. This is particularly significant when the person involved is detained while awaiting a hearing.

Additionally, there remain several questions related to the due process afforded noncitizens in immigration court, including constitutional protections such as the right to counsel. As was noted in chapter 4, this is a significant issue since the process and outcomes of cases differ between immigrants who are able to hire an attorney to represent them and those who cannot. This raises fundamental questions about the equity and fairness of the process, something federal officials have not been able to adequately resolve.

Hiring more judges and making greater use of expedited review, which essentially denies the immigrant an opportunity to present evidence disputing the charges, is not a reasonable response to the problem, particularly since the enforcement strategy has far too many incentives to arrest and detain people when such action is not really justified. In other words, people caught up in the immigration enforcement machine end up losing twice: first when they are caught up in aggressive police tactics and again when their cases are delayed and given less attention than actual assessments of the merits of the charges. Such a recipe is bound to result in significant gaps in fairness and decency for those who may or may not have committed a crime.

In this chapter, we will examine what happens after the courts have ruled against the person. Given that mandatory detention is a requirement for those who have committed criminal acts in the past, by itself a highly controversial topic, such a policy decision means the person may continue to be separated from his or her family until he or she is deported. Such a process can be years in the making and have a host of economic, social, and psychological effects on the immigrant and his or her family. It also has a resonating effect on others who witness such events and creates a climate that further makes all immigrants fearful of being vulnerable to governmental intrusion.

The Mass Incarceration of America

It might be tempting to conclude that the current immigration policy efforts, including the widespread use of detention, is part of a larger strategy designed to rid the country of illegal immigrants. While there may be some truth to such a position, the United States has been embarking on the use of incarceration as a mainstay strategy in criminal justice for decades. The term *mass incarceration*, like the phrase *sanctuary city*, has no precise meaning, and the criteria used to make assertions about what it is or how much it needs to be reduced are relatively arbitrary. As Pfaff (2017) points out, the general use of the term suggests that mass incarceration implies that we have been using jails and prisons for all manner of problems and that the rates of incarceration need to be reduced.[281]

As a starting point of this discussion, it is important to note that mass incarceration is inextricably linked to a larger discussion about race in the United States. That is, the disproportionality of African Americans, and of Hispanics and Latinos, is found at every stage of the criminal justice system. Blacks, who represent about 14 percent of the population, are more likely to be stopped, frisked, arrested, formally charged, sentenced to longer periods of incarceration, denied parole, and executed than whites, even when charged with similar crimes.[282]

While this trend can be part of a larger discussion of the role of race in crime in general, in this section, we will focus more on the role of race in incarceration trends. Parenthetically, it is worth noting that any discussion of race in criminal justice can be a source of considerable debate. Normally debates about social problems such as crime inevitably include criticisms of the data, the methodology of a given study, or its findings. However, in the case of the disproportionality of African Americans and Hispanics/Latinos in the criminal justice system, there are few if any disputes about whether the trends actually exist. Instead, it is in the explanations for why the disproportionality exists that the disagreements become heated.

As it relates to race and incarceration rates, there are essentially three schools of thought. First, there is what Pfaff (2017) calls the "Standard Story," which argues that the mass incarceration of minorities is the result of attention paid to policy decisions and practices that resulted in the incarceration of many low-level drug dealers as part of the War on Drugs. Such policies, it is argued, paid special attention to African Americans since the use, sale, and distribution of drugs typically occurred in inner-city neighborhoods where many African Americans live. Moreover, this position argues that drug transactions typically occurred in public spaces, which made them more susceptible to police surveillance.

In contrast, whites, who have similar drug use patterns and sell and distribute drugs at similar rates as African Americans, have the resources to avoid such open-air transactions and live in neighborhoods that do not attract the attention of the police. Thus, while whites are as actively involved in drug use and dealing as African Americans, they escape the attention of the police. Additionally, policies and laws created during the 1980s in response to the War on Drugs resulted in longer prison sentences, with mandatory minimums, that resulted in a dramatic increase in the prison population.

This school of thought argues that the focus on the systematic discrimination of African Americans in the justice process ensures that this group remains marginalized and prohibited from achieving any level of upward social mobility. With arrest records and felony convictions, African Americans, primarily males, are permanently unable to achieve any meaningful level of societal success and are also more likely to remain under the control of the system. This is the position most often associated with Michelle Alexander in her book *The New Jim Crow: Mass Incarceration in the Age of Colorblindness* (2012).[283]

Alexander argues that the criminal justice system imposed racially motivated social controls on African Americans through convictions for nonviolent crimes, mainly drug crimes. She also argues that the reason for these efforts was to circumvent the rights afforded to African Americans as part of the civil rights movement of the 1960s. In what is sometimes referred to as the *racial hierarchy argument*, the objective was to create a caste system whereby African Americans would be segregated from society via the criminal justice system. While not overtly racist or discriminatory, such policies and laws created under the rubric of accountability, law and order, and maintaining the safety and security of communities became the vehicle by which more subtle and nuanced forms of discrimination and racism could occur.[284]

Thus, in the racism that existed during the Jim Crow era, prejudice and discrimination were more overt, and the mistreatment of blacks was seen as justified given their status in society. Today, however, Alexander argues a more subtle form of racism has emerged. By using a law-and-order campaign, one that appeals to people's sense of reasonableness (after all, it is understandable that people want to feel safe and to hold accountable those who do not abide by the rules), blacks can still be discriminated against and relegated to a marginalized status. This is accomplished through the use of incarceration and social labeling that prohibits them from obtaining jobs, housing, the ability to vote in the democratic process, and other opportunities.

This marginalization is further accomplished by recasting minor drug offenses into major crime categories, such as President Clinton's "three strikes and you're out" laws, along with elevating possession of drug charges to distribution and trafficking offenses. It is also seen at the federal level with longer prison sentences for crack cocaine convictions compared to those for the possession of powder cocaine. Capitalizing on the public's fear, along with a rise in crime rates, these changes were seen as a reasonable response to a growing epidemic of crime and drug use.[285]

Alexander's point, along with other scholars, is that in the short-term, the fundamental problem of the mass incarceration of blacks is one of selective enforcement by concentrating on where they live and what they do. If whites and blacks use and sell drugs at similar rates, but the police focus on those places where blacks are more likely to live and engage in these activities, then this group is far more likely to end up in prison than the whites who do not live there.

In the long-term, the problems of mass incarceration become more enduring. If it becomes part of conventional wisdom that blacks are more likely to be involved in criminal activity, it is reasonable to think that the people working within the system, along with the general public, will normalize the criminalization of blacks so that they are typically seen and labeled as criminals. Once the formal label is applied and the person has a record of imprisonment, the chances that he or she will be able to participate in society as an equal is virtually eliminated. This consequence of the social labeling results in a return to crime because the person cannot obtain a good job, live in good neighborhoods, or associate with good people who can offer him or her the opportunity to succeed.[286]

Interestingly, these changes related to incarceration occurred at a time when experts and policy makers were reconsidering the purpose and value of prison as a form of punishment. Until the 1980s, most experts questioned the value of incarceration as a crime control effort, believing that prison should be a last resort for offenders because the deleterious effects of incarceration often resulted in criminals becoming worse upon their release. This is based on the notion that inmates cannot be imprisoned forever, and if an offender is more of a risk to the community upon his or her release than prior to his or her sentence, what value does prison actually have?[287]

Additionally, the 1970s witnessed the closing of several federal prisons and the elimination of mandatory minimum sentences for low-level drug offenses because the prevailing view was that drug addiction should be seen as a public health problem rather than a criminal justice one. However, the 1980s brought with it a change in perception about crime, criminals, and the value of incarceration.[288]

The philosophy of punishment shifted from one involving the notion of rehabilitation as the goal to one involving just desserts. This was politically popular since it gave politicians an opportunity to demonstrate they were being hard on criminals and holding them accountable for their actions. This was important because the country was coming off a period in which rehabilitation was seen as ineffective because it coddled criminals and gave them too many incentives to continue to commit crimes.[289]

Similar to the inaccurate perceptions of immigrants, policy makers and politicians created a climate of fear and then capitalized on it by passing laws and policies that ramped up the punishment of criminals. Such strategies also resulted in the massive construction of prisons, which was seen as a means to reduce unemployment and put people back to work. This get-tough-on-crime approach resulted in changing laws that made offenders eligible for longer prison sentences; implementing mandatory minimum sentences, particularly for drug offenses; and redefining certain offenses as eligible for incarceration. As a result of these and other changes, incarceration rates dramatically increased, leading to the need for the construction of additional prisons and jails.[290]

In sum, the racial hierarchy argument points out that the decline in economic opportunities for blacks, in part due to deindustrialization and the elimination of many semiskilled jobs, particularly in inner cities around the country, led to increases in unemployment, poverty, and other challenges. In an effort to contain and control displaced workers, who were largely African American, some of whom became involved in crime, the get tough approach to crime was seen as a reasonable reaction.[291]

However, not everyone agrees with this position best characterized in Alexander's book. For instance, Barry Latzler's book *The Rise and Fall of Violent Crime in America* takes issue with much of what Alexander offers as an explanation for why African Americans were the subject of so much discussion of the mass incarceration in America.[292] Latzler argues that the main thrust of Alexander's argument, that mass incarceration is a result of political factors rather than actual crime increases, is incongruent with other research that shows support for tougher sanctions against African Americans by black leaders.[293]

Latzler points to James Forman's book *Locking Up Our Own*, which describes how fear in the black community led many to support the punitive approach that resulted in the increases in incarceration rates among African Americans.[294] Latzler argues that the increase in incarceration rates was not simply whites attempting to control blacks. Rather, it was residents and communities responding to increases in violent crimes; those people living in poor and minority neighborhoods, along with black leaders, were concerned about the increase in crime as it related to all neighborhoods. Blacks were killing other blacks with alarming frequency, and so they needed to support a more strict law-and-order campaign.[295]

Latzler (2016) also points out, as does Forman (2017) and Pfaff (2017), that while drugs were a part of that discussion, the data suggests that drug offenses made up only a small part of the increases in incarceration. Instead, violent crime was increasing, and the longer sentences and incarceration of blacks was a reflection of and response to the data that suggested people were, and had reason to be, afraid. Perhaps more importantly, Latzler points out that homicide-victimization rates *doubled* between 1960 and 1980 and did not begin a consistent decline until the mid-1990s. Additionally, although blacks represented approximately 12 percent of the U.S. population during this period, they were nearly *half* of the homicide victims and 60 percent of the suspected perpetrators.[296]

Latzler also questions Alexander's claim about the majority of sentences being related to drug offenses. He argues that among state offenders, drug crimes were about 20 percent of all sentences, whereas sentences for violent crimes were anywhere from 46 percent to 59 percent of all sentences. Among federal offenders, drug sentences amounted to more than half of all sentences, but federal offenders make up only about 7 percent of the total prison population. More importantly, federal offenders tended to be higher-level drug dealers, not the street-level offenders, who tend to be African Americans. Finally, Latzler questions Alexander's claims that the massive increase in incarceration was an abysmal failure. He points out that while the increase in incarceration was not the only reason for reductions in crime, it had some role to play in the decrease in crime rates.[297]

A third point of view is offered by John Pfaff in his book *Locked In: The True Causes of Mass Incarceration and How to Achieve Real Reform* (2017).[298] Pfaff argues that the mass incarceration movement is characterized by two primary threads. The first narrative he calls the "Standard Story," which is best captured by assertions from scholars, such as Alexander, who suggest that the problem stems from the stigmatization of drug offenses coupled with long prison sentences and the exploitative nature and increased use of private prisons. This narrative essentially argues that there is a form of systematic racism and discrimination found within the entire criminal justice system that labels African Americans.[299]

The second narrative, as outlined by scholars such as Latzler (2016) and Heather MacDonald (2015),[300] is a conservative view that contends higher rates of incarceration are not a product of the system but rather reflect actual crime rates and offender patterns. The decision by African American offenders to commit crimes, not structural or individual racism, explains the overrepresentation of African Americans. Scholars in this camp tend to focus on crime rates in general and tend to point out that drug offenses do not explain the rise in incarceration since they represent a small percentage of those in prison.[301]

Pfaff agrees with the idea that drug offenses were not the primary driving force behind increased incarceration rates. He also argues that a thorough analysis of the data indicates that incarceration rates increased even when crime rates declined. Thus, both previous arguments have some merit and a role to play in understanding increases in the number of people in prison, but they fall short of being a compelling explanation.

Rather, Pfaff contends that the real reason for the increase in incarceration rates has to do with the unchecked discretionary authority afforded to prosecutors.[302]

As evidence of this trend, Pfaff notes that rates of reported crime decreased steadily between 1994 and 2008, along with arrests for violent crime, property crime, and drug offenses. Despite these facts, there was an increase in the number of felony cases filed in state courts during this same period. What this means is that the chance that any particular arrest would lead to a felony charge rose significantly. Once a felony case was filed, there was a very good chance that this would lead to a conviction and incarceration for the offender. Thus, the problem is not so much one of actual offending patterns since those were changing during the study period, as evidenced by the rates of crime and number of arrests.[303]

The real problem, as he sees it, is that efforts to reform the system are flawed—scholars and policy makers are focusing on the wrong dimension of the problem. Mass incarceration will not be meaningfully addressed by reducing the length of sentences since that is not what is causing the problem in the first place. Instead, the primary focus needs to be on the unfettered discretion afforded to local prosecutors, who have little oversight or accountability, and courts and legislatures are reluctant to provide it. Prosecutors play a key role in the overall justice system, but particularly as it relates to increases in incarceration rates. With fewer arrestees to choose from, and with prosecutors attempting to ramp up convictions, particularly for felony cases, the rates of incarceration dramatically increased.[304]

There is little question about the increase in incarceration rates. According to a Prison Policy Initiative report in 2019, the American criminal justice system holds almost 2.3 million people in 1,719 state prisons, 109 federal prisons, 1,772 juvenile correctional facilities, 3,163 local jails, and 80 Indian Country jails as well as in military prisons, immigration detention facilities, civil commitment centers, state psychiatric hospitals, and prisons in the U.S. territories (see figure 5-1).[305]

While the number of inmates in state-run facilities is large, despite the fact that it has seen decreases in recent years, it remains at 1.3 million people, a significantly large number by any account.

Interestingly, the Prison Policy Initiative report identifies local jails as playing a significant role in the mass incarceration phenomenon. What is important to note about local jails is that those incarcerated there often have not been convicted of a crime. Some may have just been arrested and cannot afford bail, so they remain incarcerated until their trial. According to the report, every year, over 600,000 people enter *prison*

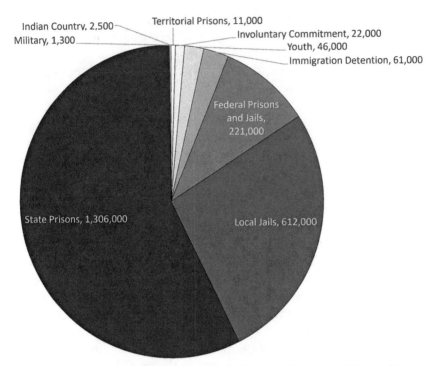

Figure 5-1 How Many People Are Locked Up in the United States (Sawyer, Wendy, and Peter Wagner. (2019). "Mass Incarceration: The Whole Pie 2019." Prison Policy Initiative, March 29. Available at https://www.prisonpolicy.org /reports/pie2019.html.)

gates, but people go to *jail* 10.6 million times each year. Only a small number (less than 150,000 on any given day) have been convicted, they and are generally serving misdemeanors sentences of under a year.[306]

The report also outlines several myths about mass incarceration, similar to what has been noted by other researchers. These include the *over-criminalization* of drug use, the use of private prisons, and the exploitation of inmates once they are incarcerated.

Myth: Releasing Drug Offenders Would Eliminate the Overrepresentation of Minorities

The Prison Policy Initiative report notes, unlike the assertions made by Alexander, that the vast majority of people in prison are incarcerated for violent and property crimes, not drug offenses, particularly in state prisons. At the federal level, there are more offenders incarcerated for drug offenses, but the number of inmates in federal custody is far smaller than the number in state prisons across the United States. Where the Prison Policy Initiative report and scholars such as Alexander agree is that the labeling that occurs as a result of incarceration has a negative and lasting impact on inmates once they are released.

Myth: Private Prisons Increase the Disproportionality of Minorities in Prison

Some experts have argued that given the profit-driven orientation of private prisons, inmates in these facilities, primarily minorities, are provided with less than optimal care while incarcerated. The Prison Policy Initiative report points out, however, that the data indicates only a small percentage of inmates are held in private facilities, less than 10 percent nationwide.

Where the issue of privatization becomes more apparent are those instances where city and county jails rent space to other agencies, including state prison systems, the U.S. Marshals Service, and Immigration and Customs Enforcement (ICE). While the argument that privatization results in a cost savings for cities and counties has not been seen in the literature, where the issue of exploitation of inmates occurs is in the outsourcing of jail and prison services. Private companies are frequently granted contracts to operate prison food and health services, and prison and jail commissary functions have spawned multi-billion-dollar private industries. By privatizing such services as phone calls, medical care, and commissary, prisons and jails offset some of the costs of incarceration by charging inmates and their families for these services.[307]

Myth: Expanding Community Supervision Is the Best Way to Reduce Incarceration

Alexander and other researchers point out that the mass incarceration of minorities extends beyond the prison and jails to the greater use of community supervision, such as probation, parole, and pretrial programs. While clearly less costly than incarceration, there remain questions about whether the structure of these programs, which can be quite restrictive and expensive for inmates, creates an environment where violations of the terms of the agreements result in a greater likelihood of incarceration. Offenders are often reincarcerated for technical violations while on parole, such as failing to pay supervision fees or violating curfew requirements.

In 2016, according to one account, this amounted to nearly 170,000 people. The report argues that probation violations lead to a significant amount of unnecessary incarceration.[308]

Myth: Violent or Sex Offenders Cannot Be Released from Prison

Finally, there is a perception that violent and sex offenders threaten the safety of the community. Further, because these are such serious offenses, many people think these types of offenders cannot be rehabilitated. The only viable option in these situations is longer sentences. In general, people who are convicted of violent offenses are less likely than virtually all other offenders to reoffend years after their release. For instance, people convicted of homicide are at low risk to repeat their offense. Similarly, people who are convicted of sexual assault have lower recidivism (or rearrest rates) than those convicted of property crimes such as larceny or motor vehicle theft. This is true despite the fact that these offenders must be assigned to sex offender registries for years after their sentences have been served. This is part of what Alexander describes in her assertions that the labeling of criminals carries with it far-reaching consequences beyond the time served.

The Mass Incarceration of Immigrants

The vast majority of people who are detained for criminal immigration offenses are there essentially for crossing the border without permission (the offense listed is illegal entry or reentry). This comprises about thirteen thousand people, with another ten thousand in pretrial detention (see figure 5-2).[309]

The data shows that about forty-nine thousand people are detained by ICE for their undocumented immigrant status. Approximately twelve thousand unaccompanied children are held in ORR custody as they wait to be placed with their parents, relatives, or others who meet the requirements to serve as legal guardians.[310]

Much of what is offered by Alexander and others regarding the increase in incarceration rates can be used to understand how it applies to the use of incarceration for immigrants. That is, the arguments used by Alexander are easily seen in the immigration debate: where certain acts are elevated in seriousness to make immigrants eligible for detention and deportation.

As previously mentioned, under the recent immigration enforcement strategy, immigrants can be detained and deported for the commission of a crime. This was originally intended to remove those immigrants who

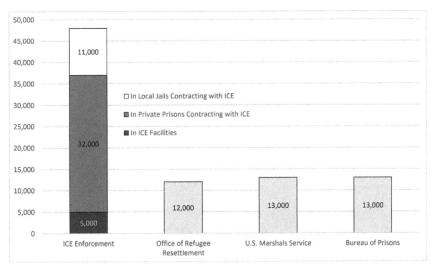

Figure 5-2   Almost Eighty-Five Thousand People Are Confined for Immigration Reasons (Sawyer, Wendy, and Peter Wagner. (2019). Mass Incarceration: The Whole Pie 2019. Prison Policy Initiative, March 29. Available at https://www .prisonpolicy.org/reports/pie2019.html.)

were seen as the greatest threat to the community. However, given that there are only a small number of these individuals (recall the discussion about the relationship between involvement in violent crime and immigrants), to justify the enormous effort and expense of the current immigration enforcement policy, a change in the definition and criteria of a crime occurred, where minor offenses, such as traffic stops or possession of small amounts of drugs, coupled with the retroactive nature of these offenses, are being used as criteria to constitute an aggravated felony. Under these circumstances, where the immigrant is now considered a violent offender, he or she is eligible to be arrested, detained, and deported.

Such a strategy sounds a lot like what Alexander describes in the criminalization of African Americans and prisons. Similarly, the aggressive enforcement undertaken during the War on Drugs, where the police targeted certain types of offenders in particular areas and engaged in an intensive form of sweeps, is strikingly familiar to what Amada (2017) offers in her assessment of police strategies toward immigrants in Tennessee.[311]

Similarly, Latzler's (2018) argument about the types of crimes that warrant incarceration can also be seen in immigration enforcement. Recall that Latzler's argument centers on incarceration for violent offenses, rather than for drug offenses; this is an important consideration in understanding the extent and characteristics of mass incarceration in the United States. The main point here is not that drug offenses are unimportant but that incarceration should be used for violent offenses that actually threaten the public. In other words, there is a significant difference between a truly violent offender and someone who is sent to prison for drug possession.[312]

In a similar way, it is one thing to incarcerate an immigrant who commits a legitimate violent crime or felony; it is another thing to manufacture a felony and identify someone as a threat to national security by crossing the border or remaining in the country without proper documentation. This is particularly true given that the same behavior was seen in the past as a technical or administrative violation.

Finally, Pfaff's (2017) argument regarding the abuse of authority by prosecutors in explaining the dramatic increases in incarceration rates for offenders can easily be applied to previous discussions of immigration courts, where prosecutorial discretion, or the lack of it, and the absence of adequate oversight of ICE and Border Patrol agents results in the abuse of suspects.[313]

As was mentioned in the discussion of the disproportionality of African Americans in the criminal justice system, where there is little debate about the existence of this trend in all phases of the system, a similar argument can be made regarding the trends related to immigration apprehensions, detentions, and deportations. That is, there have been very few debates about the number of people who have been apprehended, detained, or deported. The differences, of course, stem from the fact that many immigrants who are detained have not been convicted of a crime. However, the backlog of cases means they will likely spend a considerable amount of time waiting for the chance to refute the charges, assuming they can acquire legal representation and have the ability to collect evidence to prove their cases. Additionally, the structure of immigration detention is such that conditions under which immigrants must remain in detention are designed to encourage detainees to withdraw appeals or to give up fighting the deportation charges even before the hearing occurs.

These considerations raise many questions about the fairness and due process afforded anyone who experiences a deprivation of his or her liberty. However, because these individuals are considered noncitizens, the rules are not being applied to their situations.[314] In many ways, then, the mass incarceration of African Americans the 1980s is being replayed on immigrants. While it is a fair criticism that the United States has always used incarceration as a go-to strategy to solve many of its problems, particularly as it relates to crime and criminals, it is also a fair criticism to say that it often becomes the only solution considered.

As scholars have consistently noted, we cannot detain and deport our way out of the immigration dilemma, yet we seem determined to rid the country of certain types of immigrants. This is true despite the fact that they do not pose the threat we think they do; immigrants make significant contributions economically, socially, and culturally in this country.[315] Thus, the problem may be serious for those people who are caught up in the immigration incarceration machine, but the real danger lies in the social and moral acceptability of the mistreatment of a group of people who may be innocent and who are more than likely long-term contributors to this country by paying taxes, raising families, and making positive contributions to the culture as a whole.[316]

Viewing Immigrants as Criminals and Incarceration

As previously mentioned, the basis for the detention and deportation of immigrants is the idea that many have committed crimes. Despite the repeated claims by President Trump and ICE officials, a consistent theme in the empirical research on the relationship between immigrants and crime shows that such assertions are false.[317]

For instance, a recent study by the Marshall Project found that cities in the United States that accept large numbers of undocumented immigrants do not witness higher rates of violent and property crime. The findings of this study are in direct contrast to Trump's claim that sanctuary cities suffer as a result of allowing undocumented immigrants. In fact, this study compared crime rates and recent estimates of increases of undocumented immigrants in metropolitan areas and found that there were significant *decreases* in violent and property crime between 2007 and 2016.[318]

There are many reasons for the fluctuations in crime rates, including law enforcement efforts, community responses, changes to the economy, and other factors. This study pointed out that the decreases in crime in these areas had nothing to do with the undocumented immigrant population. However, Trump seems convinced that undocumented immigrants are a critical variable in the crime problem. Trump has stated in the past, "When Mexico sends its people, they're not sending their best. They're not sending you. . . . They're sending people that have lots of problems, and they're bringing those problems with us. They're bringing drugs. They're bringing crime. They're rapists. These aren't people. These are animals."[319]

The recent study by the Marshall Project is not the first or the only study to refute the claims about the relationship between immigration and crime. In 2018, the Cato Institute published a report showing that documented and undocumented immigrants commit fewer crimes than U.S. citizens in Texas. Other studies using national data sets found similar results.[320]

Again, the problem with President Trump's claims is not only that they are "fake news." In the absence of an equal response to refute them, they can create an impression among the public about immigrants, who may then accept the current strategies to address the problem as reasonable and acceptable. In other words, the real problem is that the public begins to believe the narrative and concludes that the current immigration policy is justified.

Even when the evidence focuses attention on those who actually have committed crimes, one needs to be very careful in how the data is interpreted. According to ICE statistics, at the end of fiscal year 2018, there were 158,581 arrests, an increase of about 15,000 arrests from the previous year (143,470) and a 40 percent increase from fiscal year 2016 (110,104). However, the number of arrests does not tell the entire story.[321]

In their assessment of the problem, ICE included those convicted of crimes and those who were arrested for crimes. Of course, an arrest of someone does not guaranteed a conviction. Under normal circumstances, however, the combination of those arrested and those convicted results in a misleading figure about the extent of the increases.[322] In addition, the data shows that the largest number of convictions and pending charges were for nonviolent crimes, such as traffic violations, immigration offenses, and minor crimes, such as liquor law violations, health and safety offenses, public peace, and invasion of privacy offenses, none of which are not adequately defined. Including immigration offenses is debatable since it has been recalibrated to be a criminal offense when historically it was treated as an administrative violation, not a crime.

Moreover, DHS claims that immigration proceedings are not criminal trials but administrative or civil hearings, thereby bypassing the constitutional protections afforded to all criminals under the due process of law. If that is true, then including it as a criminal offense for data collection purposes seems inconsistent—it is either a crime or it is not—and if it is, then the people who are charged with a crime, whether citizen or noncitizen, should be entitled to protection under the U.S. Constitution because jeopardy is attached (meaning the person could lose access to life, liberty, and property under the equal protection clause of the Fourteenth Amendment).[323]

Finally, even according to its own data, ICE reports that a significant percent of the individuals arrested in 2018 had neither criminal convictions nor criminal charges pending. Thus, there are many questions about the immigration and crime connection, including who gets arrested by ICE and the charges assigned to that individual. The data suggests that these are not the violent predators that President Trump claims them to be because they have been arrested for noncriminal offenses or for minor crimes that many citizens have likely committed.[324]

What Is the Value in Detaining Immigrants?

As pointed out by several scholars, the mass incarceration strategy employed by the United States had political, economic, and ideological purposes. It gave politicians an opportunity to demonstrate that they were "tough" on crime and criminals, and they were taking demonstrable steps to protect the public from the threat of criminal victimization. Economically, the massive increase in incarceration rates resulted in significant overcrowding issues within prisons, thereby necessitating the construction of new facilities. This was a boom for many rural areas, where prisons are typically built and where employment opportunities tend to be limited. It is also the least expensive way to build prisons, so politicians could assert that they were being responsible stewards of taxpayers' money.

Ideologically, the shift in priorities about incarceration is consistent with the larger notion of neoliberal economic policies, which are designed to keep a stable supply of compliant and obedient workers in the lowest-paying sectors of the economy. As noted by Alexander (2012), in the 1980s, just as the War on Drugs was escalating, economic changes had a significant impact on inner-city neighborhoods, as many factory jobs were eliminated due to deindustrialization. Prior to 1970, people living in those communities could find jobs without the benefit of a college education, and the jobs were in close proximity to their homes. Globalization changed that, and manufacturing jobs were moved to other developing countries, where workers were paid a fraction of what their American counterparts had made.[325]

In his book *When Work Disappears* (1997), William Julius Wilson offers the observation that the overwhelming majority of people living in inner-city neighborhoods were African Americans who were ill-equipped to transition to a technology-based job market. As a result, these communities had high rates of unemployment and poverty. The few manufacturing jobs that African Americans could perform were located in the suburbs. Given that many poor blacks did not have access to transportation, these jobs might have as well been located in another country.

This disconnect between the loss of jobs, the concentration of lower-skilled workers, and the high rates of unemployment and poverty is known as the *spatial mismatch hypothesis*.[326] One of the consequences of the lack of access to jobs was involvement in the drug trade. Couple that with the intense law enforcement effort as a result of the War on Drugs and the relationship between deindustrialization, unemployment, and incarceration is easily seen. As Golash-Boza (2015) points out, increases in funding for social control along with decreases in social services are all a part of the neoliberal reforms.[327] All of these strategies resulted in higher rates of incarceration and, arguably, higher rates of crime as well.

An added feature to this trend as it relates to undocumented immigrants is the fact that many legal and illegal immigrants are parents, often to U.S.-born citizens. It is estimated that of the 5.1 million children who have at least one undocumented parent, about 4 million are native-born citizens. The current strategy, which appears less interested in distinguishing immigrants who pose a real threat to national security from any immigrant who has ever committed any type of offense, has resulted in dramatic increases in the number who are incarcerated. Cracks are appearing in such a strategy, as the limited number of facilities that can accommodate such a large number of detainees are filled to capacity, along with several examples of abuse and deaths while under the supervision of the Border Patrol or ICE. Such episodes and trends indicate that changes in the effort to deport all 11 million undocumented immigrants are needed.[328]

Immigration Detention

The immigration detention effort in the United States is made up of detention centers, county and city jails, and privately owned prisons used to hold immigrants awaiting a hearing in immigration court or deportation. The people experiencing immigration detention are not serving time for a violation of the criminal law per se. Instead, they are detainees awaiting trial or deportation. In other words, a person cannot be sentenced to a fixed amount of time in immigration detention. If the immigrant had committed a criminal act, at the completion of his or her prison or jail sentence, he or she would then be detained in an immigration detention center while awaiting a removal hearing. This is what makes the backlog of cases so significant: the longer the wait for the hearing, the longer the noncitizen must remain in detention—in some cases after having already served time for the criminal offense.

Differences between Immigration Detention and Traditional Incarceration

While immigrants in detention centers may be similar to traditional criminals who are incarcerated, in that they are confined to a cell and subject to a host of rules and regulations that dictate their freedom of movement, in many ways, immigration detention is very different from criminal detention. As mentioned in chapter 4, the criminal law protects suspects and those convicted of offenses in many ways that are not available to immigrants. For example, people charged with a criminal offense in the United States have an opportunity for legal representation, even if they cannot afford an attorney.

Additionally, the Fifth Amendment to the U.S. Constitution ensures that a person cannot be deprived of life, liberty, or property without due process of law. However, people held by DHS do not have those same rights, even though they are being similarly deprived. DHS can detain people to ensure their deportation or their appearance at a removal hearing, but DHS does not have the authority to hold someone as a form of punishment.[329] The importance of due process and protections against unfair or unlawful imprisonment is well-known and a foundation of the U.S. justice system, but the current U.S. immigration system of detention does not provide these protections.

Other examples include placing the burden of proof on the immigrant to prove his or her case instead of the government as well as allowing the government to deny bail hearings. The latter is the primary mechanism to ensure the suspect appears before the court at trial, unless there is a compelling reason to think he or she will not show up. The rationale behind DHS's strategy is that the current system allows them to detain people to make sure they appear at their hearing and they will leave the country if they are deported. Denial of bail under U.S. immigration law is considered acceptable since the government does not consider detention as a form of incarceration. However, the characteristics of detention facilities, which share many of the same characteristics as prisons, leave many unanswered questions as to the actual differences between the two.[330]

There are some differences between detention centers for immigrants and prisons for inmates, however. While prisons typically have exercise programs, rehabilitative services, and educational opportunities, detention centers for immigrants have none of these features. Additionally, there are reports that the conditions of detention facilities for immigrants are designed to make the experience particularly uncomfortable. Examples include keeping the temperature in facilities very cold, overcrowding, and limiting opportunities for detainees to communicate with family and attorneys.[331] All of these efforts are said to be designed to encourage detainees to agree to deportation or to withdraw their appeals. Moreover, because immigrant detainees are doing time with no sense of how long they will remain (with caseloads backlogged an average of two years), the pains of imprisonment are more severe than what is offered in prisons for people who have committed crimes.[332]

Thus, even those immigrants who have valid claims and may be able to fight a deportation order are faced with the loss of income due to being incarcerated, the costs involved in hiring an attorney, the challenges of being separated from family members, and the deleterious conditions of detention facilities, and they have no sense of how long they will remain in detention. Under these circumstances, it is easy to imagine how such a climate prompts immigrants to simply accept deportation as a solution.[333]

The Privatization of Detention—A Conflict of Interest?

The idea of privatization of detention services is that private companies can do a better job of providing services than the government. While such an argument is debatable, from the outset, there remain questions about the privatization of detention for immigrants based on the mandate that requires a specific number of beds in facilities for immigration violations. That is, if DHS continues to raise the number of available detention beds, it is likely that ICE officials have an incentive to fill them by making more apprehensions of immigrants.

As previously mentioned, part of what Pfaff (2017) describes regarding the disproportionality of African Americans in prisons around the country is in part explained by the expanded use of private prisons. For instance, in 2018, the Sentencing Project produced a report on the growth of private prisons. The study reported that the United States has the world's largest private prison population. Of the 1.5 million people in state and federal prisons in 2016, 8.5 percent, or 128,063, were incarcerated in private prisons.[334]

As noted by Latzler (2018) and Pfaff (2017), 8 percent or 9 percent does not make up a large proportion of all people in prisons, and the vast majority of people who are incarcerated are still housed in public facilities. This is a fair point, but what is not highlighted in such commentary is the fact that the growth in the use of private facilities has been steadily increasing, particularly as cities and states realize the enormous costs involved in operating and managing detention and correctional facilities. Given that incarceration is, and will continue to be, a primary solution for many problems in this country, this growth should be expected to continue. This is particularly true for immigration cases, where 73 percent of all people in detention for immigration violations were housed in privately run facilities in 2017.[335]

As an illustration of this growth, according to the Sentencing Project report, from 2000 to 2016, the number of people housed in private prisons increased five times faster than the total prison population. In addition to the federal government's use of private prisons, 27 states used them as well in 2017. New Mexico and Montana relied most heavily on private prisons, which housed 43 percent and 39 percent, respectively, of their prison populations.[336] According to the Sentencing Project report, the private prison population reached a peak of 137,220 in 2012 and then declined to 126,272 in 2015 before rising again in 2016 to 128,063.[337]

Such growth should not be taken solely as evidence that the privatization of incarceration and detention is more effective than what is offered in the public sector. For instance, in 2016, a report issued by the Department of Justice's Office of Inspector General raised several concerns about the operation of private facilities, including safety issues, concerns about inmate discipline, and other issues. This led President Obama to phase out federal private prison contracts.[338]

However, since taking office, President Trump has largely supported a greater use of private for-profit prisons, particularly as it relates to immigration detention. Such a decision is considered by many observers to be consistent with Trump's policies regarding the use of detention as a general strategy as well as a greater level of intensity by prosecutors to leverage the most serious charges in federal cases, particularly those that carry long prison sentences. Such a move is also expected to result in an expansion of private prison contracts with the federal government.[339]

Evidence of the greater use of private prisons at the federal level are particularly noteworthy as it relates to immigration enforcement. In January 2018, the Bureau of Prisons (BOP) issued a new directive that encouraged BOP officials to transfer eligible offenders, particularly immigration and low-level drug offenders, to privately run facilities.

Concerns about Privatization

While the notion of outsourcing has become a rather common feature for many parts of the economy in this country, including the use of private companies to manage those who are detained or incarcerated, there are several concerns about the use of private prisons. While the rationale behind their use is primarily related to cost savings for states, decades of research point to the fact that the use of private prisons has not resulted in any meaningful cost benefits to either the federal government or the states that make use of them.

For instance, in 2016, the U.S. Office of Inspector General conducted an assessment of the costs related to the use of private prisons. The report found that few cost savings were ever realized. Similarly, other research has consistently found that private prisons do not result in higher levels of efficiency in operating a facility compared to a publicly funded one, nor are the cost savings assured by using companies to do the work of managing a facility.[340]

Other areas of concern in the use of private prisons relate to the quality of the services provided as well as the safety of the employees and inmates within the facilities. As with any for-profit company, a balancing act must be maintained between keeping costs low to maximize profits while still providing adequate services to maintain the safety of the institution. Since wages are the largest expense for any company that has employees, this is the primary area where private prisons attempt to cut costs. Compared to salaries and benefits offered to employees in publicly run facilities, those working in private prisons are routinely paid less.[341]

High turnover, poor training, and low morale are problematic in any organization, but in a prison, such trends can have a significant impact on the safety of employees and inmates. Studies have found that assaults in private prisons occur at double the rate found in public facilities. Researchers also find that public facilities tend to be safer than their private counterparts, and privately operated prisons encounter significant difficulty in maintaining order within the facility.[342]

Other concerns about the privatization of prisons stem from the fact that many of the companies that offer these services, such as Corrections Corporation of America, since renamed Core Civic, make a concerted effort to lobby members of Congress and the White House in an effort to escalate the enforcement of laws that result in greater use of detention as a strategy.[343] The reason for this, quite simply, is that a decline in incarceration as a strategy has a significant impact on the profit margins of these companies.

Private Detention and Immigration Cases

In 2002, approximately 4,800 ICE detainees were held in privately run facilities. By 2017, that number had jumped to 26,249 people, and in 2018, it was 32,000.[344] In 2009, Congress linked DHS funding to creating and maintaining over 33,400 beds in detention facilities. This figure was increased to 34,000 beds in 2014. This number was again increased to 52,000 beds in President Trump's proposed budget in 2020, with a goal of 60,000 beds in the future.[345]

It seems fairly apparent that the realities of the Trump approach to immigration enforcement are becoming problematic—the system is overwhelmed with people who are being detained. In response, in early 2019, President Trump threatened to release detained immigrants into sanctuary cities as a form of punishment for not supporting his immigration efforts. Such a move was politically unpopular and raised many questions about the real issue surrounding immigration. After all, releasing illegal immigrants into the very cities that welcome them in the first place is inconsistent with the notion that these individuals represent a threat to national security. In fact, such an act would technically constitute negligence if one takes President Trump's characterizations and descriptions of immigrants as valid.

However, in May 2019, a *USA Today* article revealed that the president was following through on his threat. In Broward and Palm Beach Counties in Florida, more than a thousand migrants from Central America who had been detained in Texas were transported to a Border Patrol facility in Florida with the goal of releasing them into the community. No accommodations were made to house, feed, or provide any support services for these individuals, and no additional federal funding was provided to the state.[346]

Moreover, the Border Patrol informed the Florida governor that the state could expect upward of one thousand new detainees every month for the foreseeable future. The reason? The federal government claims that existing detention facilities are at capacity, and the decision to relocate detainees to a different facility was based on that county's or state's capacity to accommodate them. However, state officials argue that such a move will severely tax the ability of the government to provide the funds needed to support the detainees. Given that immigration enforcement is seen as a federal responsibility, the federal government should bear the costs of such actions. However, no mention of additional funds was planned, according to federal officials.[347]

Such a strategy may be political in nature; perhaps the Trump administration is attempting to leverage sanctuary cities and other communities with supporting federal immigration efforts. However, another explanation may be that the federal government is actually experiencing an overcrowding problem. That is, an aggressive enforcement effort coupled with an effort to increase the number of people occupying detention beds in federal facilities may have actually worked—and the system is being overloaded as a result.

Given the incentive for private correctional companies to profit from the increase, it is unlikely that this is the main reason for the decision, but it is reasonable to think that increases in the number of people who experience detention may temporarily tax the system until more spaces are built. More likely, there is a political agenda being played out, with detained immigrants being used as pawns in an effort to get cities and states to comply with federal policies regarding undocumented immigrants.

In addition, as the 2020 election looms, President Trump recently unveiled a new immigration plan that focuses attention on legal immigrants. In an attempt to attract highly skilled workers, Trump announced a plan that made it easier for these workers to secure permission to reside in the country as legal immigrants. Missing from the narrative, however, is a discussion of a comprehensive immigration strategy that includes a solution to those who are undocumented or who attempt to enter the country illegally. To be fair, this is a much more complicated problem and is not simply the result of a squabble between Democrats and Republicans. In the meantime, the current climate of aggressive enforcement, detention, and deportation, both at the border and with internal immigration enforcement, continues.

In chapter 6, we will move from the macrolevel discussions that have been the main focus of previous chapters to a more microlevel analysis of the challenges and consequences of the effects of the current immigration strategy. Included in this discussion will be an overview of the problems that immigrants and their families experience once they are affected by the immigration policies currently being deployed across the country.

CHAPTER SIX

The Consequences of Criminalizing Immigration

- "We cannot address this crisis by simply shifting more resources or building more facilities. It's like holding a bucket under a faucet: it doesn't matter how many buckets you give me if we can't turn off the flow."
  —Border Patrol chief Carla Provost[348]

- "It's beyond the pale to threaten to take away the most basic protections [for children]. Once again this administration is using children as pawns for their broader political goals."
  —Neha Desai, director of immigration at the National Center for Youth Law[349]

- "You have an administration that proactively killed DACA, TPS and DED to put these communities at risk of deportation. They've been hell bent on using ICE and CBP to go after our communities."
  —Bruna Bouhid, a twenty-seven-year-old DACA recipient about the recently passed immigration bill in the House

Much of the discussion up to this point has focused on the process and strategies used to implement the federal government's immigration policy. It seems apparent that there is an agenda in place to limit all immigrants access to the United States, whether they attempt to cross the border illegally, seek asylum due to the overwhelming conditions in their native countries, or legally enter and remain in the United States. The number of asylum-seeking Central American families crossing the southern border broke a record in April 2019, with Border Patrol agents apprehending 58,474 members of family units during the month, an all-time high. The flood of migrants has overwhelmed federal facilities, forcing immigration agents to release migrants directly into U.S. border communities and hope they will appear at their immigration court hearings. Such a policy seems to suggest the federal government is perhaps beginning to recognize its inability to stem the flow of immigrants into the United States.[350]

While the impact of policies that focus on detention and deportation are rather self-evident for the person who experiences them, there are also a host of negative consequences for their families as well. In response to the issues generated from detention and deportation, some people may assert that the person made the decision to commit a criminal act, crossing the border illegally, and the fallout from that decision is not the government's responsibility to remedy. Some may disagree with such a position.

A primary focus of this chapter will be the impact of detention and deportation on the children in those families, who had no say or influence in any decisions related to their immigration status or that of their families. Additionally, we will also explore the issues stemming from those youth who cross the border illegally by themselves. These *unaccompanied minors*, as they are sometimes called, are symbolic of the larger problems related to immigration: what reasonable parent would allow his or her child to be placed in such a vulnerable position by crossing the border into the United States alone or with younger siblings unless the conditions in their home country were far worse than the chance of being victimized in the journey? By itself, the presence of unaccompanied minors should signify the severity of the problem and call attention to the need to fix what is obviously broken in Central America. This issue will be further discussed in chapter 7. For now, we will focus on the effects of immigration on children and families.

An added dimension of the discussion of children and the issue of deportation is the children who were born in the United States, making them U.S. citizens. That one or more parents or extended family members are undocumented places those children in a difficult position, particularly if life in the United States is the only one they have known. Given that this affects millions of children, the scope of the problem is significant and warrants serious consideration.

How Are Children Impacted by Immigration?

As was mentioned in chapter 5, as of 2018, there were more than eight million people living in the United States with at least one family member who is undocumented. The majority of people in this group, according to the American Immigration Council, are children—almost six million children under the age of eighteen live with a parent or family member who is undocumented. Additionally, about four million children who are U.S. citizens under the age of eighteen live with at least one undocumented parent. What are the consequences of the current immigration enforcement strategy for these children?[351]

Physical and Emotional Health

According to the research on this topic, physicians and service providers have found that a child's risk of mental health issues, such as depression, anxiety, and severe psychological distress, increases as a result of a parent's deportation or detention. Children experiencing the deportation of a parent or family member have also exhibited a range of psychological disorders, including symptoms of more severe problems, such as *toxic stress*.[352] Additionally, a 2017 study of Latino children found higher levels of posttraumatic stress disorder (PTSD) symptoms among children who had at least one detained or deported parent.

Moreover, the experience of witnessing the arrest of a parent had a significant impact on the children's overall psychological and emotional well-being. According to one study, the majority of children studied had significant behavioral changes as long as six months after the arrest of a parent in the home or workplace or when the parents were caught in an ICE raid. Compared to other children and to the previous six-month period before the arrest, children who experienced the arrest of a parent cried more often; expressed fear; exhibited changes to their eating and sleeping habits; were more anxious, angry, or aggressive; or suffered from separation anxiety.[353]

These reactions can have a significant impact on the child's social, emotional, and academic performance. In fact, one study points out that the impact of an aggressive immigration enforcement plan even has an influence on children before they are born. According to one study, a raid in Iowa in 2008, heralded to be the largest single-site raid in U.S. history, was linked to premature and underweight birth rates and childbearing complications that increased babies' risk for sudden infant death syndrome (SIDS) and long-term health problems. The study found that babies born to Latina mothers in the area within nine months of the raid were more likely to be underweight compared to the previous year. Such a risk was not evident in babies born to non-Latina white mothers in the same area during the same period.[354] Thus, at many levels, the experiences involved in having a parent arrested, detained, or deported has a significant impact on a child.

Academic Achievement

Parents who are undocumented often move frequently in search of work. As a result, their children may end up changing schools several times. The research on the effects of school mobility indicates that when a child frequently changes schools, there is a negative effect on academic performance. Unauthorized parents are also less likely to interact with teachers or allow their children to participate in field trips or after-school events because they require, among other documentation, health forms that could expose the parents' immigration status.[355]

Research on the cognitive development of young children who have undocumented parents shows that they tend to be at greater risk of lower school performance and a host of academic-related problems, such as dropping out and behavioral problems, when compared to legal immigrant children.[356]

Economic Instability

It makes sense that the arrest, detention, and deportation of a parent, particularly if that parent is the primary breadwinner for the family, puts the child and the family as a whole in financial jeopardy. For example, research estimates that an immigrant family's income decreases as much as 90 percent following the arrest, detention, or deportation of a parent. A study of immigration enforcement in several cities noted that families typically lost 40–90 percent of the family income, or an average of 70 percent, within six months of an arrest, detention, or deportation.[357]

The loss of income is significant in such situations, and it can also lead to the loss of housing for the remaining family members. A study in 2016 showed that the deportation of the primary provider often led to the loss of the family home and increased the number of relocations for the remaining family members. Such a situation increases the likelihood of changing schools for the children, thereby putting them at risk for academic vulnerability and failure.[358]

Another study showed that an aggressive immigration enforcement strategy resulted in higher rates of home foreclosures among Latinos. This makes sense; if the family loses an average of 70 percent of its income as a result of a detention or deportation, it is unlikely the remaining parent or family members will be able to continue to meet the mortgage payment or other housing expenses. Additionally, counties that had 287(g) agreements, in which local police collaborate with ICE officials on immigration enforcement, had the highest rates of foreclosures among Latinos.[359]

One of the challenges of the deportation of a father is that the remaining parent must then find a way to survive without the husband's income. According to the Transactional Records Access Clearinghouse (TRAC) at Syracuse University, 95 percent of detainees and deportations are men. This means the wife/mother must often attempt to access a variety of social services, including food stamps, subsidized housing, health care, and other programs.[360] Yet, the climate created by the aggressive enforcement strategy has made parents reluctant to apply for assistance out of a fear that they too may be arrested and deported.

Parental Rights and Custody of Children

Another consequence of the economic challenges for families with a parent who is arrested, detained, or deported is that this can increase the likelihood that a minor child in the household ends up in the child welfare system. Federal law provides all parents, citizen or noncitizen, with a constitutional right to the custody of their children unless it is determined by a court that they are unable or unwilling to care for them. However, the challenges related to an aggressive immigration enforcement policy often interfere with the process by which immigrant parents are able to exercise that right.

Thus, immigration policies can actually interfere with the protections afforded to all parents, regardless of their immigration status, and such policies can further adversely impact the children of immigrants. The primary problems relate to differing timelines for actions in each respective agency. Decisions about custody are time sensitive, and these timelines are often not compatible with the pace of immigration court decisions. Additionally, there is generally a lack of coordination between child welfare, immigration, and criminal justice agencies, which can lead to family separation and the termination of parental rights for immigrant parents.[361]

In 2013, in an effort to address the issue of parental rights, particularly as it relates to minor children and custody, ICE issued a memo called the Parental Interests Directive. One aspect of this directive included how ICE prosecutors were to use their discretion in the handling of parental rights in immigration cases. The directive instructed prosecutors to act "in the best interests of the child" and to use discretion in cases involving children and parental rights.[362]

As discussed in chapter 4, much of what was outlined as policy during the Obama administration was routinely ignored by ICE officials, and the use of prosecutorial discretion, ostensibly designed to improve efficiencies and effectiveness in the resolution of immigration cases, has been replaced with a zero tolerance policy of immigration enforcement. Consistent with such a shift, in 2017, ICE issued a Detained Parents Directive, which instructs ICE officials to "remain cognizant of the impact" enforcement efforts have on children and families. All language related to the best interests of the child and references to parental rights were eliminated from the new memo—meaning it is not a guiding principle in the handling of immigration cases.

For example, the Detained Parents Directive outlines that ICE agents should "generally accommodate" the parent's or legal guardian's efforts to make child care arrangements before contacting local child welfare agencies or the police department to take temporary custody of children.[363] However, there is no real definition of what "generally accommodate" means, which gives a great deal of latitude to agents in how they should proceed. In those instances where a parent or legal guardian cannot arrange child care or custody before the parent is detained or deported, the child may then be taken into the custody of the state's Child Protective Services agency.

What usually occurs is that the child is placed in an emergency shelter, group home, or foster care until permanent custody is determined by a family court. While there is not a lot of solid data regarding this trend, the best estimate offered of the number of U.S. children in foster care who entered the system as a result of a detained or deported parent is approximately five thousand, but most experts note that this number extremely underrepresents the extent of the problem.[364] Immigrant children are also more likely to enter the foster care system if they live in a county that has a 287(g) agreement compared to those counties that do not.[365]

The problem with children being placed in foster care is troubling on many levels, largely because of the challenges the system currently experiences. However, there is an added component for children of deported or detained parents since their parental rights are often invalidated, even when the parents are able and willing to reunite the family. It is here that the lack of communication and coordination between immigration and child welfare agencies becomes most evident.

As part of the family court system, parents who are at risk of losing custody of their children have a right to receive a notification of proceedings that affect their children and family status. They also have the right to attend these hearings and receive copies of court documents that are being used as evidence in the case.[366] According to federal law, if a child has been out of a parent's custody for fifteen of the past twenty-two months, his or her parental rights are in jeopardy and can be terminated.

While each state has its own laws and protocols about how parental rights are terminated, along with procedures for how parents can regain custody of their children, generally speaking, there is some type of reunification plan that outlines parental contact with the children and requirements the parents have to fulfill for custody to be awarded. Attendance at family court hearings about the case is included in these actions.[367]

However, parents who are detained or deported are not always given the opportunity to meet these requirements while they are involved in immigration proceedings. Parents who are being detained by ICE may request that they be allowed to attend these hearings and interactions with their children, but under its new directive, ICE no longer has clearly stated protocols about how this is accomplished.

While the new directive states ICE agents should attempt to facilitate visitations, the policy no longer puts an emphasis on this as a standard practice. Another problem is that ICE is not obligated to inform child welfare officials of the whereabouts of the parent of a child in its custody. This makes it difficult for child welfare providers to locate the parent or properly notify the parent of developments in the custody case.[368]

In many cases, child welfare officials take the absence of parents in visitation or court proceedings as a lack of interest in the case when it may be due to their incarceration or the parents were unaware of when the hearings and visits were scheduled to occur. Additionally, because of a lack of understanding of the implications of failing to meet the requirements of the treatment plan, ICE officials may underestimate the impact of a parent's lack of attendance at court hearings or visitations. The problems stemming from lack of attendance at court hearings and visitations becomes particularly troubling for those parents who have already been deported, even when court attendance is required. Such action means the parent may have their parental rights terminated because ICE does not allow a deported parent back into the country to participate in the hearings.[369]

Finally, parents facing deportation are often faced with the difficult decision of what to do with their children, particularly if the child is a U.S. citizen and has never been to the parent's home country. According to the Center for Public Integrity, ICE collects data on people who are being deported and whether they have minor children who are U.S. citizens. In 2018, ICE reported 87,351 people who claimed to have at least one child who was a U.S. citizen between 2015 and 2017.[370]

Parents who have already been deported can be reunited with their children outside the United States as long as there is a reunification plan and if the parents can demonstrate that they have the capacity to provide a safe and stable environment for the children. This is problematic at a number of levels, largely because the reason the parents left their native country in the first place is because the circumstances are not stable.

Such a task also requires the intervention of multiple agencies in the United States as well as the native country's consulate. Thus, a critical decision for parents who are being deported is whether to bring their children with them, even if they are U.S. citizens, or risk losing custody if they remain in the United States after the parent is deported.

Unaccompanied Minors Who Cross the Border

It is one thing to consider the plight of those youth who were brought to the United States illegally or who were born in the United States but have undocumented parents. The challenges they face are considerable, even if they qualify as U.S. citizens. But what about those individuals—whose numbers are increasing—who attempt to cross the border without their parents? The responsibility for unaccompanied minors who cross the border involves several agencies and a variety of federal laws since there are a host of issues related to this segment of the immigrant population.

Unaccompanied alien children (UAC) are defined as children under the age of eighteen who do not have a legal right to reside in the United States and who are either without a parent or legal guardian in the United States or without someone who can provide for their care and physical custody.[371] Several DHS agencies, such as the Border Patrol and ICE, handle the apprehension, processing, and repatriation of UACs, and the Office of Refugee Resettlement (ORR) and the Department of Health and Human Services (HHS) are responsible for the care and custody of UACs. The Executive Office for Immigration Review (EOIR) in the U.S. Department of Justice conducts immigration removal proceedings, and the U.S. Citizenship and Immigration Services (USCIS) is responsible for the initial adjudication of asylum applications filed by UACs. Thus, addressing UACs involves a process with many moving parts for the federal government.

For instance, the Border Patrol is responsible for apprehending, processing, and detaining the majority of UACs arrested along the U.S. border. When Border Patrol agents confirm a juvenile or child has entered the country illegally and unaccompanied, he or she is classified as a UAC and processed for immigration violations, and the appropriate country's consulate is notified that the juvenile is being detained by DHS. With the exception of Mexican and Canadian UACs, who have a separate processing protocol, the Border Patrol has to turn UACs over to ICE for transport to ORR within seventy-two hours.[372]

In the case of UACs who are from a contiguous country, such as Mexico and Canada, agents must screen the UAC within forty-eight hours of apprehension to determine whether he or she has been a victim of human trafficking and whether the juvenile or child is at risk by being returned his or her country of origin. The Border Patrol must also determine whether the UAC has a possible asylum claim and whether he or she is able to make the decision to voluntarily return to his or her home country.[373]

In 2019, the Border Patrol witnessed a steady and dramatic increase in the number of UACs and families crossing the border. In the past, the trend had been for individual males to attempt to cross the border illegally, but today, the majority of illegal crossings involve families and UACs (see table 6-1). As table 6-1 shows, the number of UACs and family units have nearly doubled in the span of one fiscal year. From October 2018 to April 2019, the percentage of UACs increased nearly 80 percent, from 4,968 to 8,897. Similarly, the increase in the number of families apprehended increased 1.5 times between October and April, from 23,116 to 58,474. Single adults also saw an increase of 37 percent, from 22,924 in October to 31,606 in April.

As it relates to UACs, ICE is responsible for physically transporting them either from the Border Patrol to the custody of the Office of Refugee Resettlement (ORR) or repatriating them to their country of origin if there is a final order of removal (or if the UAC voluntarily elects to return home). ICE follows certain procedures for returning UACs, which includes requirements that government officials for that UAC's country sign for him or her upon return as well as giving UACs the opportunity to communicate with those officials prior to their return. Consular officials are also required to issue travel documents for the UAC so that transportation

Table 6-1 U.S. Border Patrol Southwest Border Apprehensions, FY 2019

	Oct	Nov	Dec	Jan	Feb	Mar	Apr
Unaccompanied Child	4,968	5,259	4,754	5,107	6,821	8,973	8,897
Family Unit	23,116	25,164	27,507	24,200	36,531	53,205	58,474
Single Adult	22,924	21,443	18,487	18,684	23,531	30,653	31,606

Source: U.S. Border Patrol. (2019). *Southwest Border Apprehensions, FY 2019.* Available at https://www.cbp.gov/newsroom/stats/sw-border-migration.

by ICE can be arranged. With regard to Mexican UACs, the protocols are similar with a few minor differences.

ORR is responsible for detaining and sheltering UACs who are from noncontiguous countries, or who may be victims of trafficking, or those who have an asylum claim while they await an immigration hearing. ORR provides care for the children either by reuniting them with a family member, by placing them in foster care with a sponsoring family, or by housing them in an approved shelter. The majority of youths are placed in state-licensed facilities that provide counseling, case management, and educational and recreational opportunities.

The shelters, run by nonprofit organizations and funded through federal grants, are responsible for assessing the child's needs and providing services such as medical care and classroom education. As is the case with most juveniles who are detained in the juvenile justice system, juveniles who are detained for an immigration violation may be held in a more restrictive facility if they have committed a violent act or represent a risk to themselves or others around them. They may also be held in a more secure facility if they represent a risk of escape or if there are not sufficient spaces in a traditional detention facility.

ORR is also tasked with finding and screening suitable adult sponsors, which may include parents or friends of family who can take custody of the child in the United States. Upon release to a sponsor, the children are directed to pro bono attorneys who can represent them in deportation proceedings.[374] It is worth noting that in June 2019, the Trump administration made the decision to terminate educational services to youths who are detained, citing the need to shift resources to other priorities related to immigration enforcement.[375]

Such a move may be illegal, as outlined in the *Flores* agreement regarding the treatment of children in immigrant detention. Under the court settlement in the *Flores* case, immigrant children are entitled to English classes five days a week, one hour of recreation time per day, and access to legal counsel. Some critics of the latest decision about providing services to children argue that such a move is designed to leverage Congress to approve additional funding for the border wall and other enforcement efforts. Other critics point out that the government has manufactured this problem because of the continued practice of separating children from their families means more space and services are needed for UACs.[376]

Other critics contend that if shelters maintained by ORR ran efficiently and released kids promptly, it would free up money for the kinds of programs the department is now cutting. Instead, children are spending an average of sixty-six days in detention, nearly twice the length of time prior to Trump's election. The amount of time children spend in detention began increasing in May 2018 after the government began separating families, which resulted in about 3,000 children being sent to unaccompanied children's shelters. Though the zero tolerance policy ended in June 2018, the government is still separating families on a smaller scale.[377] If the current trends continue, referrals of unaccompanied children to the ORR could surpass the record 2016 figures, when 59,171 minors were referred for care. Prior to fiscal year 2012, the number of children sent to the program each year hovered under 8,000.[378]

In making placement determinations for UACs, ORR conducts a background investigation on prospective sponsors to ensure the identity of the adult assuming legal guardianship for the UAC and that the adult does not have a record of abusive behavior. ORR may consult with the consulate of the UAC's country of origin as well as interview the UAC to ensure he or she also agrees with the proposed placement. If such background checks reveal evidence of actual or potential abuse or trafficking, ORR may require a home study as an additional precaution.[379]

Home studies are required by law in those instances in which a child has been a victim of trafficking, for children with disabilities, in instances where the child has been a victim of physical or sexual abuse, and when the sponsor clearly presents a risk of abuse, maltreatment, exploitation, or trafficking to the child. In addition, a home study is required for any child going to a nonrelative sponsor who is seeking to sponsor multiple children or has previously sponsored or sought to sponsor a child and is seeking to sponsor additional children. In 2018, ORR conducted 3,641 home studies.[380]

U.S. Citizenship and Immigration Services (USCIS) is responsible for the initial adjudication of asylum applications filed by UAC. If the Border Patrol or ICE determines a youth is a UAC and transfers him or her to ORR custody, USCIS will generally take jurisdiction over any asylum application, even when evidence shows that the child reunited with a parent or legal guardian. USCIS also has initial jurisdiction over any claims made by the UAC regarding his or her case in immigration court or with appeals to the Board of Immigration Appeals.[381]

As mentioned in chapter 4, the Executive Office for Immigration Review (EOIR) is responsible for hearing and resolving immigration cases. Federal law requires that the Department of Health and Human Services (HHS) ensures that UACs have access to attorneys and child advocates. EOIR also has established specific policies in removal hearings to ensure that UACs are able to present their cases and understand how the proceedings occur. This includes special dockets for UACs; using child-sensitive questioning, informal protocols, and explanations; and encouraging the use of pro bono representation.[382]

Challenges to the System

In the past decade, Mexico has been the main source for UACs into the United States, with over 80 percent of UACs coming in from that country. In comparison, El Salvador, Guatemala, and Honduras account for less than 20 percent of UACS. However, since 2014, those figures have essentially reversed, with Mexico now accounting for about 23 percent of UACs while the three Central American countries account for approximately 77 percent. These trends have largely continued because economic prospects in Mexico have improved for many families and the birth rate in Mexico has declined. Thus, there is less urgency for many Mexican families to cross the border illegally. However, this is not the case for people from Central American countries.

In the first four months of 2019, about 60 percent of all the aliens apprehended along the southwest border were UACs and aliens traveling in family units (parents or legal guardians traveling with children). In 2019, of the UACs who were apprehended along the southwest border in the first five months of this year, almost 47 percent were from Guatemala, 25 percent were from Honduras, and about 12 percent were from El Salvador. Of the family-unit apprehensions along the southwest border in 2019, almost half were from Guatemala, nearly 40 percent were from Honduras, and about 10 percent were from El Salvador.

Improper Handling of UACs

According to a 2015 report issued by the U.S. Government Accountability Office, the interagency process involved in handling UACs was said to be "inefficient and vulnerable to error." Among the problems cited in that report was that federal officials were not properly identifying and screening potential sponsors before releasing children to them.

Additionally, as is the case with adults, while all children are entitled to have access to an attorney in immigration cases, and while HHS is supposed to provide UACs with legal advocates, in reality, only a small percentage of UACs ever secure legal representation. In fact, most UACS do not even appear at their removal hearings. According to the Congressional Accounting Office, only about 58 percent of the children showed up at their hearings in 2018.[383] Attorneys are supposed to play an important role in the process by helping ensure that children comply with immigration court proceedings and fulfill their responsibilities, but if UACs are not provided with attorneys from the beginning, the attorneys cannot reasonably advise their clients on how to proceed.

This lack of representation is critically important for UACs, perhaps more so than for adults. According to Syracuse University's TRAC system, approximately 30 percent of unaccompanied children whose cases began in 2015 are still without legal representation, and of those cases that began in 2018, 76 percent have no legal counsel. It seems readily apparent that few UACs have the financial resources to hire an attorney, and the law only requires HHS to ensure legal representation "to the greatest extent practicable"—which in many cases simply involves giving the children and their sponsors a list of pro bono lawyers.

The sizable increases in UAC referrals since 2008 have challenged ORR to meet the demand for its services while maintaining child welfare protocols and administrative standards. In January 2016, a Senate investigation indicated that in 2014, some UACs who had originally been placed with distant relatives and approved guardians were abused, and there were other serious deficiencies discovered in the safe placement of children.

The investigation also found the postplacement process lacking. This was part of a series of highlighted news stories about DHS "losing" children who have been in their care. In actuality, an official from ORR/HHS reported to the Senate committee that 1,475 children (out of the 7,635 children the agency was responsible for) could not be accounted for as part of their follow-up protocol after they had been placed with approved parents or guardians.[384]

Separating Children from Families

Some immigration advocates have pointed to new ORR/HHS data that indicates the number of migrant children taken into U.S. custody has increased by 21 percent since April 2019 as well as evidence that border agents are more frequently separating parents from their children at the border. The Trump administration said the focus of its recent crackdown is on illegal border crossings, not separating families.

When the White House announced a zero tolerance policy toward illegal immigration in spring 2018, meaning immigration officials were ordered to prosecute anyone caught crossing the border illegally, one of the consequences of such a decision meant that children traveling with parents were separated while their parents were placed in detention.

Within thirteen days of instituting this policy, 658 children were separated from their parents. These children did not arrive at the border alone, but they are essentially rendered unaccompanied by the government when they are separated from their parents and taken in by HHS.[385]

This policy drew widespread condemnation, prompting President Trump to halt the practice in late June 2018 after a federal judge prohibited the Trump administration from separating parents and children. A year later, government data shows nearly 250 parents have been separated from their children. The problem becomes even more complicated when a child crosses the border with a relative who is not a parent.

A report released by the Texas Civil Rights Project found that children are often separated from relatives and even younger siblings. These types of separations are a growing issue; children are increasingly being brought across the border by other relatives, such as siblings, grandparents, and cousins. In those instances, when they are apprehended, the children are considered UACs—by definition, a family unit can only consist of a parent or legal guardian and a minor child. If a minor child crosses the border with a relative and is apprehended, the two are separated, and the child is treated as a UAC and the adult as a single individual immigrant. In those instances where both are minors, they are treated as UACs and may still be separated when they are placed in different facilities.[386]

While a federal court prohibited the government from separating families under most circumstances and mandated that the families that had been separated be reunited, there are a few exceptions. According to immigration officials, under the current policy, when families are separated, it is because the parent has a criminal history, there is a "law enforcement purpose" that justifies the separation, there is a medical necessity for separating the child from his or her parents (such as hospitalization), or the adult with the child is not the parent or legal guardian. In the vast majority of cases, however, "law enforcement separations" are the primary reason for the separation (92% of cases). In the report issued by the Texas Civil Rights Project, only 58 percent of parents interviewed had criminal convictions. While some of these were undoubtedly for serious crimes, for others, the offense had been elevated from a minor crime or violation to a felony.[387]

Separations of families that are not a parent and child are not included in the court order or counted in separation statistics. The DHS maintains that it is required by law to treat any child entering the United States without a parent or legal guardian as "unaccompanied" and to send him or her to the custody of HHS. The Texas Civil Rights Project report is the first data on family separations to come from outside the government.

They found 38 parents who had been separated from children as well as 228 siblings and other relatives who had traveled with children and were separated once they were apprehended. Children are not allowed to be held in immigration custody; instead, UACs are supposed to be referred to HHS for placement.[388]

This latest trend is one of the reasons it has become so difficult to reunite families, even after the court's ruling. It is also why the statistics offered by DHS do not necessarily reflect the extent of the problem. Ironically, as was mentioned, once a UAC is referred to HHS, officials work to find a relative living in the United States who can house the child while the child's immigration case is pending. If the child does not have a parent living in the United States, an adult sibling, aunt, uncle, or grandparent is usually considered eligible to be a sponsor. A significant problem, however, is that the person who could easily qualify as the UAC's sponsor is also likely to be the person with whom the child was with when the group was apprehended in the first place. In fact, that person may still be in detention or fast-tracked for deportation. As a result, many of these children are placed in a detention facility.

To put the impact of the separation of children from their families into perspective, as part of a lawsuit filed in district court by the American Civil Liberties Union, the advocacy group argues that the Trump administration must do more to reunite children separated from their families as part of its aggressive enforcement efforts. In fact, the government currently estimates that it will take up to two years to identify the parents of the nearly forty-seven thousand children who were apprehended by immigration officials between 2017 and 2018 along the U.S.-Mexico border.[389] In March 2019, the Office of Inspector General issued a report documenting that the Trump administration had a family separation pilot program in July 2017 that it failed to disclose to the court, despite the fact that U.S. district judge ordered the government to stop family separations as part of its zero tolerance policies.[390]

Risks of Exploitation

The risks UACs take in an effort to cross the border should not be overlooked. The cost of the trip is quite expensive, sometimes as much as $5,000 or more, and smugglers often bring children across the border and leave them in locations where they think Border Patrol agents will find them. However, this is risky as agency resources are spread thin due to overcrowding and addressing health issues for detained migrants. This means agents are not patrolling as frequently or in remote areas, which can leave UACs vulnerable to the elements as they make the journey. Exposing children to these types of risks is significant, particularly in remote areas of the desert, where children can suffer from exposure and other challenges.

In addition to avoiding the risks presented by the environment, these children and juveniles face the risk of sexual assault and other forms of violence against them. In May 2017, Doctors without Borders reported that more than two-thirds of the migrant and refugee populations entering Mexico reported being victims of violence during their journey to the United States and that almost one-third of women surveyed had been sexually abused during that trip. The United Nations has also reported that the smuggling of aliens is big business for criminal organizations, valued at $3.7 billion to $4.2 billion a year.[391]

Life, Death, and Health Issues for Detainees

Prior to 2018, it had been ten years since a child had died while in the custody of the Border Patrol. However, in late 2018, several children died either while in custody or shortly after being released by the Border Patrol. The details of the cases involving children in custody gained national attention and called into question the ability of the Border Patrol to manage people in such large numbers while remaining in compliance with federal regulations regarding the detention of immigrants in general and children in particular. As details of the cases became known, it was obvious that the Border Patrol had violated some of those regulations, such as the standard of holding migrants for no more than seventy-two hours before they must be transferred to ORR or ICE, particularly if they are UACs.

There are actually two related problems that create serious health concerns and put all detainees, but particularly children, at risk. The first is the sheer number of people being held in detention. In June 2019, a news report surfaced that in one particular Border Patrol processing center, there were upward of 900 people being held in a facility that had a maximum capacity of 125. This facility was so crowded that detainees were standing on toilets to get some relief from the small confines of their internment.[392]

These migrants were required to remain in this facility, with only room to stand, for days, with no efficient or effective protocol to clean the facilities or to provide showers, laundry, or other amenities. In some facilities, the overcrowding is so severe that a flu outbreak often results in a closing of the entire facility, essentially quarantining it. In other facilities, children are held outside and forced to sleep on the ground, which is a dangerous tactic given the summer temperatures in places like Texas and Florida.[393] It also appears that more people who are suffering from health problems are making their way to the border, thereby bringing their health conditions with them when they are detained.

The emergence of bus smuggling routes through Mexico allows people to be brought to the United States more quickly and comfortably than before; therefore, those who would not have attempted to cross into the United States using traditional methods are now able to do so. The immigration enforcement system in the United States cannot care for these types of people. The system is set up for people who can be apprehended, detained, and deported quickly (even though there appear to be significant challenges with this approach).[394]

It seems evident that the system is being overwhelmed in terms of the number of people entering and remaining in it, and adding an increased number of people with health-related problems only exacerbates an already dangerous situation. As a result, standard protocols are not being followed. The volume of people entering the immigration system means that migrants may not be transferred to an ORR shelter or an ICE facility because they are already at capacity. As a result, more people remain in Border Patrol custody for longer periods of time than the guidelines allow and under more adverse conditions. Add to this situation an increase in the number of people with health issues and it becomes quite clear that the Border Patrol does not have the capacity to handle the volume of people.[395]

To illustrate the significance of the health-related issue regarding the handling of immigrants, the Border Patrol asserts that the number of people who require medical assistance is taxing the ability of the agency to staff the detention facilities since most agents are at hospitals with migrants suffering from a variety of illnesses. Moreover, the logistics of transporting people to receive the care they need are significant. It takes people, vehicles, and time to take people to the hospital. From December through February 2019, agents spent a combined fifty-seven thousand hours at hospitals; at one point, a Border Patrol official said that half of all agents were on duty at hospitals with migrants seeking care. That results in fewer people checking on the migrants staying behind and a limited ability for agents to quickly respond if someone else is showing signs of illness at the facility.[396]

In other words, children are dying in the custody of the Border Patrol in part because there are more children in custody, some of whom have health issues of their own, and there are more sick people who come into

---

IMMIGRANT CHILDREN WHO HAVE DIED IN CUSTODY, 2018–2019[i]

- **Carlos Hernandez Vazquez,** a sixteen-year-old Guatemalan boy, died in a Border Patrol facility after a long bout with the flu. He remained in custody for several days.
- **Felipe Gomez Alonso,** an eight-year-old Guatemalan boy, died in a New Mexico hospital on December 24, 2018. He was suffering from the flu. He remained in custody for several days.
- **Jakelin Caal Maquin,** a seven-year-old Guatemalan girl, died while in custody from an undisclosed illness.
- **Juan de Leon Gutierrez,** a sixteen-year-old Guatemalan boy, died while in custody from a severe brain infection.
- **A two-year-old Guatemalan boy,** who has not yet been identified, died from a severe case of pneumonia.

[i] Lind, Dara. (2019). "The Crisis of Children Dying in Custody at the Border, Explained." *Vox*, May 22. Available at https://www.vox.com/2019/5/22/18632936/child-died-border -toddler-patrol-three-five.

---

contact with them. In response to the long delays in processing cases, the Border Patrol has begun releasing families after they have been apprehended. However, after the deaths that occurred in December, the Border Patrol is now required to conduct a medical examination of children in custody as well as ensuring that they have not been trafficked. This is in addition to the standard procedure that requires Border Patrol agents to issue the families a notice to appear in immigration court at a future date. This can only be done efficiently, of course, if agents are at the facility and can complete the tasks.

The Trump administration's response to this problem is to prevent children from coming into this country in the first place. Deporting families quickly has a deterrent effect that will convince others not to cross the border into the United States. Such an argument is compelling only if the risks of remaining at home are lower than those presented by attempting to cross the border. For most UACs, this is simply not the case.

Are Immigrants Gaming the System for UACs?

Migrants generally have a grasp of basic facts about immigration policy related to their status once they cross the border. Some immigrants are given advice by smugglers to request asylum either when they are caught by Border Patrol agents or when they voluntarily surrender at official ports of entry. Immigrants making this perilous journey also know their chances of being released or avoiding deportation are increased if they travel with a child. Federal law articulates that the government cannot keep migrant families in holding facilities for more than seventy-two hours. After that time, they must either transfer them to an immigration detention facility that is suitable for children or release them.

The Trump administration and federal officials have argued that the special considerations given to UACs creates a climate in which many immigrants bring their own children, or any child for that matter, and claim they are a family unit. Officials contend that parents often think they will be released if they are apprehended at the border if children are with them at the time. Additionally, immigration officials argue that smugglers often assign children to adult travelers posing as their parents so they can be treated differently and released from custody after being apprehended.[397]

The Trump administration has also claimed that most migrants are trying to flood the system with invalid asylum claims. According to one report, in 2008, just under five thousand applicants claimed they had a credible fear of persecution, the first legal step toward obtaining asylum, to avoid being returned to their homeland. Last year, nearly one hundred thousand claimed a credible fear. In recent years, immigration judges have granted fewer than 20 percent of asylum requests, a proportion that is even lower for Central Americans.[398] Critics of the Trump administration's position argue that the increase in requests is not the result of a "gaming" of the system as much as it is an escalation of the problems in those countries that force people to flee.

Many asylum seekers from Central America claim they have been victims of gangs, which is harder to prove than political and other types of persecution. Poverty is not among the grounds for receiving asylum, and if they are denied, asylum seekers can be deported. But since many are released while their case is pending, some never return to court and evade deportation.[399] The U.S. attorney general determined that the threat of victimization by gangs or poverty is not a sufficient reason to grant asylum. Instead, the United States has redefined the criteria used to grant asylum to consist of very narrow and carefully articulated reasons that must be demonstrated by the applicant during the credible fear interview. The result is that there are fewer applications and fewer approvals of asylum applications.

The Trump administration has proposed several changes to how the United States handles unaccompanied minors trying to enter the country, including those that would make it easier to detain and deport migrant children and harder for those children to seek asylum. According to the *Washington Post*, the proposed changes would give immigration judges more discretion in determining whether a child deserves the special status of UAC.[400] Whether such loopholes exist in the system and thereby exacerbate the scope of the problem, the real issue is how immigrants are perceived and treated and the unintended consequences of a determined effort to eliminate all undocumented immigrants and prevent more from entering the country. The overwhelming number of people coming into the system is at least in part a consequence of the intentional effort to detain and deport them.

It is clear by any reasonable assessment that ICE, the Border Patrol, ORR, and DHS are ill equipped to handle the immigration problem, despite additional resources and the construction of holding facilities or "the big beautiful wall" that President Trump has promised. Overwhelmed courts, the child welfare system, and detention and holding facilities are at least in part products of the efforts made to redefine behaviors as crimes and felonies, and making them retroactive only increases the volume of people who can be swept up in the immigration enforcement net that was created. Further, the overcrowding of the system also brings with it a host of public health issues, some of which are contributing to highlighted cases of child deaths. One way to frame these challenges is to not conceptualize it as an immigration issue at all—this is a humanitarian/public health/economic challenge that one agency or set of agencies are unable to resolve on their own.

In response to the obvious problems, the Trump administration has doubled down on its enforcement efforts with predictable results. While this may sound politically popular, particularly as an election looms in 2020, increases in funding, personnel, and buildings are not the solution to the problem. We have already seen that strategy fail on a variety of other issues, and immigration is no different.

In chapter 7, we will examine the *why* portion of the immigration problem in the United States. In that discussion, I attempt to offer insight into why there are so many people attempting to enter the United States and why so much time, effort, and energy is being spent trying to curtail it.

CHAPTER SEVEN

Framing the Immigration Problem

- In a discussion about passing the DREAM Act, President Trump said, "Why do we want all these people from shithole countries? We should have people from places like Norway."[401]

- "The heart and soul of Europe is tolerance. It has taken us centuries to understand this. We have persecuted and annihilated one another. We have laid our own country to waste. . . . The worst period of hatred, devastation, and destruction happened not even a generation ago. It was done in the name of my people."[402]
  —Angela Merkel, chancellor of Germany

- To find peace, migrants and refugees are willing to "risk their lives" on long and dangerous trips, often enduring hardship and suffering, "and to encounter fences and walls built to keep them far from their goal."[403]
  —Pope Francis

In the previous chapters, we examined the value and purpose of immigration to the social, political and economic importance to the United States as well as the recent efforts to curb the latest "threat" to the country and the culture: immigrants from Mexico and Central America. The policy changes that have occurred, which are predicated on preventing immigrants from these countries from entering the United States along with removing the ones who have remained illegally, have been the foundation of the Trump administration.

The *criminalization of immigration* is the term often used to describe how the government targets the behavior of certain groups and elevates certain behaviors by members of the groups for criminal prosecution.

Criminalizing the behavior of certain groups is not a new idea; as documented by the National Law Center, we have seen evidence of a criminalization of the homeless population, where the goal was to remove or at least eliminate the visibility of homeless people from certain locations and communities by targeting typical behaviors of this population and making them criminal offenses. The criminalization of certain groups has been used on other populations as well.[404]

While the criminalization of Latinos and Mexican immigrants is not a new idea, its impact reaches beyond those individuals immediately targeted. In addition to detaining and deporting immigrants, there is a series of intended and unintended victims of such an approach, including an enormous allocation of resources to manage the volume of people participating in the immigration and incarceration machine.

As we have seen, stepped-up enforcement of immigration laws has resulted in the misguided targeting of Latinos and Mexicans in the form of proactive law enforcement campaigns, a heated and hostile debate about sanctuary cities, a backlog of cases in immigration court, and overcrowded detention facilities that have witnessed the abuse and deaths of immigrants. Clearly, the immigration machine that has been constructed during the Obama and Trump administrations is not equipped to manage the problem, nor does it appear to be fixable under the current model.

The current immigration policy, with its focus on incarceration and deportation as its driving themes, also resembles the efforts in the past, when mass incarceration for criminal offenders was seen as the solution to rising crime rates. Such an approach has not produced the intended effect, and experts question the value of prison as a long-term solution for inappropriate behavior. In a similar way, detaining and deporting undocumented immigrants, attempting to prevent people from seeking asylum into the United States, and building walls along the border seem to be an overly simplistic solution to a far more complicated problem.

In addition to the debate about the process of immigration and the rationale behind the current policy, along with whether or not the problem is being characterized accurately, two questions have been largely overlooked in the immigration discussion and debate. The first question is how the problem has become so significant, particularly since Mexican workers have been crossing the border for decades to work in various industries in the United States. A second and related question focuses on whether the immigration issues seen in the United States are found in other countries around the world. This is important because as white nationalism in the United States becomes more visible, it is reasonable to consider whether this is a product of a unique experience in the United States or whether the problem is understood more globally.

This chapter explores two primary issues. The first is why the United States is facing enormous challenges at the U.S.-Mexico border. As we will see, the problem did not suddenly emerge but has been the product of a series of political and economic decisions in countries that comprise Central America. That is, there is a reason why so many migrants from Central America are coming to the United States and seeking asylum. An understanding of this issue is pivotal to addressing the immigration challenges facing this country in the present as well as in the future.

While there are many factors that contribute to the current situation in Central America, most experts note that U.S. interventions in the economic and political decision making in those countries, driven largely by profits, have allowed the exploitation of the people of many Central American countries. As we will see, like it or not, the immigration problem we are facing in the United States is linked to these decisions, which means we are largely responsible for the circumstances that allowed the civil unrest, violence, corruption, and extreme poverty that is forcing people in those countries to flee their homes and come to the United States.

A second issue that will be discussed in this chapter is the global context of the immigration problem in the United States. The United States is not the only country wrestling with what do to about immigration, and many of the strategies used by the Trump administration, and even some of the rhetoric to support them, are similar in scope and content to what other countries and their leaders have used to address their burgeoning immigrant and refugee populations. While a full discussion of the global refugee problem is beyond the scope of this book in general and this chapter in particular, a description of the global immigration problem places U.S. policy into a context of understanding.

Immigration and Central America

Similar to the discussion of African American involvement in the criminal justice system, there is little, if any, debate about the trends in the migration of citizens from countries in Central America to the United States. That is, no one really disputes that thousands of people are fleeing these countries, nor is there much debate about why they need to leave their homes.

Central America is made up of several countries, and the ones most frequently mentioned in the U.S. immigration discussion are Honduras,

El Salvador, and Guatemala. The bulk of the immigrants who are attempting to cross the border into the United States come from these three countries. As such, the current and historical conditions in these countries,
particularly the involvement of the United States in their affairs, is an
important feature in understanding the U.S. immigration challenges.

Honduras

A key aspect of the history of the Honduran-U.S. relationship involves
the U.S. military. The Honduran story began in the late 1890s, when U.S.-
based banana companies were established there.[405] As a result, these companies built railroads, established a banking system, and generally created
several industries that exported their goods to the United States. The
banana companies were also instrumental in developing agricultural and
mining industries.

Another common feature of the history of Honduras was the use of
bribery and the corruption of its officials. In fact, the banana companies
were so influential that by the beginning of World War I, they owned
almost a million acres of the best land in Honduras. Few complained
about the extent to which these companies essentially took over the country, and given its history of poverty and disenchantment, the economic
influence of the multinational banana companies was seen by citizens
and government officials as a positive one in Honduras.[406]

These private interests were augmented by a U.S. military presence,
which was designed to protect the country's booming agricultural trade
and the corporate interests there. Political influence was also a part of the
landscape, with the United States playing a significant role in elections
and placing democratic leaders in key positions in Honduras. Moreover,
the ruling class of Honduras, which was dominated by members of the
Honduran military, became heavily dependent on the United States for
economic, political, and military support. By the 1960s, the military was
a significant political force in the country's decision making.[407]

By the 1980s, there was significant U.S. involvement in Honduran
affairs. During the Reagan administration's efforts to rid neighboring
Nicaragua of the Sandinista government and reduce leftist movements in
the region, President Reagan deployed several hundred U.S. soldiers to
Honduras. The U.S. military was also responsible for training and sustaining Nicaragua's "contra" rebels in Honduras. It was during this time
that the United States provided substantial military aid and created joint
military bases and installations with Honduras. One consequence of this
development was the militarization of Honduras socially, politically, and

economically. As a result, there was greater willingness to engage in political repression, assassinations, illegal detentions, and the common practice of people simply disappearing if they challenged the status quo.[408]

Economically, the Reagan administration also took steps to develop and enhance manufacturing industries in Honduras and to disrupt traditional forms of agriculture, including the deregulation of the coffee industry, upon which Honduras depended for economic stability. By expanding opportunities to engage in globalization, Honduras was able to attract more global capital. In addition, as Reagan did in the United States, funding for programs to address the pervasive poverty in Honduras was significantly scaled back. These factors, consistent with the neoliberal reforms seen in other countries, resulted in higher levels of poverty, unemployment, and significant human rights violations by military and political leaders.

Reformists in Honduras made concerted efforts in the late 1980s and 1990s to improve conditions in Honduras, but the stranglehold the ruling class had on the economy and the political institution made social change difficult. One feature of this regime was the increase in the number of Hondurans immigrating to the United States. Given the lack of jobs, extreme poverty, few safety nets to help the poor, and excessive human rights violations, many families felt they had no choice but to leave their homeland.[409]

A glimmer of reform occurred with the election of Manuel Zelaya, a liberal, who was elected in 2006. Zelaya attempted to effect meaningful change in Honduras, including raising the minimum wage and establishing social services programs for the poor, and he even brought together a group who wanted to change the country's constitution, which had given power to the ruling classes during a military government. Such dramatic changes led to Zelaya's overthrow in a military coup in 2009.[410]

This coup was an important moment for Honduras since it ultimately led to a dramatic increase in the number of people fleeing the country and the realization that meaningful change was unlikely. While denouncing the overthrow of Zelaya's administration, the Obama administration stopped short of calling it an actual coup, largely because doing so would require the United States to terminate most of the aid to the country. Given the corporate and business interests in Honduras, economic and military support continued.[411]

To ensure that Zelaya did not return to power, the United States supported a series of other elections and continued to overlook corruption, fraud, and violence in Honduras because the ruling class continued to support U.S. economic and geopolitical interests. Because policies and decisions by country leaders typically favored only the ruling classes and U.S. multinational corporations, the region has remained unstable, creating power gaps into which drug cartels, gangs, and paramilitary groups have emerged.

The extensive violence is also a current feature in Honduras. In 2017, Global Witness, an international nongovernmental agency, declared Honduras as the most violent and deadliest country in the world.[412] This is largely due to the existence of violent gangs that operate in urban neighborhoods, but also because political dissent is often met with assassination, imprisonment, or the aforementioned "disappearances," which are presumed to be homicides.

In addition to the deeply disturbing political and social dimensions of life in Honduras, with humanitarian violations becoming far too common, the United States has continued to support a free market form of capitalism that is essentially unregulated. Such a climate results in significant forms of socioeconomic inequality, issues of worker safety and exploitation, and decreases in health care, education, and other forms of social services. The result of these efforts is that the poverty rate in Honduras has dramatically increased in recent years.[413]

The Dominican Republic–Central American Free Trade Agreement (CAFTA-DR), which is an agreement between the United States and five Central American countries and the Dominican Republic, is designed to improve the economic opportunities in those countries. However, the language of the agreement contains stipulations that virtually ensure economic dependence on the United States and U.S. multinational corporations. This one-sided agreement, particularly in agriculture and the manufacturing sector of the Honduran economy, limits the stimulation of domestic business activity and the creation of a self-supporting economy. This is one of the reasons so many farmers and union advocates voted against it.[414]

According to an AFL-CIO report in 2015, while the agreement was intended to provide stabilization and opportunities for workers to be treated fairly, nearly 70 percent of all employers in Honduras had violated employee rights in regard to minimum wage and overtime requirements. In addition, retaliatory firings for engaging in labor activism, intimidation by employers, and other forms of violence remain features in the lives of workers.[415]

A critical component of this agreement is that under the CAFTA-DR, all U.S. industrial and commercial goods enter Honduras duty free, yet Honduran goods coming to the United States must pay a 3 percent duty on the goods. The result is that, as of 2018, Honduras and other Central

American nations had a negative trade balance of more than $4 billion.[416] Such disadvantaged agreements, continued exploitation of workers, and extreme poverty, coupled with military dictatorships and criminal organizations that operate with the continued support of the United States, create a climate in which many families come to realize they are at risk on several fronts: economically in the lack of job opportunities, the lack of any meaningful safety net should the family need assistance, and the threat of violence from criminal gangs. The result is that many families realize that they cannot remain, and so they migrate north to the United States.

El Salvador

Similar in many ways to the historical account of Honduras, the story of El Salvador begins earlier, with the influence of military dictatorships and the threat of communism. It also includes U.S. involvement in the form of military aid, political influence, and humanitarian support, even when coups occurred. Life in El Salvador also includes the frequent use of political assassinations, disappearances of rebel and religious leaders, and the execution of civilians who are seen as dissidents.

El Salvador is also a good example of the tendency of the United States to ignore political leaders and regimes that engage in civil unrest and the victimization of innocent civilians. During the Reagan administration, for instance, while a civil war raged in El Salvador between the military-led government and leftist rebels, the United States continued to provide military support for the authoritarian government. The United States trained members of the Salvadoran army and provided so much equipment and other forms of support that by 1983, some experts noted the United States was essentially funding the civil war in El Salvador.

One example of the extreme violence and victimization of civilians occurred in 1981 in the village of El Mozote. The Atlacatl Battalion of the Salvadoran army, trained by U.S. soldiers, was responsible for killing between seven hundred and one thousand unarmed civilians, including women and children. Further evidence of the violence was the estimated eighty thousand people who were killed. About 85 percent of those killings were committed by the army and its "death squads," according to a United Nations report.[417]

In response to the massacre in El Mozote as well as the murder of four Catholic nuns by Salvadoran soldiers, the Reagan administration claimed that the El Mozote incident was political propaganda and that the nuns who were executed were actually acting outside the capacity of their roles as church leaders.[418] Even after a State Department report in 1981 documented the existence of the massacre at the hands of government soldiers, the U.S. government did not admit its error, and it has never acknowledged its role in the funding and support of the El Salvadoran government during that time.[419]

Perhaps even more telling was the U.S. response to asylum applications by families and individuals who attempted to flee the violence in El Salvador. The Reagan administration claimed that those who fled El Salvador during this time were not the result of human rights violations but were instead "economic migrants." It should not be surprising to learn that the United States granted only 3 percent of all the asylum applications from El Salvador during this time.

As pointed out by Garcia (2006), it was also during this time that religious groups and other nongovernmental organizations provided asylum to many Salvadoran citizens. This occurred despite the U.S. denials of the atrocities occurring in El Salvador and in violation of existing U.S. policy on granting asylum.[420] It is worth noting that during this period, the United States continued its financial, political, and public support of existing Salvadoran political parties that were instrumental in ensuring that U.S.-backed politicians continued to remain in power.[421] It was also during this time that thousands of young men deserted from the army or the guerillas during the war and fled to the United States.

In the mid-1990s, President Clinton allowed temporary protected status for tens of thousands of Salvadorans who had fled to the United States to expire. This meant that those young men were required to return to El Salvador, even though there was little in the way of legitimate economic opportunities for them. These men quickly realized that the absence of the rule of law coupled with their fighting skills learned in the war created an opportunity to form criminal gangs. Consequently, the homicide and violent crime rates skyrocketed as gangs attempted to control urban neighborhoods.[422]

El Salvador and the MS-13 Gang

For some people, a discussion of El Salvador and its history conjures up images of the famous MS-13 gang. Such a perception is fueled by President Trump's repeated references to the gang as part of his claims about the invasion of immigrants from Central America. Other policy makers often make reference to MS-13 as one of the most violent street gangs, particularly because of some of the more graphic acts of violence by gang members. As we will see, while the gang is a real entity, and while some members do engage in extreme forms of violence, its impact on the crime problem or even the gang problem in this country is in contrast to the actual facts. Moreover, despite Trump's assertions, the gang actually emerged in California, and its growth came as a result of changes in immigration law that forced many Salvadorans back to their native country despite the fact that many of these teens had never spent any time there.

In 2018, President Trump said, "We have people coming into the country, or trying to come in—and we're stopping a lot of them. You wouldn't believe how bad these people are. These aren't people. These are animals."[423] In June 2018, then Homeland Security secretary Kirstjen Nielsen said, "Large criminal organizations such as MS-13 have violated our borders and gained a deadly foothold within the United States."[424] The Trump administration often invokes MS-13's acts of violence to justify hard-line policies against immigration. The president said, "This is a crisis. You have human trafficking, you have drugs, you have criminals coming in, you have gangs, MS-13. We're taking them out by the thousands and bringing 'em back."[425]

The Origins of MS-13

There is little debate that El Salvador is a dangerous place. In 2017, there were close to 4,000 homicides in El Salvador, a significant decline from the 6,600 killings in 2015, but El Salvador still has one of the highest murder rates in the world. The problems in El Salvador are chronic ones, with corruption and poverty a consistent feature of the landscape. It is in this climate of lawlessness and the resulting migration to the United States that MS-13 originated. MS-13, or *"Mara Salvatrucha"* (roughly translated, *Mara* means "gang" in Spanish, and *Salvatrucha* means "Salvadoran peasant guerilla," from which many members originated), is one of the largest gangs in the world, and its influence in Central America is one of the factors that drives thousands of migrants to flee to the United States. Despite commentary by President Trump about MS-13 members migrating from El Salvador into the United States, the gang actually originated in Los Angeles, California.[426]

During El Salvador's civil war in 1980s, government forces were responsible for thousands of human rights violations, and hundreds of thousands of Salvadorans fled the country and migrated to the United States. The immigration policies during the Reagan era made it especially difficult for Salvadorans to obtain asylum status or temporary legal status. Those undocumented migrants who came to the United States in the

1980s found themselves in the middle of the anti-immigration boom of the 1990s. With the civil war in El Salvador finally over, and with the passage of the Illegal Immigration Reform and Immigrant Responsibility Act (IIRIRA) in 1996, the federal government began deporting tens of thousands of Salvadoran immigrants. This volume of migrants taxed the Salvadoran government's ability to take them back and integrate them into the existing social structures of the country. This was particularly true given that the United States did not identify which deportees were criminals. In reality, the vast majority of deportees to El Salvador were not MS-13 gang members.[427]

Social Factors and the Rise of MS-13

During the period prior to the mass deportation of Salvadoran immigrants, many settled with relatives in communities that already had large numbers of Guatemalan, Honduran, or Salvadoran immigrants. In these low-income neighborhoods, Salvadoran teens faced hostility from other ethnic groups and from other youths, some of whom were involved in local gangs. Many of these youths had already suffered a host of traumatic experiences. They had a limited understanding of English and were socially and physically isolated. In those instances where children and teens were separated from their families, the HHS often placed them with other immigrant children, and sometimes the sponsoring families provided inadequate care. Adding to the problem, social service agencies were not prepared or equipped to work with school officials or local governments to address the needs of migrant families or their children once they arrived.[428] In addition, school authorities were not always willing or able to help: some officials misidentified gang intimidation as bullying, and others were simply afraid of the gangs and ignored the problem all together. When school officials did make an effort to eliminate gangs from the schools, local police officers were often unable to distinguish gang members from their victims.

In an attempt to cope with all these challenges, Salvadoran youths began to cluster together to provide some level of protection from local gangs. MS-13 initially began as MSS, a group or gang made up of teenage immigrants who used drugs and listened to heavy metal music. The group originally called themselves the Stoners and later Mara Salvatrucha. When and why the Stoners became a hardened violent gang is not clearly understood. Some observers note that it had more to do with confrontations with other L.A. gangs, but others argue it had more to do with newer Salvadoran immigrants who had experienced the violence of civil war in their home country and were more prone to violence themselves. Still others argue that the Salvadoran government's get tough response to delinquent youth, in which even minor offenders were sent to over-crowded jails and prisons, had had the predictable result of creating hardened criminals. These individuals then migrated to the United States, where there was a greater willingness to engage in vicious acts of violence and engage in crimes as part of an organized gang.[429]

Once the deportations of Salvadoran immigrants from the United States began, the response by the Salvadoran government was similar to a strategy used in Honduras, known as *mano dura* ("firm hand"), a form of zero tolerance that resulted in the imprisonment of thirty-one thousand young people from 2003 to 2005 simply on the suspicion that they were members of gangs. Such a policy had limited effects: according to one estimate, about 84 percent of those imprisoned were released because the government lacked sufficient evidence to charge them with a crime. For those actual gang members who were incarcerated in El Salvador, prison officials decided to keep members of the same gang together in dedicated prisons. Such an approach may have reduced violent confrontations between rival gang members, but it also made it a lot easier for gang lead-ers to consolidate and plan criminal activity.[430]

Media Hype and the Moral Panic of MS-13

Currently, the U.S. Department of the Treasury officially designates MS-13 as a "transnational criminal organization"; however, most experts have concluded that this is an inaccurate description of the gang and its structure for two primary reasons. First, MS-13 does not operate like an international crime organization; instead, the structure tends to reflect more of a franchise model, with individual and independent "owners" of a particular gang clique. That is, there is not a great deal of communica-tion, trust, or opportunities for collaboration between cliques under the umbrella of MS-13. In fact, efforts to consolidate different factions within MS-13 have been ineffective.[431]

Second, MS-13 fails to meet the criteria of a transnational criminal organization based on its activities, which tend to focus on low-level drug dealing and simple extortion. Thus, MS-13 lacks the diversity of revenue streams found in other transnational organizations. What seems to garner the most notoriety for MS-13 is its extreme use of violence. However, homicide rates have declined even in places where MS-13 has a presence. The real reason MS-13 has garnered so much of the public's attention is that cliques tend to establish in major metropolitan areas, such as New

York and Washington, DC, where media coverage tends to be widespread and has a national platform. Thus, while the gang does engage in some gruesome acts of violence, its actual impact on crime and the community are largely overblown. While ten thousand members is a considerable number, when compared to other gangs, along with the types of activities MS-13 members engage in, the impact is actually rather limited.[432]

As previously mentioned, the more troubling problems at the border are the gang violence, street crime, and civil unrest that force many parents to send their children to the United States alone or with siblings. There were approximately 260,000 unaccompanied alien children (UACs) who migrated to the United States from 2012 to mid-2017. For some politicians and policy makers, such a large number of migrants who crossed into the United States and then were released gave the appearance of a type of invasion. The Trump administration has consistently pointed to MS-13 to describe this influx of UACs, characterizing it as an invasion of violent immigrant gang members intent on harming citizens.[433]

In reality, there was no large-scale infiltration of the United States by MS-13 members. In June 2017, the chief of Customs and Border Protection, Carla Provost, told the Senate Judiciary Committee that 159 unaccompanied minors who had been processed by Border Patrol between September 2011 and June 2017 were "confirmed or suspected" to have gang ties—a "very low" number given that about 260,000 unaccompanied children were processed during that time. Of the 159 who were confirmed or suspected to have gang ties, only 56 were "confirmed or suspected" to be affiliated with MS-13.[434]

It is important to remember that this count contains an element of subjectivity. That is, Border Patrol agents may have incorrectly concluded a particular person was a member of MS-13 because they misunderstood or misidentified the person's tattoos or perhaps the person had family members who were involved in MS-13. A third possibility is that a particular immigrant may have been coerced to join MS-13 and traveled to the United States to escape the gang's influence. There could be other reasons, of course, but the fact that there are so few MS-13 members identified in this data suggests that calling it an "invasion" is an exaggeration. It also suggests that the influence of MS-13 in terms of its impact on crime, violence, and immigration is symptomatic of a type of moral panic outlined in chapter 2.

The debate about the threat posed by the MS-13 gang occurs within the criminal justice system as well. What needs to be remembered is that regardless of which side of the immigration debate one might align with, it is important to note that there are incentives for agencies to adopt a particular stance on immigration (that it is an invasion by gang members, for example, can be an important and potentially effective reelection campaign message). These can be based on a number of factors, but the politics of immigration and the way it is being presented to the general public can easily shape public policy.

For instance, prosecutors can sometimes focus too much attention on the threat the gang poses largely because incarcerating people is a large part of what prosecutors do, and if they are elected officials, they must give the appearance that they are tough on crime. In contrast, police agencies and their officers tend to downplay the significance and threat from gangs (if the gang is running rampant, it suggests that the police are not doing their job of protecting citizens). Additionally, a significant part of the challenge for law enforcement is identifying gang members and distinguishing them from their potential victims—the community. The only realistic way the police can accomplish this goal is by interacting and collaborating with community members.

As discussed in chapter 3, the immigrant community has become distrustful of the police, which is largely a product of Trump's assertions that local law enforcement should be involved in immigration enforcement. This means that immigrants, both documented and undocumented, are unlikely to provide insight about gang activity, and they are not likely to report being victimized by gang members. As one police official put it, "The community's silence is the gang's strength."[435] In other words, the reluctance of immigrants to collaborate with the police limits the ability of the department to actually have an impact on reducing gang-related crime.

A review of the statements by President Trump make it evident that he has used the popular perceptions of MS-13 to stigmatize all immigrants and assert that people from other Latin American countries come to the United States for the purpose of committing crimes and violence against the American people. Missing from that narrative, of course, are the facts that there are very low numbers of immigrants who are affiliated with MS-13; the gang actually originated in California, not El Salvador; and Reagan-era immigration policy created the problem of MS-13 members growing in size and influence in El Salvador.[436]

Guatemala

As with the other Central American countries mentioned, the history and current situation in Guatemala is characterized by a steady stream of military dictators, poverty, civil unrest, and violence. The most significant wars in Guatemala began in 1954 when a CIA-sponsored military coup overthrew the existing democratically controlled government that had attempted to effect reforms.[437]

Until the 1990s, Guatemala was ruled by a series of military officers, and while opposition groups emerged during this time, power and economic control continued to rest with a small segment of the population. In fact, the inequalities that existed in Guatemala were arguably worse than in Honduras or El Salvador. For example, in Guatemala, 2 percent of the population controlled nearly three-quarters of the private land. At the same time, almost two-thirds of the population earned less than $2 per day working in the agricultural fields, harvesting coffee, cotton, and sugar cane. Many homes did not have indoor plumbing or electricity, and there was limited access to health care and education for children.[438] Of particular note were the Maya Indians who lived in the highlands of Guatemala. With a population of more than eight million, this group was particularly hard hit by the influx of multinational corporations who confiscated Indian land for its oil, minerals, and ranching.[439]

As is often the case, such conditions are ripe for unionization, worker advocacy groups, and even insurgency. In the early 1960s, the government had the army move into the highlands to undertake a campaign of violence, kidnapping, and murder of those who attempted to effect change. Guerilla groups operated during the 1960s and 1970s in an effort to overthrow or undermine sitting dictators. In response, the level of violence escalated during the 1980s. The army burned crops and fields and killed livestock in an effort to attack insurgents' food supplies.[440] The soldiers also killed women and children, and engaged in torture, rape, and the mutilation of civilians. Such actions were deemed "scientific killings" designed to eliminate the rebels' influence over the people of the region.

In 1981, the Guatemalan Army launched Operation Ceniza in response to growing Marxist guerilla efforts. Calling them "counterattacks" against guerillas, the army bombed entire villages and executed civilians using U.S.-supplied equipment. During this time, the Reagan administration approved a $2 billion covert CIA program in Guatemala as well as nearly $25 million worth of military helicopters, trucks, and other equipment.[441]

Between 1978 and 1984, approximately 100,000 Guatemalans were killed, 40,000 more "disappeared," over four hundred villages were destroyed, and more than 700,000 people were displaced from their lands. It was also noted during this time that more than 250,000 people fled the country.[442] As was the case with other Central American countries, the United States continued to train Guatemalan soldiers and provide military and humanitarian relief to the country along with promoting corporate development.

Such continued support of an oppressive and violent regime by the United States, especially when instances of violence were inflicted upon citizens, drew international condemnation from other countries. Yet, U.S. support for those in power in Guatemala was essentially unaffected. In 2006, Guatemala, like the other countries discussed in this chapter, entered into the CAFTA-DR free trade deal with the United States, and like other countries, virtually all U.S agricultural exports enter Guatemala duty-free.[443]

Central Americans as Immigrants or Refugees

As a result of the chaos and civil unrest in various countries in Central America, Mexico and the United States became hosts to many Central American refugees. These countries, particularly the United States, offered greater stability and economic opportunities than what was available in their home countries, so many immigrants made the difficult decision to make the dangerous journey north.

In the 1970s, many officials in the United States argued that there was a wave of anti-immigration sentiment by the public because of concerns that millions of additional immigrants would drain the economy that had only recently recovered from a recession. Politicians, then and now, also argued that Americans were suffering from "compassion fatigue" about the problems in Central America. They argued that while helping the refugees might be the right thing to do, the volume, intensity, and duration of the crisis was causing people to be fearful of the impact so many Central Americans would have on the cultural and economic fabric of the country.

This sentiment led to a series of immigration laws during the 1980s and 1990s that attempted to restrict the flow of immigrants into the United States. However, such a perception by politicians was not borne out by public opinion polls, nor was there a concerted effort to force politicians to "do" something about the increase of Central American immigrants into this country. These decisions were based on the perception of the problem by politicians, not the public.

One way the United States could limit the arrival of so many immigrants from Central America, particularly those who were seeking asylum, was to change the criteria used to determine their application. Prior to 1980, when the United States was most concerned about the threat of communism, U.S. policies rewarded those individuals who fled communist countries. Generally speaking, if a person came from Cuba or one of the Eastern Bloc countries, that fact alone would often automatically qualify them for asylum since it was generally accepted that the person had escaped an authoritarian regime and qualified for consideration.

In 1980, however, the United States adopted the 1980 Refugee Act, which followed the United Nations' definition of *refugees* in an effort to standardize the process by which people were recognized as refugees and asylees. Under this new law, if someone petitioned for asylum, the person had to prove that there was a well-founded fear of persecution based on race, religion, nationality, or membership in a particular political or social group that warranted assistance by the host country. How one determines whether a fear is "well founded," however, became a critical talking point in the discussion and in the application of the policy.

As a result, even after the passage of the 1980 act, most Central Americans did not qualify for asylum. Instead, the United States continued to treat Central Americans as economic migrants, meaning they were making the decision to come to the United States in search of a better life. This is an important distinction because the United States was not obligated to accept economic immigrants as asylum seekers. Experts argue that one of the reasons the United States continued to see Central Americans this way was because such a categorization relieved the government of the obligation to do something about their plight.[444]

In addition to altering the eligibility criteria for asylum seekers, the United States argued that those who migrated through Mexico had ample opportunities to find safety, security, and economic opportunities in that country. During this period, Mexico had a clearly defined asylum policy and was receptive to the plight of Central Americans. Thus, U.S. officials argued that there was no real danger presented to Central Americans in Mexico, so if someone decided to continue their journey to the United States, it had more to do with seeking better economic opportunities than efforts to flee persecution.[445]

Trump's Modeling of Reagan's Policies

Immigration reform became a priority for the Reagan administration. As part of a task force that reviewed practices and policies on immigration, along with years of debate and controversy, Congress passed the Immigration Reform and Control Act (IRCA) in 1986, increased funding to the Border Patrol, and penalized employers who knowingly hired undocumented workers. As was discussed in chapters 1 and 2, IRCA also granted amnesty to undocumented workers if they could prove they had entered the United States prior to January 1, 1982. This resulted in about 280,000 Central Americans legalizing their status, most of which were from El Salvador and Guatemala. However, the majority of Central Americans arrived after the deadline, making them ineligible.[446]

At about the same time, the Reagan administration became concerned about what it called "frivolous petitions" for asylum that tied up the court dockets. Officials claimed that many Central Americans applied for asylum regardless of their status because this could delay their hearing for up to two years while they lived in the United States. The goal for the Reagan administration was to expedite the deportation process with a concerted immigration enforcement effort that used detention as a strategy while attempting to fast-track the deportation process.

As a result, in the 1980s, detention centers along the U.S. border filled to capacity with immigrants, particularly what the Border Patrol called OTMs (other than Mexicans). Many of the facilities housed detainees in far greater numbers than their maximum capacity, causing an overcrowding problem.[447] Immigration advocates and legal representatives called attention to human rights violations and deplorable conditions in the detention centers and a systematic denial of due process and civil liberties in the court proceedings. This included the physical and sexual abuse of women and the mistreatment of children. Many detainees were denied access to an attorney, if they had one, and many Central Americans were tricked into signing voluntary deportation papers. Another common strategy was to separate family members.[448]

All these tactics should sound familiar because they are the basis of the Trump administration's approach to solving the immigration problem. In fact, a persuasive argument could be made that Trump has simply copied the efforts of the Reagan administration in its approach to immigration.

Interestingly, the general public did not appear to have a firm grasp on the immigration debates or strategies used to address the issue during the Reagan administration. Public opinion polls in the 1980s showed that immigration and the plight of Central American refugees was not high on the list of concerns for most Americans. For example, a 1984 CBS News poll showed that only about 25 percent of Americans knew which side the United States was on in the conflicts in El Salvador, and only about 13 percent knew that the United States was supporting the contra rebels in Nicaragua. That said, there was a segment of the population that was very vocal about the failure of the United States to address the humanitarian crisis that was occurring and the U.S. foreign policy with regard to Central America.[449]

This group argued that the United States had a moral and legal obligation to protect the refugees coming to the United States from Central America. The basis of this approach was the history of involvement by the United States in supporting the corrupt and oppressive military regimes that exploited the country's resources and forced millions of people into poverty and violence. This group also argued that the United States was responsible for the fact that much of the aid that went into Central America never really reached the people it was designed to help. Instead, the money went to corrupt government officials who used it for their own gain and to support the status quo. Given these developments, this group argued that the United States should at least accept the consequences of such misguided actions by receiving the refugees as a by-product of those decisions.[450]

Thus, the problems experienced by many people in Central America, both in the past and in the present, stem from oppressive and corrupt regimes that routinely ignore the plight of most citizens and the poverty they experience. As military rulers continue to create a climate in which organized crime, gang activity, and corruption flourish, many people feel that they have no choice but to flee their countries. As many experts note, the United States has supported, encouraged, and profited from such regimes in the form of military aid, equipment, training of the military, and humanitarian aid that often never reaches the people who needed it most.[451]

Advocates argue that the United States was not only aware of these developments but actively participated in the construction of one of the greatest humanitarian crises in human history. To that end, as in the 1980s, the United States today has a moral, legal, and ethical obligation to address the immigration issue from Central America because it is a direct result of the misguided decisions of the past. As one expert, Oscar Martinez, noted, it is incorrect to identify the caravans of people in Central America as migrants; these people are not migrating based on the traditional pursuit of better economic opportunities characteristic of globalization. Rather, these are people who are fleeing their countries based on the fear of persecution, victimization, or the threat of torture, execution, and murder.[452]

Immigration as a Global Problem

The problems described in this book have focused on the issues and challenges related to the United States; however, immigration is not simply a domestic problem between the United States and Mexico or Central

America. Similarly, the strategies used by U.S. federal agencies are not unique to this problem either. In fact, while the United States has faced considerable criticism for its current approach to immigration, many other countries have passed anti-immigration laws and are employing a similar type of alt-right logic as a justification for these decisions.

By almost any account, the world is facing an enormous refugee crisis. According to a recent report by the United Nations High Commissioner for Refugees (UNHCR), the conflicts that are taking place around the globe have resulted in more than sixty million people being displaced from their homes. Much of this problem stems from the conflict in Syria, but other conflicts have contributed to the growth of the refugee population as well.

According to the UNHCR, in 2018, the number of *displaced persons*, the term used to define people forced from their homes as a result of conflict or insecurity, was 68.5 million. This is almost 3 million more than in 2016, the largest increase UNHCR has ever seen in a single year. New displacement is also growing, with 16.2 million people displaced during 2017 for the first time.[453]

Actually, the majority of these people, about forty million of the total, are *internally displaced persons*, or IDPs. This refers to people who have been forced from their homes but have not left their countries. In contrast, refugees and asylum seekers are those who have been forced from both their homes and their countries. This is important because it means many people are forced into displacement camps in their home countries while the problems are still taking place. In other words, they literally cannot go "back home." The number of asylum seekers awaiting the outcome of their applications for refugee status had risen by about 300,000, to 3.1 million, by December 2017.[454]

When the problems are so severe, people have no choice but to flee to the safety of other countries. However, because the people forced to flee are poor, often with little or no money and only the belongings they can carry, they can usually only flee to a country on the border of their own. Thus, in the vast majority of cases, refugees and asylum seekers go from one poor country to another with little hope that there will be chances for a better life there. However, such conditions are still better than remaining in their home countries. As seen in figure 7-1, while Turkey has the world's largest refugee population, Lebanon and Jordan are hosting the highest number relative to population size. In Lebanon, there are 164 refugees per 1,000 inhabitants, which equates to 1 in 6 people. In Jordan, 1 in every 14 people is a refugee under the responsibility of the UNHCR (see figure 7-1).[455]

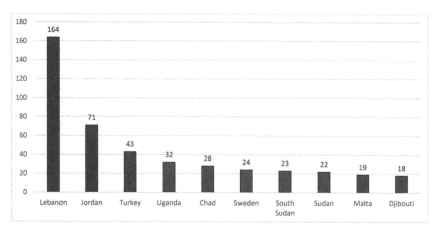

Figure 7-1 Number of refugees per 1,000 inhabitants (end of 2017) (UNHCR. (2018). *Global Trends: Forced Displacement in 2017.* Geneva, Switzerland: UNHCR, 21. Available online at https://www.unhcr.org/5b27be547.pdf.)[456]

The War in Syria

When most people think of the global refugee crisis, they think of the problems in Syria. It is true that the Syrian Civil War is the largest source of refugees around the world. The war essentially started as a result of many of the problems identified in the discussion of Central America: poverty, unemployment, corruption, and a lack of political freedom. In March 2011, in the city of Deraa, a prodemocracy demonstration occurred that quickly escalated in intensity.[457] The government intervened, and the violence ended in the deaths of several protesters.

In response, many people demanded the resignation of Syrian president Bashar al-Assad. Protests continued, and the government's response was to crackdown on the dissenters. The violence between protestors and the government escalated as protestors used weapons to defend themselves and to force soldiers out of neighborhoods. Calling it "foreign-backed terrorism," President Assad took an aggressive approach, and the violence escalated into a civil war across the country. According to some accounts, the level of violence had resulted in more than a half million deaths by December 2018 along with many accounts of human rights violations of civilians by government officials.[458]

However, the war has escalated beyond a contest of wills between protestors and the government. Many groups and even other countries have used the conflict in Syria as a backdrop to further their own agendas, including fostering conflict between religious groups, and jihadist groups such as Islamic State (IS) and al-Qaeda have gained a foothold in Syria.[459]

Internationally, some countries, such as Russia and Iran, have supported the Syrian government in the struggle, while others, such as Turkey, several Gulf Arab states, and some Western countries have supported the opposition. This complicates matters further since those countries have their own conflicts with each other and those agendas become entangled in the Syrian conflict. For instance, Israel is concerned about the growing influence of Iran, which has deployed hundreds of soldiers and billions of dollars in aid to Syria along with shipments of Iranian weapons to Hezbollah. In response, Israel has conducted hundreds of air strikes in Syria. Russia has also conducted air strikes in support of the government, ostensibly of "terrorist" targets, but reports exist of civilian casualties as well.[460]

The United States, Great Britain, and France provide support for rebel groups, but the type of help has changed to the nonlethal variety since jihadists became involved in the opposition forces. A U.S. coalition has carried out air strikes on IS factions in Syria since 2014 and helped the Syrian Democratic Forces recover territory once held by jihadists.[461]

All these complex dynamics have affected the people of Syria, where at least 6.3 million Syrians are internally displaced and another 5.7 million have fled abroad. Lebanon, Jordan, and Turkey, which are hosting 93 percent of the Syrian refugees, have struggled to cope with the volume of people coming into their countries.[462] In February 2019, approximately 13 million people were estimated to be in need of humanitarian assistance, including 5.2 million in acute need.[463]

While efforts have been made to effect some type of peace agreement, little progress has been made in resolving the conflict, and it does not appear one will be forthcoming in the foreseeable future. The main point of contention is that President Assad appears unwilling to negotiate, and the rebels still insist that any peace accord must contain his resignation.[464]

Refugees from Other Countries

Despite the enormity of the problem in Syria, Syrians make up only about a third of the world's sixteen million refugees. Other conflicts, such as the violence in the South Sudan of Africa, the Myanmarese government's violent actions against the Rohingya Muslims in that country, or even the Taliban's efforts against the Afghan government, also contribute to people fleeing their homes.[465] In fact, in 2017, 68 percent of all refugees

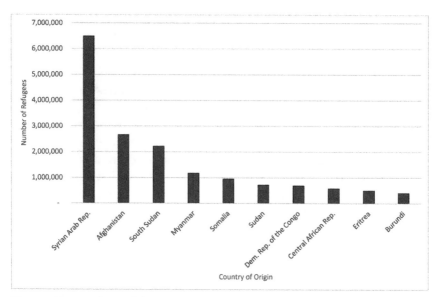

Figure 7-2   Ranking of the Major Source Countries of Refugees, 2017 (UNHCR. (2019). Asylum Trends Report (Latest Monthly Data, accessed September 6, 2019). Available online at https://www.unhcr.org/en-us/figures-at-a-glance.html.)[466]

came from five countries: Syria, Afghanistan, South Sudan, Myanmar, and Somalia (see figure 7-2).[467]

Such staggering numbers have resulted in some countries refusing to accept refugees based on an inability to accommodate them. Other countries have accepted refugees, but the backlash has resulted in the growth of an alt-right populist movement based on citizens' fears that they will be outnumbered and lose control. For example, Jordan, a country with about 6 million people, has become home to more than 600,000 Syrian refugees. Turkey, with a population of about 76 million, has taken in more than 3.5 million refugees (see table 7-1).

At the other end of the spectrum is Hungary, which has constructed a border wall to keep refugees out, and the United States, where President Trump barred all refugees from entering the United States for 120 days in 2017 and limited refugee access from "high-risk" countries such as Syria.[468]

Consistent with his policies regarding immigration in general, President Trump undertook several executive orders, policies changes, directive memos, and other actions to limit the flow of immigrants and refugees

Table 7-1   **Countries That Host Syrian Refugees**[469]

Country	Percent of Refugees	Number of Immigrants
Turkey	64.1%	3,606,737
Lebanon	16.6%	935,454
Jordan	11.8%	664,330
Iraq	4.5%	252,987
Egypt	2.4%	132,473
N. Africa	0.6%	35,713
Total		5,627,694

Source: UN High Commissioner for Refugees. (2019). "Syria Regional Refugee Response." June 3. Available at https://data2.unhcr.org/en/situations/syria.

Table 7-2   **U.S. Refugee Ceilings and Actual Admissions**[470]

Year	Ceiling	Number of Actual Admissions
FY 2017	50,000	53,716
FY 2018	45,000	22,491
FY 2019	30,000	12,154 (first six months of FY)

Source: Pierce, Sarah. (2019). *Changes in the First Two Years of Trump Administration.* Migration Policy Institute. May. Available at https://www.migrationpolicy.org/research/immigration-policy-changes-two-years-trump-administration.

into the United States. As it relates specifically to refugees, President Trump initially suspended all refugee admissions for 120 days and instructed federal officials to reduce the refugee ceiling from the 110,000 in 2016 to 30,000 in 2019 (see table 7-2). The Trump administration also directed officials to increase the criteria used in vetting refugees who attempted to enter the United States. As seen in table 7-2, the refugee ceiling and actual number of refugees admitted has been dramatically reduced.

As seen in the data, there is an uneven distribution of refugees by various countries; for example, Lebanon, a rather small country, has taken in almost a million refugees when it has a total population of about five million. Smaller countries simply cannot sustain the influx of refugees; the refugees strain the infrastructure and resources of these nations despite their best intentions.

In such situations, international agencies such as the United Nations (UN) are, theoretically, supposed to support those countries that want to help refugees but cannot. However, funding for the UN humanitarian relief for refugees has not kept up with the volume of people needing it. According to one account, in 2014, at about the time when the refugee crisis began in earnest, the United Nations received about half of its requested funding for humanitarian aid. In 2017, President Trump threatened to cut the U.S. contribution to the United Nations by 40 percent. This, coupled with the ban on refugees entering the country, put an enormous burden on other countries to accommodate those in need.[471]

In an effort to find some level of relief, many refugees attempted to flee to Europe. However, many European countries have limited the number of asylum seekers and attempted to restrict refugee movement through their borders. In some cases, countries simply cannot afford to process many asylum applications. One such example is Greece, which has its own financial challenges and cannot process large numbers of applications. The result is that many asylum seekers are forced into resettlement camps while they wait for their applications to be determined. Other countries, such as Hungary, have made the decision not to offer any help to refugees.

All of this comes at a time when the anti-immigrant/refugee movement has changed the political landscape in many European countries. As in the United States, many European countries have seen an increase in what is known as *far-right populism*, which involves white voters who are fearful of the growing diversity in their country, particularly as it relates to Muslim minorities. This group has voted for political candidates who promise to restrict immigration in their countries. Hungary has built a border wall, and other European leaders have espoused some of the same rhetoric as President Trump about the "invasion" of immigrants and the dilution of the culture in their countries, which is then used as a justification for restricting access for immigrants.

Recall the discussion of neoliberalism in chapter 2 where many countries embraced the idea of globalization and the theoretical benefits of labor migration as a consequence of living and working in a globalized world. The reality of globalism, however, is that while some countries have benefited from the expansion of consumer markets, others have not fared as well. For workers, the freedom of movement to pursue better job opportunities has not been realized, and the economic benefits of globalization have not been seen in all countries. This is, in part, one of the reasons for the unrest in those countries, as corruption, crime, and dictatorships have continued to rule the day. It is also one of the reasons for the refugee and immigration crisis.

Proposed Solutions to the U.S. Immigration Problem

The complexity of the problems related to immigration in the United States make it difficult to reach consensus on solutions. The fact that Congress has been unable to pass meaningful and comprehensive immigration reform suggests there are significant divisions about what to do and how to do it. Perhaps this is a function of party politics, where each side feels the need to remain loyal to their particular ideology on immigration, or perhaps it is based on fear by politicians about the need to demonstrate they are doing something, even if it has only a limited effect.

While there are some groups that have made their feelings clear about the threats that immigrants present to the U.S. culture, for the most part, questions remain about the public's overall stance on immigration, which may be quite different from how politicians see the issue. Still, as previously mentioned in the opening chapter of this book, the media and the rhetoric about the "threat" that immigrants represent can influence people's understanding of the issues as well as their perceptions of this particular group of "others."

If opinion polls are any indication of where people stand on immigration, it seems evident that the public does not view the problem as a threat to national security, and most Americans are still not in favor of the construction of the border wall. Somewhere in this debate, then, there has been a disconnect between what policy makers and politicians see as the problem and how the people they represent understand it. However, such an incongruence has not prevented politicians from consistently promoting the negative narrative about the problems immigrants present.

That said, there have been some efforts in the past to find a bipartisan solution to the challenges presented by immigration that seek a balance between humanitarian compassion on one hand and reasonable concerns about security and legitimate threats to the nation on the other. One example was proposed by Peter King, a member of Congress, in March 2019.

King's plan creates a pathway to citizenship for about two million younger immigrants, better known as *Dreamers*. To be eligible, they must have graduated from high school, have no record of criminal activity, and be serving in the military, working full-time for at least three years, or attending college. King's plan would extend similar coverage to those individuals, approximately four hundred thousand people who were given temporary protective status (TPS) by the United States.[472]

In addressing relatives of Dreamers and TPS recipients and other undocumented immigrants, which make up nearly three million more people, they would be eligible for three years of protective status, which is renewable, if they have been in the United States for a number of years and have no record of criminal activity. In total, over five million people would be given protected status. To offset some of the costs of the increased number of immigrants who would make greater use of social services under this plan, the cost of which is estimated to be approximately $1.4 billion, an undocumented person would be required to pay a $2,000 fee. If all five million paid, that would result in $10 billion in revenue.[473]

The remaining $8.6 billion would be allocated to improve border security and to address the economic and political issues in Central America. Specifically, $4.3 billion would improve physical structures and technological advances along the Mexican border, as proposed by the Department of Homeland Security, and another $4.3 billion would be designated in aid to the three Central American countries that generate the largest group of immigrants into the United States: Honduras, El Salvador, and Guatemala.[474]

Such a plan attempts to balance the need for border security and the ability of federal agencies to target, detain, and deport undocumented immigrants who present a clear threat to the United States with a humanitarian approach to resolving the challenges for children and immigrants who would make constructive and meaningful contributions to the country and economy despite their undocumented status.

Missing from this proposal, however, is how all five million people would generate the money necessary for the entrance fee, especially if they are children. While such an idea has some merit in that it appears to be more bipartisan than what has been proposed in the past, many questions remain about its logistics.

Other Thoughts on Current Immigration Policy

Inconsistency in Thinking and Action

As discussed in chapter 3, the logic behind the use of an aggressive law enforcement strategy is based on the broken windows theory. This theory has been the basis of many strategies in law enforcement, including the larger expansion of community policing across the country. It was also a critical component of President Clinton's crime control strategies, in which there was a general belief in the idea that solving quality-of-life issues and larger social problems such as crime could be achieved by identifying the causes of problems and preventing them before they become bigger ones.

Thus, repairing the broken windows in abandoned buildings, cleaning up the trash in a community, and eliminating graffiti and other forms of disorder are key steps to solving the larger crime problems in an area. Community policing is also based on the idea that policy makers, police officers, and the general public, working collaboratively, can collectively solve large-scale problems by examining the causes of a problem rather than simply treating its symptoms. It is also based on the logic that a traditional law enforcement approach, with a heavy emphasis on arrests, citations, and aggressive efforts under the rubric of "proactive" policing, does little to solve the problem. This is especially true if the particular strategies morph into a form of zero tolerance policing.

While the data may offer insight into the accountability by officers, as evidenced by workload analysis and perhaps even reductions in some types of crime, those data do not tell the entire story—fluctuations in crime occur for a number of reasons and rarely can be attributed to only police activity. The end result of zero tolerance policing is dissatisfaction by community members and a concern by policy makers that they have not done enough to solve community problems.

What is particularly fascinating is that while many policy makers, politicians, police chiefs, and researchers have embraced the idea of community policing and the broken windows theory, policy makers and politicians seem to be unable to divest themselves from the limits of the traditional law enforcement model as it relates to immigration. That is, we seem determined to resolve the immigration challenges in this country through aggressive and zero tolerance enforcement that puts an emphasis on arrests, citations, detentions, and deportations. In short, we are treating the *symptom* of immigration with border walls, fencing, and aggressive enforcement.

What we are not addressing are the *causes* of the problem, such as why migrants from Central America and Mexico are coming to this country in the first place. As previously discussed, the problems are complex and multilayered, but we cannot deport our way out of them. Even thirty years ago, there was a recognition that if we fixed the problems occurring in the countries that present the largest number of immigrants, such as Honduras, El Salvador, Guatemala, and Nicaragua, the need to migrate would be significantly reduced. We have already seen this occur in Mexico, where the number of people in that country who feel they need to leave has decreased, in large part because the Mexican economy is improving and people are finding work at home.

The billions of dollars being spent on immigration enforcement, detention, and deportation could also be used to address the situation in

Central America. It is fair, though, to assert that this does not mean we leave our borders unprotected; there needs to be a reasonable response to the issue of border security. But it seems fairly evident that much of what we are currently doing is not working, and it is an enormously expensive undertaking.

Part of the solution would likely involve the United States asserting its will over Central American countries and their leadership in an effort to quell the unrest and implement fair and reasonable economic incentives that would allow those countries the ability to grow their domestic and international trade. Such a dramatic step would force multinational companies to exercise fair and reasonable work conditions and practices, and it would also require ending the corrupt and long-standing regimes that currently exist. Some might balk at this approach, arguing that this constitutes meddling in the affairs of sovereign nations; however, part of the reason the situation in Central America is so dire is *because* of U.S. involvement in the politics and economic development in those countries.

The United States has a long history of leveraging its position to its advantage as the situation dictates. A recent example of this was the decision by President Trump to institute a steep and graduated tariff on all goods coming out of Mexico and into the United States unless Mexico took dramatic steps to reduce the number of immigrants who came through that country on their way to the U.S. border.[475] Such a decision came on the heels of a trade agreement with Mexico, and the tariffs were projected to cost an estimated $612 billion per year.[476]

So it is not beyond reason to think that the United States could exert sufficient control and influence on stimulating the economies and leadership of many Central American countries in an effort to improve the conditions in those countries that are forcing people to migrate to the United States.

Recent Legislation

In May 2019, the House of Representatives passed the latest attempt to find a solution to immigration reform. The legislation is likely stall in the Republican-controlled Senate, and even if it somehow passed both houses of Congress, President Trump has promised to veto it if it reaches his desk. However, the bill is an honest attempt to create pathways for immigrants to obtain citizenship in the United States, provided they meet certain criteria and benchmarks.

The logic behind the legislation is that, in addition to the humanitarian considerations, where the United States has a moral and legal obligation to help immigrants from Central American countries, there is an economic element that could benefit the United States over time. This is particularly true given that the combination of low birth rates in the United States, the aging of the U.S. population, and the fact that fewer people are migrating to the United States from Mexico means there will be a critical shortage of workers in certain industries that will need to be filled somehow. The support of the U.S. Chamber of Commerce and the AFL-CIO organization for this legislation suggests that they are not concerned about immigrants taking jobs away from U.S. citizens. Rather, they see it as a form of long-term economic development.[477]

What Kind of Country Are We?

In the larger sense, the immigration challenges facing the United States require its citizens to really examine their values, mission, and goals as a world leader. This is not a Republican, Democrat, or Independent issue, and the problem was not created by Presidents Trump, Obama, Bush, Clinton, or Reagan. As discussed in the opening chapter, we are all to blame for the problem, and we cannot simply deport our way out of it or invalidate the needs of a group of people because we do not think they are valuable enough to extend help to them.

Immigrants drive the economy of this country, and we have always placed a high value on the labor they provide. Moreover, they are not a drain on our system; the research has consistently pointed out that they make substantial economic, political, and social contributions over time. Our history of mistreatment of those who are different is a long-standing one, and it seems we consistently find one group or another to be the target of our animosity.

It is worth remembering that, other than Native Americans, we are all immigrants in one form or another, and the current fabric of this country is the result of the efforts of those people who came to this country, for whatever reason: seeking a better life, fleeing oppression of various types, or being forced to come as slaves or indentured servants. It is far too easy to become a strict gatekeeper once we have been allowed inside those gates and to allow our sense of entitlement to restrict the next generation similar opportunities to create a better life.

Thus, while we cannot leave the borders unprotected, what type of policy makes sense given our history, our values, and our responsibility as a world leader? That should be driving the discussion, not party politics, irrational fears, or narrow views about whether one group or another is worthy of admission to a country that is predicated on its diversity, its compassion for others, and its willingness to do what is right.

In July 2019, amid media reports of overcrowding and unsanitary and unsafe conditions at detention camps for immigrants, President Trump responded to these concerns by blaming Democrats for their failure to pass immigration legislation and by tweeting: "If Illegal Immigrants are unhappy with the conditions in the quickly built or refitted detentions centers, just tell them not to come. All problems solved!"

The comment came one day after a Department of Homeland Security (DHS) report warned of "dangerous overcrowding" in the facilities along with the lack of running water and access to needed medication, unsanitary conditions, human waste, and spoiled food. Further, an Office of Inspector General report was recently released that characterized the severe conditions of the camps, which often hold thousands of migrants across the country, including children and families, in cage-like holding cells, often with little or no room.[478]

The president's comments come after a recent statement where he asserted that the United States was pushing Guatemala to enter into a safe third country agreement, in which people seeking asylum would remain in that country (along with Mexico, which has been under intense pressure to sign a safe third country agreement with the United States) while their cases were being reviewed. The irony of such a decision is that many of those who are seeking asylum into the United States are citizens of Guatemala who are attempting to flee that country. The fact that the United States would require people fleeing a country because of persecution and violence to remain in that same country while their application is being reviewed (which involves longer delays than ever) seems a bit incongruent with the idea of asylum in general. In fact, there were stipulations in the proposed Guatemalan agreement that would allow the United States to send asylum seekers to Guatemala even if the person had never been to that country.

Additionally, a recent report noted that a separate document contained language in which the Guatemalan agreement would primarily apply to asylum seekers from Honduras and El Salvador as well. In response, the Guatemalan Congress rejected the deal and claimed that the President of Guatemala, Jimmy Morales, had acted without their involvement or guidance. When the country's Constitutional Court agreed to hear three separate petitions to block the deal, President Morales terminated the agreement.[479]

The proposed asylum agreements, along with the commentary about the deplorable and inhumane conditions in detention facilities, raise questions about President Trump's motives. On one hand, it could be that Trump's comments and agreements are politically strategic, in that they reflect a public message and position to other countries and immigrant advocate groups about his firm stance on immigration, but in reality, such threats and comments are designed to leverage Democrats into passing a more strict immigration law.

On the other hand, it could be that President Trump's comments are symptomatic of a blunted sensitivity or even a sense of apathy to the plight of those involved; he may really believe this is a reasonable and appropriate strategy, and he is responding to what he thinks his supporters want. Perhaps the explanation is a combination of both possibilities, but let's remember, we created this problem by developing a narrative of immigrants as criminals and use it as a justification for arrest and detention. Moreover, we continue to ignore the positive and constructive contributions immigrants from these countries make to our economy.

In addition to the many questionable strategies employed by the Trump administration to rid the country of Hispanic and Latino immigrants, in July 2019, the Trump administration announced that it was providing Border Patrol and ICE agents with the authority to deport illegal immigrants without appearing before an immigration judge. The rationale behind this decision was that the federal government cannot manage the nearly one million immigrants who are awaiting a hearing, and expedited removals will also reduce the length of stays in detention facilities, which is currently at an average of 114 days. The American Civil Liberties Union is expected to sue the federal government to prevent the government from implementing this new policy.[480]

The expanded use of expedited removals comes on the heels of the Trump administration's decision to refuse to consider asylum applications unless the applicants have attempted to seek asylum in the countries they pass through on the way to the United States. This decision is under legal review, but it is reflective of the inability of the federal government to manage the immigration problem in this country.

The Culture of Fear

In 1999, sociologist Barry Glassner wrote *The Culture of Fear*. Glassner argued that whether it is a fear of crime, dangerous chemicals and additives in food, the quality of water, shark attacks, flesh-eating bacteria, or the dangers of cell phones and sexual predators on social media, when people are afraid, they will do almost anything to reduce or eliminate that fear—even things they rationally know will not resolve the problem. Like a strong addiction, fear can paralyze people or cause them to act in rash ways, and they may use extraordinarily poor judgment in their decision making. Once the notion of fear is created, it is very difficult to divest from that emotion, even when the person wants to be rid of this form of irrational thought and action. Glassner also points out that there is actually an incentive for some groups to promote and even escalate people's fear levels. Entire industries profit from people being afraid because they will buy products and services that attempt to reduce their fears and concerns.[481]

While Glassner's book is nearly two decades old, the concepts are no less relevant today and offer important insight into the nature of immigration in this country. Glassner's observations also offer an understanding of the development of the alt-right movement and white nationalism. In fact, much of what can be called white nationalism/white supremacy is a fear-based strategy designed to highlight the loss of white control. This exaggerated form of white privilege leads to all manner of disparaging other groups, including references to their lack of intelligence and how the celebration of those differences threatens the status and value of white culture.

In the end, the current mistreatment of Latinos and Hispanics is based on the fear of a group of people who are different in characteristics from whites. The criminalization of immigration is similar in nature, scope, and intensity to the vilification of other minority groups over the sweep of history in this country. This, it seems, is the real danger: it is not the influx of undocumented immigrants or even the aggressive means used to enforce policies regarding immigration that pose the greatest risk to the United States. Rather, the danger is in allowing these fears to shape public policy and laws that justify all manner of mistreatment of a group of people who want to come to this country and make significant, even extraordinary, economic, social, and political contributions to it.

Epilogue

As the preceding pages highlight, the current approach to immigration enforcement has been, by all accounts, dramatic, extraordinary, and extreme. Despite criticisms for the manner in which President Trump has managed the challenges of increased immigration to the United States, particularly by people from Central America and Mexico, one has to acknowledge that the policies and strategies used by the Trump administration are nothing if not consistent. This may be due to racist ideology or an extraordinary fear of a group of people, or it may be that Trump is simply planting a political flag that defines his presidency; however, there is little doubt where he stands on this issue.

As was mentioned in the preface, immigration is a topic that is quite dynamic; it seems like every day there is a new wrinkle in the attempt to rid the country of immigrants from the Northern Triangle of Central America or a new strategy to deter them from trying to enter the United States. The fact that none of these strategies has worked suggests a lack of understanding of the extreme circumstances immigrants are facing or an unwillingness to address the problem in a meaningful way.

To date, what appears to be the U.S. policy on immigration is an increase in the severity of the punishment for illegally entering the country without any concern or recognition of the fact that deterrence as a behavioral control strategy only works if the punishment is certain, swift, and severe—that it outweighs whatever benefits are offered in committing the crime.

In the summer of 2019, after several years of aggressive enforcement, stepped-up efforts to detain, and extensive use of executive privilege to skirt federal laws regarding immigration, the Trump administration embarked on a new set of tactics designed to address the immigration problem. As of September 2019, the following are a few noteworthy examples that highlight both the philosophy and practice of immigration enforcement under the Trump administration.

ICE Raids

In July and August 2019, the Trump administration announced that ICE would be conducting a series of raids that were designed to escalate the enforcement of current immigration policy. While a large number of raids failed to materialize, one particular event in Mississippi garnered significant media attention.

On August 7, in Morton, Mississippi, ICE agents raided several food processing plants to arrest undocumented workers as well as their employers for hiring them. In one of the largest ICE raids in a decade, 680 people were arrested at the Koch Foods Inc. plant in this small town near Jackson. Workers who could confirm they had legal status to work in the United States were allowed to leave after a search of their vehicles was conducted. About 300 of those arrested were released but are currently required to appear in court on immigration violations at a future date.

Koch Foods is one of the largest poultry producers in the United States with operations in Alabama, Georgia, Ohio, Tennessee, and Illinois as well as Mississippi. Forbes ranks Koch Foods Inc. as the 135th-largest privately held company in the United States, with an estimated $3 billion in annual revenue. In the Morton plant, the company employs thirteen thousand workers and produces more than seven hundred thousand tons of poultry feed each year.[482] While one of the objectives of the raids was to hold employers accountable for employing undocumented workers, there were no charges filed, nor were there any arrests of Koch officials during the raids, at their conclusion, or at any time since.

This is a chronic problem and reflects the tendency for the government to allow employers to use the cheap labor that undocumented workers provide but at little or no risk to themselves, despite federal laws that prohibit employers from doing so. While many employers claim that undocumented workers often have fake documents when they apply, one account of the Morton raids indicated that the employers were aware that many of their employees were using them. Another indicator was workers wearing ankle bracelets, indicating they had been charged with an immigration offense, but Koch employers continued to employ them. Despite this evidence, no charges have been filed against Koch Foods or its officials.[483]

Koch Foods is not the only culprit when it comes to hiring undocumented workers, and it is not unusual for employers to go unpunished for these violations. One report indicated that between April 2018 and March 2019, only eleven employers had been prosecuted for hiring undocumented workers, and only three had been sentenced to any form of jail time for those offenses. In comparison, over 120,000 immigrants were prosecuted for illegal entry into the United States during that same period.

Such a trend leaves many questions unanswered about such a strict and intensive immigration policy, where the government seems to be focusing on the workers and not the employers who hire them. This is another example of treating the symptom of a problem rather than its root causes. If employers ever stopped hiring workers, the incentive to cross the border illegally would be dramatically reduced. However, the history of immigration policy in this country reflects this thorny problem; companies need the cheap labor immigrants provide and their impact on the economy. Somewhere in that discussion, however, this trend seems to outweigh the threat of the "invasion" of violent immigrants who put American citizens at risk.[484]

It is also the case that large-scale ICE raids are not a new or recent strategy. Such efforts were used during the George W. Bush administration, particularly a noteworthy raid in Postville, Iowa, in 2008, which had similar features to the Mississippi raids in 2019. The Obama administration did not make use of ICE raids, preferring a low-profile approach to immigration enforcement that did not garner a lot of public attention. When Trump was elected, he embraced the idea of large-scale raids, but such efforts require an extensive allocation of time and resources. As a result, such raids have become a relatively rare feature of immigration enforcement.[485]

Detaining Immigrant Families Indefinitely

In late August 2019, the Trump administration unveiled a new strategy to address the influx of undocumented immigrants from Central America to the United States. This policy, which will be explained in greater detail below, essentially allows the government to detain immigrant children and their families indefinitely or until their immigration cases are resolved. To understand the significance of this new directive, which is already being challenged in court, it is important to understand the guiding principles behind the existing rules regarding the detention of children.

In the 1980s, Alma Cruz and Jenny Flores were fifteen-year-old undocumented immigrants whose parents brought them to the United States because the civil war in Central America made them fearful for their daughters' safety. During the 1980s, Los Angeles found itself hosting thousands of immigrants fleeing the guerillas of El Salvador. After their parents made the difficult decision to send them across the border to the United States, Alma and Jenny were apprehended by the Border Patrol and transferred to a detention facility in Pasadena, California.[486]

The girls' mothers were afraid to retrieve their daughters from custody out of a fear that they would be deported. As one attorney for the families noted, children were being indefinitely detained, and the government was using them as bait to arrest the parents. Because immigration officials would not allow anyone else to take custody of the two girls, they remained in custody. In an old motel, surrounded by razor wire, migrants were locked in overcrowded rooms with children and adults living side by side. For weeks, the girls remained there, with no recreation, no medical care, no visits from relatives, and no educational opportunities. Advocates who discovered such conditions, along with volunteer attorneys, began visiting the facilities and documenting the extreme conditions, which included body cavity searches on migrant children by immigration agents.[487]

As a result of these conditions, a class-action lawsuit was filed on behalf of Cruz and Flores along with two other adolescent girls. The lawsuit filed on July 11, 1985, argued that the government should be required to meet basic child welfare standards that included education, recreation, and medical examinations. It also said the authorities should release children to competent and available adults, rather than indefinitely detaining them until a parent or legal guardian could come forward. While the lawsuit resulted in the release of the particular girls named in the lawsuit, attorneys sought an injunction that applied these criteria to all children in federal custody. The settlement that came from the case was a consent decree in 1997 known as the *Flores* agreement.[488]

Included in the agreement were stipulations that required the government to refrain from indefinitely detaining children. Instead, they had to be released quickly to a family member or guardian. If that was not possible, the children had to be transferred to a licensed care facility that did not function like a jail. A later interpretation of the agreement limited the time children could spend in detention to no more than twenty days.[489]

In 2014, Central American families and unaccompanied children began pushing across the border in large numbers, largely for the reasons outlined earlier. In response, the Obama administration attempted to gain relief from the criteria outlined by the *Flores* agreement but was not successful. Facing considerable numbers of families with no meaningful way to handle the volume of people, the Obama administration responded by establishing large detention centers for families. In early 2015, after attorneys filed a motion in federal court that required the federal government to follow the rules established in the *Flores* agreement, a federal judge responsible for overseeing the agreement ruled that the agreement also applied to children who were apprehended with a parent. The upshot of this ruling meant that the twenty-day limit for release applied to families with children as well as those unaccompanied minors who crossed the border alone or with siblings.[490]

Upon taking office in 2016, the Trump administration attempted to circumvent the *Flores* agreement by arguing the twenty-day limit created an incentive for families to cross the border illegally because they knew they would be released after only twenty days. As immigration officials argued, the *Flores* agreement provided what amounted to a guaranteed admission into the United States. This was based on the conclusion that, once released, undocumented parents would not show up for their immigration hearing and would remain in the United States illegally.

When the Trump administration was unsuccessful in its attempts to gain relief from the requirements of the *Flores* agreement, in 2017, immigration officials began separating children from their parents to detain the parents alone. The resulting backlash against this policy by the general public and advocacy groups led the Trump administration to rescind the policy. While this strategy was never completely eliminated, immigration officials have tried to gain permission from the courts to keep children with their parents in detention for longer than twenty days. When the federal judge who oversees the agreement denied the government's request, the Trump administration published a new set of regulations regarding detention of children in violation of the *Flores* agreement.[491]

Trump's New Directive

In response to claims of loopholes in the *Flores* agreement, which Trump administration officials argue provides a free passport into the United States if a family illegally crosses the border with children, the goal of this new directive is deterrence. Its message to immigrants considering crossing the border is that their indefinite detention may outweigh the decision to come into the United States illegally. As President Trump noted, "One of the things that will happen, when they realize the borders are closing—the wall is being built, we are building tremendous numbers of miles of wall right now in different locations—it all comes together like a beautiful puzzle."[492] Trump also pointed out that this new rule would make it "almost impossible for people to come into our country illegally."[493]

If the new rule goes into effect, the administration would be free to send families who are caught crossing the border illegally to a family residential center to be held for as long as it takes for their immigration cases to be decided.

In addition to allowing the government to detain children and families indefinitely, the directive creates new minimum standards for the conditions of detention centers where families will be housed. The directive would also eliminate a requirement that federal detention centers for immigrant families be licensed by states. Instead, the three centers built to house hundreds of immigrant families in Texas and Pennsylvania would have to meet standards set by ICE, the agency that operates them.[494]

Immigration rights advocates argue that the new regulation ignores the long-term consequences of detention on children and does nothing to change the current conditions of existing detention facilities. Several reports have noted that children are currently being kept in overcrowded cells and are sometimes being deprived of basic needs, such as showers, toiletries, or hot meals. Advocates, attorneys, and lawmakers who have visited these facilities have also noted long waits for medical care, spoiled food, and limited or no educational opportunities for children.[495] How, they ask, would any of these conditions change if ICE were responsible for meeting its own standards, given that they have not been able to do so under the current climate?

While the new directive must be approved by the federal judge who oversees the *Flores* agreement, it is likely that the decision would be appealed by either side of the debate, making the likelihood of its implementation unlikely in the near future. In response to this new directive, nineteen states filed a lawsuit in August 2019, calling attention to the long-term harm to children and the fact that the new directive interferes with a state's ability to ensure the health, safety, and welfare of children by undermining state licensing requirements for facilities where children are held.[496]

Safe Third Country Agreements

Another strategy employed by the Trump administration to stem the flow of immigrants into the United States is the use of safe third country agreements. These agreements require asylum seekers to remain outside the United States while their cases are being reviewed. As the name suggests, these countries are supposed to be safe places where asylees, who are often fleeing some type of persecution or violence, can wait while their cases are being heard. The Trump administration has pressured Mexico to sign such an agreement, but so far that country has resisted.

In early July 2019, President Trump also attempted to convince the Guatemalan president to sign a similar agreement. However, there was a considerable backlash from members of the Guatemalan Congress, who felt the president of their country had acted inappropriately. The country's Constitutional Court ruled that the president did not have the authority to enter into such an agreement. However, in late July 2019, Guatemala agreed to enter into the agreement. Trump stated, "We have long been working with Guatemala, and now we can do it the right way. This landmark agreement will put the coyotes and smugglers out of business. These are bad people."[497]

The Guatemalan government said the agreement would specifically apply to Hondurans and Salvadorans, who typically travel through Guatemala to Mexico and then to the United States. Under the agreement, they would be required to seek asylum in Guatemala first and only after being denied refuge there could they then claim asylum in the United States. Hondurans currently account for about 30 percent of all those apprehended at the U.S. southern border, about 205,000 people, while Salvadorans make up about 10 percent.

Whether the same rules would apply to asylum seekers from elsewhere in the world was left unclear. Typically, safe third country agreements apply to all asylum seekers. Trump implied that the agreement would also allow the United States to send back Guatemalan asylum seekers, who make up about one-third of all those apprehended at the U.S. border. Such a development is curious since safe third country agreements do not apply to nationals of the countries making the agreement, only to those from other countries.

Critics of the agreement argue that Guatemala does not meet the legal definition of a "safe" country. Given its homicide rates, which are among the highest in the world, along with its widespread poverty and corruption, the country seems incapable of providing safe haven for hundreds of thousands of asylum seekers from other countries. Such an agreement actually raises many questions about the integrity of safe third party agreements since many Guatemalans who are fleeing the violence in their country would be forced to remain in Guatemala while the United States evaluates their asylum application.[498]

Given the lowered ceilings of approved applications as well as the long delays in processing them, it is likely that those migrants would simply be forced to remain in their country indefinitely, all the while being exposed to the very conditions that led them to make the decision to seek asylum in the first place. Trump also announced that he planned to sign similar agreements with Honduras, El Salvador, and Panama. There may be many reasons why these countries would agree to enter into such agreements with the United States, but the end result is that immigrants who are seeking legal means to come to the United States will be prevented from doing so at great risk to themselves and their families. Such agreements seem to negate the very purpose of seeking asylum in favor of keeping people from these countries from coming into the United States for any reason.

Building the Wall

As a critical piece to his campaign promise, and despite several legal challenges regarding its funding, the Trump administration has attempted to move forward with the construction of a border wall along the U.S.-Mexico border. In actuality, much of the current construction activity focuses on replacing or upgrading existing fencing along the border. Currently, the U.S. Army Corps of Engineers has completed about sixty miles of replacement barriers during Trump's presidency, all of it in areas where there was preexisting structure in place to prevent illegal immigrants from crossing into the United States.[499] While Trump has promised to complete five hundred miles of fencing by 2020, there is a substantial amount of work to complete to meet that goal. In fact, some experts note that none of the money spent on a border wall has resulted in any new or additional fencing.

Part of the challenge in such a large-scale endeavor is the process needed to acquire the land as well as the logistics involved in the construction. Trump has been described by White House officials as so eager to have a wall constructed prior to the 2020 presidential election that he has ignored the protocols used to select contractors as well as seized private lands through eminent domain. He has also instructed aides to have contractors ignore environmental protections of the land.

One White House official expressed concern that this need to hand out contracts as quickly as possible comes at the expense of obtaining competent providers. Not only has this led to the Army Corps of Engineers having to take corrective action for two existing contracts, because the protocols for awarding contracts have been essentially ignored, many contractors have protested the current procedures being used.[500]

From an environmental standpoint, the companies building the fencing and access roads have been taking heavy earth-moving equipment into environmentally sensitive border areas adjacent to U.S. national parks and wildlife preserves, but the administration has waived procedural safeguards and impact studies, citing national security concerns. In response to concerns by White House officials as well as those involved in the project, Trump has promised to pardon them should they violate federal laws to complete the project under his timeline.[501]

In addition to a hard deadline to complete the wall, Trump has ordered the Army Corps of Engineers and DHS to paint the structure black so that it absorbs the heat and makes it too hot to climb. In addition, he has instructed contractors to top the fencing with sharpened tips to discourage people from climbing it. Painting or coating 175 miles of barriers adds between $70 million and $133 million to the overall cost of the project, which will mean between four and seven fewer miles of fencing can be erected. The height of the structure will vary between 18 and 30 feet, high enough to inflict severe injury or death from a fall.

Trump conceded last year in an immigration meeting with lawmakers that a wall or barrier is not the most effective mechanism to curb illegal immigration. But his argument for a wall was that his supporters wanted a wall, and so he has to deliver one.[502]

Trump and Limits for Legal Immigrants

In August 2019, the Trump administration added another component to its immigration policy, this time focusing on legal immigrants and their future opportunities to become citizens. This new directive not only limits the number of immigrants who will be allowed to enter or stay in the United States but also makes it easier to reject visa and green card applications. That is, applicants who have low incomes, low levels of education, and have used Medicaid, food stamps, or housing vouchers can be denied because the use of these programs indicates that they would be more likely to need government assistance in the future. There are exceptions to the rule, such as benefits received by an active duty member of the military, Medicaid for pregnant women, children under twenty-one years old, and emergency medical care.[503]

As previously mentioned, the research on the use of public assistance programs by immigrants shows that, over time, allowing this type of help is a short-term strategy that is more than returned when immigrants remain in the country. The vast majority go on to pay taxes and make other economic contributions that outweigh the investment needed to get them started. What the new directive also does not mention is that the vast majority of immigrants and refugees are likely coming from countries that are poor. Thus, the chance that an immigrant will have enough resources to immediately become self-sufficient is unrealistic for virtually any immigrant.[504]

Critics of this new directive point out that such a decision could result in children without food, medical care, or housing. It would also penalize even hard-working immigrants who need temporary help from the government to become more independent. In fact, one could argue that the entire welfare program in the United States was designed to be a stopgap measure designed to help people get back on their feet. Thus, whether they are citizens or noncitizens, public assistance is a key component to economic growth and financial security. Such a change in policy means that many immigrants will not make use of these programs out of a fear that it might jeopardize their opportunities for a green card or visa in the future.[505]

Are Mass Shootings Related to Immigration?

On August 3, 2019, in a Walmart in El Paso, Texas, around 10:30 a.m., a twenty-one-year-old man named Patrick Crusius, from Dallas, Texas, walked into the store armed with an assault weapon and opened fire. He killed at least twenty people and injured another thirty-six. About thirty minutes prior to the shooting, Crusius posted a four-page manifesto outlining his white supremacist stance and racial remarks about immigrants and Latinos. He also blamed immigrants and first-generation Americans for taking away jobs from other citizens. Crusius also stated he was concerned that the Hispanic population in Texas would transform his state into a "Democratic stronghold," meaning it would result in increased immigration. The suspect was arrested, and the U.S. attorney for the Western District of Texas said he was treating the shooting as an act of domestic terrorism and that he intended to bring federal hate crime charges against Crusius, which carry the death penalty.[506]

The next morning, around 1:00 a.m., in Dayton, Ohio, a gunman named Connor Betts, age twenty-four, armed with body armor, an assault rifle, and extra ammunition, opened fire at the entrance of a bar as patrons were exiting the establishment. At least nine were killed, and twenty-seven people were injured in the attack. Police arrived on the scene about a minute after the attack began and shot and killed the suspect. Police still do not have a motive for the killing, and there was nothing in Betts's record that prevented him from legally purchasing the weapon and ammunition used in the attack. However, after the attack, high school classmates of Betts informed the police that he had composed a "hit list" and a "rape list" of students at his high school in 2012. Betts caused a school lockdown in 2012 when he wrote a hit list on a bathroom wall inside the school.[507] While the investigation continues, it does not appear that this particular shooting was racially motivated or linked in any way to Latinos or immigrants.

In the immediate aftermath of the shootings, President Trump promised to visit El Paso and Dayton, and he tweeted against the bigotry and hatred that seemed to be the motivating factors behind the killings. Trump also attempted to link the mass shootings to immigration by improving background checks for those who wished to purchase weapons. He said, "Republicans and Democrats must come together and get strong background checks, perhaps marrying this legislation with desperately needed immigration reform." Trump also tweeted, "We must have something good, if not GREAT, come out of these two tragic events!"[508]

Trump's response elicited a strong reaction from Democrats and other critics, who pointed out that some of the language used by Crusius in his manifesto was similar in content to the language used by the president in his characterizations of immigrants, calling them rapists, criminals, and referring to immigration as an "invasion." In other words, some have tried to place the blame for the events on the president for inspiring hatred and the use of violence. For example, Senator Cory Booker of New Jersey argues that Trump's rhetoric and blunted sensitivity has created a climate of hate in this country that promotes the type of violence seen in the August mass shootings. He said, "In my faith, you have this idea that you reap what you sow, and he is sowing seeds of hatred in this country. This harvest of hate violence that we are seeing right now lies at his feet. There is a complicity in the president's hatred that undermines the goodness and decency of Americans."[509]

Julian Castro, a former secretary for the Department of Housing and Urban Development, argued that there is a link between Trump's anti-immigrant commentary and the "toxic brew of white nationalism" in America. He said, "When he didn't step up right away and condemn the neo-Nazis after Charlottesville, allowing that crowd for 13 seconds to chant 'send her back' a couple of weekends ago, he doesn't have any credibility anymore." Castro points to Trump's blaming both sides comment in the Charlottesville rally as well as the racist language in telling four minority lawmakers to "go back" to the countries of their ancestors, even though all four are U.S. citizens, as further evidence of Trump's tendencies to foment hate.[510]

Other politicians are critical of Trump's efforts to link gun control to immigration legislation, calling it an absurd connection that demonstrates his desperate attempts to rid the country of all immigrants. Senator Kirsten Gillibrand said, "He's linking the issue of basic, commonsense gun reform, that we should be going back into the Senate today to vote on, with this issue of immigration because again he continues to try to demonize people seeking asylum, people needing our help."[511]

Based on the available evidence, it seems reasonable to think there is a link between white nationalism and some of the mass shootings and other violence against minority groups in the United States. It also seems reasonable that inflammatory comments by the president against certain groups could lead some people to take those comments as motivating factors in the decision to inflict violence against those same groups. While President Trump cannot be blamed for the actions and decisions of others, he is responsible for what he says, and he should understand that his position requires an extra degree of circumspection when he makes negative and derogatory statements such as the ones he has made in the past about immigrants and minorities in general.

"Do Something" and Gun Control

While the debate continues about whether President Trump has encouraged the growth of white nationalism and its associated acts of racism and hatred against Latinos and Mexicans, another issue that has emerged from the mass shootings and immigration is the emotional response to gun control. As a number of advocates and politicians who favored gun control took advantage of the opportunity the mass shootings presented to urge Congress to pass more stringent laws regarding gun ownership, the tag line in the media was "Do Something!"

Politicians heard this chant during vigils for the victims of the mass shootings; a soccer star for the Philadelphia Union took to a public microphone after scoring a goal in a professional soccer match and yelled, "Hey, Congress, do something. End gun violence now!" Singer Kacey Musgraves took advantage of a Lollapalooza concert to shout, "Somebody f***ing do something! I don't know what the answer is, but obviously something has to be f***ing done." A *New York Post* issue was quick to point out that the mass shootings have made people afraid and directed its opinion at President Trump by saying, "America is scared and we need bold action. It's time to ban weapons of war."[512]

In response to the shootings, President Trump addressed the nation in a brief speech from the White House. Calling for better treatment for mental health and confinement for people who pose a risk to the community, President Trump stated, "Mental illness and hatred pulls the trigger, not the gun."[513] Such a statement seems to make sense at one level; clearly, the people who are engaging in such senseless acts are not emotionally balanced. However, to argue that the problem of gun violence is related to mental illness is simply not supported by the available data.

In fact, a statement by the American Psychological Association took exception to Trump's comments: "Blaming mental illness for the gun violence in our country is simplistic and inaccurate and goes against the scientific evidence currently available."[514] That is, not everyone who suffers from mental illness can be lumped together with those who commit violent acts. Doing so stigmatizes everyone who suffers from any type of emotional disorder and presumes that they are capable and inclined to commit violence against others.

Regardless of which side of the debate on gun control one takes, and to be fair, this is a long-standing and hotly contested issue, the response by the general public to "do something" suggests that many people are afraid. As we have seen, when emotions, particularly fear, drive decision making, it is usually the case that poor choices are made. This is not to say that gun control should or should not occur, but making decisions out of fear is a poorly conceived and ill-timed strategy that has a long history of failure. As we have seen in this book, fears of immigrants or perceived invasions by them has led to numerous examples of denying the rights of citizens, including incarcerating and denying them equal protection under the law. One could even argue that the reactions to the mass shootings are a good illustration of the moral panics that were discussed in chapter 2.

Making Sense of Immigration

Despite the inflammatory commentary by President Trump and the existing rhetoric and exaggerated narratives about immigrants as criminals, it is time to separate fact from fiction, to recognize that politics are part of the problem, and to understand how and in what ways the public has been misled about immigration and its challenges. What we need is a balanced and uncluttered response to this issue, and such a position cannot be based on fear, misinformation, a dislike for differences, or allowing the noise of a political election to sway the American people from making a decision based on principles that transcend affiliation with a particular group. Instead, we need to use the values and principles that define us as a nation, as a culture, and as a people with an understanding of the role of immigration in our heritage and history within a framework of compassion and empathy.

We live in a democracy, which means people have the right to form their own opinions and to express them. It is okay to disagree; that is what makes democracy work. But we cannot launch attacks on people who do not agree with us, and we cannot villainize people because they see and understand the world differently. While creating a villain makes for good copy in media outlets, and perhaps such denigration of others makes us feel a little better about ourselves, we know the contributions that immigrants make to this country, and we know they are important ones.

Immigrants cannot change the way they look, where they came from, or the conditions under which they come to our borders, but perhaps we can reconsider the way we see them. They are not the villains they are made out to be, and they are not the threat we have been told they present. While it is understandable that people are sometimes afraid of things they do not understand, maybe the solution to finding a reasonable stance on immigration, one that contains compassion and accountability, is found by improving our ability to see the commonality in others instead of their differences.

Notes

Chapter 1

1. Samuels, Brett. (2018). "Trump: 'You Know What I Am? I'm a Nationalist.'" *The Hill*, October 12. Available at https://thehill.com/homenews/admini stration/412649-trump-you-know-what-i-am-im-a-nationalist.

2. Klein, Rick. (2018). "Trump Said 'Blame on Both Sides' in Charlottesville, Now the Anniversary Puts Him on the Spot." ABC News, August 12. Available at https://abcnews.go.com/Politics/trump-blame-sides-charlottesville-now -anniversary-puts-spot/story?id=57141612.

3. Knowles, David. (2019). "Trump Threatens to Shut Border with Mexico Next Week." Yahoo News, March 29. Available at https://news.yahoo.com/trump -mexico-border-closing-would-be-a-good-thing-165712851.html.

4. Southern Poverty Law Center. (2019). "White Nationalist." Available at https://www.splcenter.org/fighting-hate/extremist-files/ideology/white -nationalist.

5. Ibid.

6. Stewart, Emily. (2018). "Trump Again Says He's the Least Racist Person There Is." Vox, January 15. Available at https://www.vox.com/policy-and-politics /2018/1/15/16891996/trump-least-racist.

7. Zeitz, Joshua. (2017). "The Real History of American Immigration." *Politico Magazine*, August 6. Available at https://www.politico.com/magazine/story/2017 /08/06/trump-history-of-american-immigration-215464.

8. Serwer, Adam. (2018). "White Nationalism's Deep American Roots." *The Atlantic*, April. Available at https://www.theatlantic.com/magazine/archive/2019 /04/adam-serwer-madison-grant-white-nationalism/583258.

9. Taub, Amanda. (2016). "White Nationalism, Explained." *New York Times*, November 21. Available at https://www.nytimes.com/2016/11/22/world/ameri cas/white-nationalism-explained.html.

10. Serwer (2018).

11. Taub (2016).

12. Ibid.

13. Srikantiah, Jayashri, and Sinnar Shirin. (2019). "White Nationalism as Immigration Policy." *Stanford Law Review*, March. Available at https://www.stanfordlawreview.org/online/white-nationalism-as-immigration-policy.

14. Ibid.

15. Ibid.

16. Ibid.

17. Ibid.

18. Ibid.

19. Ibid.

20. Baker, Peter. 2019. "Trump Declares a National Emergency and Creates a Constitutional Clash." *New York Times*, February 15. Available at https://www.nytimes.com/2019/02/15/us/politics/national-emergency-trump.html.

21. Antisemitism Defense League. (n.d.). "Alt-Right: A Primer about the New White Supremacy." Available at https://www.adl.org/resources/backgrounders/alt-right-a-primer-about-the-new-white-supremacy.

22. See, for instance, Gonzalez O'Brien, Benjamin. (2018). *Handcuffs and Chain Link: Criminalizing the Undocumented in America*. Charlottesville: University of Virginia Press; Golazh-Boza, Tanya Maria. (2015). *Deported: Immigrant Policing, Disposable Labor, and Global Capitalism*. New York: NYU Press; Brotherton, David C., and Philip Kretsedemas, eds. (2017). *Immigration Policy in the Age of Punishment*. New York: Columbia University Press.

23. See, for instance, Borger, Julian. (2018). "Trump Urges World to Reject Globalism in U.N. Speech That Draws Mocking Laughter." *The Guardian*, September 26. Available at https://www.theguardian.com/us-news/2018/sep/25/trump-united-nations-general-assembly-speech-globalism-america.

24. Timm, Jane C. (2018). "Fact Check: Trump Says His Wall Is under Construction. It Is Not." NBC News, July 3. Available at https://www.nbcnews.com/politics/donald-trump/fact-check-trump-say-his-border-wall-under-construction-it-n888371.

25. Beech, Eric. (2019). "U.S. Judge Denies Democrats' Lawsuit to Stop Border Wall Funds." Reuters, June 4. Available at https://news.yahoo.com/u-judge-denies-democrats-suit-012109670.html.

26. Baker (2019).

27. Ibid.

28. Ibid.

29. Ibid.

30. Ibid.

31. Ibid.

32. Jordan, Miriam. (2019). "More Migrants Are Crossing the Border This Year. What's Changed?" *New York Times*, March 5. Available at https://www.nytimes.com/2019/03/05/us/crossing-the-border-statistics.html.

33. Ibid.

34. Ibid.

35. Ibid.

36. McGraw, Meredith, and Jordyn Phelps. (2019). "Trump Backs Off Threat to Close Border, Gives Mexico One Year Warning." ABC News, April 4. Available at https://abcnews.go.com/Politics/trump-backs-off-threat-close-border-mexico-year/story?id=62170562.

37. Ibid.

38. Holland, Steve, and Dave Graham. (2019). "Trump Says U.S. Likely to Go Ahead with Tariffs on Mexico over Immigration." Reuters, June 4. Available at https://www.yahoo.com/finance/news/mexicos-ebrard-eyes-common-ground-124018622.html.

39. Finnegan, Conor. (2019). "Trump Cuts All Direct Assistance to Northern Triangle Countries: Honduras, El Salvador, Guatemala. *Good Morning America*, March 30. Available at https://www.yahoo.com/gma/trump-cuts-direct-assistance-northern-triangle-countries-honduras-043000627--abc-news-topstories.html.

40. Rosales, Paula. (2019). "New President Pledges to Cure 'Sick Child' El Salvador." Reuters, June 1. Available at https://news.yahoo.com/president-pledges-cure-sick-child-200333080.html.

41. Ibid.

42. History.com Editors. (n.d.). "U.S. Immigration before 1965." Available at https://www.history.com/topics/immigration/u-s-immigration-before-1965-video.

43. Ibid.

44. Ibid.

45. Ibid.

46. History.com Editors. (n.d.). "U.S. Immigration after 1965." Available at https://www.history.com/topics/immigration/us-immigration-since-1965.

47. Ibid.

48. Ibid.

49. Ibid.

50. Ibid.

51. American Immigration Council. (2017). "Fact Sheet: The Dream Act, DACA, and Other Policies Designed to Protect Dreamers." September 6. Available at https://americanimmigrationcouncil.org/research/dream-act-daca-and-other-policies-designed-protect-dreamers.

52. Ibid.

53. Golash-Boza, Tanya. (2015). *Deported: Immigrant Policing, Disposable Labor, and Global Capitalism*. New York: New York University Press.

54. Ibid.

55. Felter, Claire, and Danielle Renwick. (2018). "The U.S. Immigration Debate." Council on Foreign Affairs, July 2. Available at https://www.cfr.org/backgrounder/us-immigration-debate-0.

56. Ibid.

57. Ibid.

58. Ibid.

59. Ibid.

60. Radford, Jynnah. (2019). "Key Findings about U.S. Immigrants." Pew Research Center, June 17. Available at https://www.pewresearch.org/fact-tank/2019/06/17/key-findings-about-u-s-immigrants.

61. Ibid. See also McCarthy, Justin. (2018). "Immigration Up Sharply as Most Important Problem." Gallup, November 20. Available at https://news.gallup.com/poll/244925/immigration-sharply-important-problem.aspx.

62. Radford (2019).

63. Ibid.

64. Ibid.

65. Ibid.

66. Ibid.

67. Ibid.

68. Ibid.

69. Ibid.

70. Ibid.

71. Ibid.

72. Winter, Jana. (2017). "Trump Says Border Wall Will Stop Drugs. Here's What a DEA Intel Report Says." Foreign Policy, August 29. Available at https://foreignpolicy.com/2017/08/29/trump-says-border-wall-will-stop-drugs-heres-what-a-dea-intel-report-says; See also Bier, David. (2018). "New CATO Report: A Border Wall Won't Stop Drug Smuggling: Marijuana Legalization Has." CATO Institute, December 19. Available at https://www.cato.org/blog/new-cato-report-border-wall-wont-stop-drug-smuggling-marijuana-legalization-has.

73. Korte, Gregory, and Alan Gomez. (2018). "Trump Ramps Up Rhetoric on Undocumented Immigrants 'These Aren't People, These Are Animals.'" *USA Today*, May 16. Available at https://www.usatoday.com/story/news/politics/2018/05/16/trump-immigrants-animals-mexico-democrats-sanctuary-cities/617252002.

74. Ye Hee Lee, Michelle. (2019). "Donald Trump's False Comments Connecting Mexican Immigration and Crime." *Washington Post*, July 8. Available at https://www.washingtonpost.com/news/fact-checker/wp/2015/07/08/donald-trumps-false-comments-connecting-mexican-immigrants-and-crime.

75. Epstein, Jennifer, and Justin Sink. (2018). "Trump Admits He Has No Proof Terrorists Are in the Migrant Caravan." *Time*, October 23. Available at http://time.com/5432702/trump-no-proof-terrorists-migrant-caravan.

76. See Gonzalez O'Brien (2018); Golash-Boza (2015); Brotherton and Kretsedemas (2017).

77. Finnegan (2019).

78. Jordan (2019).

Chapter 2

79. CitizenPath.com. (n.d.) Presidential Quotes on Immigration. https://citizenpath.com/immigration-quotes-great-americans.

80. Ibid.

81. Ibid.

82. Long, Colleen, and Jill Colvin. (2019). "Trump: Not Looking to Reinstate Family Separation Policy." Associated Press, April 10. Available at https://news.yahoo.com/trump-says-not-looking-reinstate-family-separation-policy-164139863--politics.html.

83. Rahim, Zamira. (2019). "Trump Told Border Agents to Break the Law but Bosses Told Them to Ignore Him, Report Claims." *The Independent*, April 9. Available at https://www.yahoo.com/news/trump-told-border-agents-break-0845 55838.html.

84. Lopez, Gustavo, Kristen Bialik, and Jynnah Radford. (2018). "Key Facts about U.S. Immigration." Pew Research Center, November 30. Available at http://www.pewresearch.org/fact-tank/2018/11/30/key-findings-about-u-s-immigrants.

85. Zong, Jie, Jeanne Batalova, and Micayla Burrows. (2019). "Frequently Requested Statistics on Immigrants and Immigration in the United States." Migration Policy Institute, March 14. Available at https://www.migrationpolicy.org/article/frequently-requested-statistics-immigrants-and-immigration-united-states#Enforcement.

86. Ibid.

87. Ibid.

88. Radford, Jynnah. (2019). "Key Findings about U.S. Immigrants." Pew Research Center, June 17. Available at https://www.pewresearch.org/fact-tank/2019/06/17/key-findings-about-u-s-immigrants.

89. Lopez, Bialik, and Radford (2018).

90. Sullivan, Katie, and Jeff Mason. (2019). "Immigration Detention in the United States—A Primer." Bipartisan Policy Center, April 24. Available at https://bipartisanpolicy.org/blog/immigration-detention-in-the-united-states-a-primer.

91. Clemens, Michael. (2017). "What the Mariel Boatlift of Cuban Refugees Can Teach Us about the Economics of Immigration: An Explainer and a Revelation." Center for Global Development, May 22. Available at https://www.cgdev.org/blog/what-mariel-boatlift-cuban-refugees-can-teach-us-about-economics-immigration.

92. Ibid.

93. Ibid.

94. Ibid.

95. Sullivan and Mason (2019).

96. Hoose, Bob. Review of *Smallfoot*, directed by Karey Kirkpatrick. Plugged In. Available at https://www.pluggedin.com/movie-reviews/smallfoot-2018.

97. Cole, Nicki Lisa. (2019). "Moral Panics." ThoughtCo. Available at https://www.thoughtco.com/moral-panic-3026420.

98. Goode, Erich. (2009). *Moral Panics: The Social Construction of Deviance.* 2nd ed. New York: Wiley.

99. Cohen, Stanley. (1972). *Folk Devils and Moral Panics.* New York: Routledge.

100. McLuhan, Marshall. (1966). *Understanding Media: The Extensions of Man.* New York: Signet Books.

101. Hall, Stuart. (1978). *Policing the Crisis: Mugging, the State, and Law and Order.* London: Macmillan.

102. Golash-Boza, Tanya. (2015). *Deported: Immigrant Policing, Disposable Labor, and Global Capitalism.* New York: New York University Press.

103. Powell, John A., and Stephen Menendian. (2017). "The Problem of Othering: Towards Inclusiveness and Belonging." Othering & Belonging, June 29. Available at http://www.otheringandbelonging.org/the-problem-of-othering.

104. Powell, John A. (2017). "Us vs. Them: The Sinister Techniques of Othering and how to Avoid Them." *The Guardian*, November 8. Available at https://www.theguardian.com/inequality/2017/nov/08/us-vs-them-the-sinister-techniques-of-othering-and-how-to-avoid-them.

105. Bizumia, Boris. (2014). "Who Coined the Term Ethnocentrism?" *Journal of Social and Political Psychology* 2 (1): 3–10.

106. Heer, Jeet. (2016). "How the Southern Strategy Made Donald Trump Possible." *New Republic*, February 18. Available at https://newrepublic.com/article/130039/southern-strategy-made-donald-trump-possible.

107. Yglesais, Matthew. (2007). "The Origins of the Southern Strategy." *The Atlantic*, November 20. Available at https://www.theatlantic.com/politics/archive/2007/11/origins-of-the-southern-strategy/47093.

108. Monterroso, Violeta. (2019). "Dividing Lines: The Human Face of Global Migration." *Time*, February 4–11: 22–46.

109. Ibid.

110. Ibid.

111. Ibid.

112. Tichenor, D. (2002). *Dividing Lines: The Politics of Immigration in America.* Princeton, NJ: Princeton University Press.

113. Gonzalez O'Brien (2018).

114. Ibid.

115. Ibid.

116. Ibid.

117. Calavita, Kitty. (2010). *Inside the State: The Bracero Program, Immigration, and the I.N.S.* London: Quo Pro Publishers.

118. Ngai, M. (2004). *Impossible Subjects: Illegal Aliens and the Making of Modern America.* Princeton, NJ: Princeton University Press.

119. Massey, D. (2007). *Categorically Unequal: The American Stratification System.* New York: Russell Sage Foundation.

120. Gonzalez O'Brien (2018).

121. Ibid.

122. Jacobsen, R. (2008). *The New Nativism: Proposition 187 and the Debate over Immigration*. Minneapolis: University of Minnesota Press.

123. Gonzalez O'Brien (2018).

124. Ibid.

125. See, for instance, Gonzalez O'Brien, Benjamin, Loren Collingwood, and Stephen El-Khatib. (2017). "The Politics of Refuge: Sanctuary Cities, Crime, and Undocumented Immigration." *Urban Affairs Review*, May 7. Available at http://journals.sagepub.com/doi/abs/10.1177/1078087417704974; see also Lyons, C.; Velez, M. and Santoro, W. (2013). "Neighborhood Immigration. Violence and City-Level immigrant Political Opportunities." *American Sociological Review* 78 (4): 604–632; Martinez, R., J. Stowell, and M. Lee. (2010). "Immigration and Crime in an Era of Transformation: A Longitudinal Analysis of Homicides in San Diego Neighborhoods, 1980–2000." *Criminology* 48 (3): 797–829.

126. Golash-Boza (2015).

127. Ibid.

128. Ibid.

129. Ibid.

130. Ibid.

131. Ibid.

132. Singer, Audrey. (2012). *Investing in the Human Capital of Immigrants: Strengthening Regional Economies*. Washington, DC: Brookings Institute.

133. Harvey, David. (2005). *A Brief History of Neoliberalism*. New York: Oxford University Press.

134. Ibid.

135. Golash-Boza (2015).

136. See, for instance, Brotherton, David C., and Phillip Kretsedemas, eds. (2017). *Immigration Policy in the Age of Punishment*, 1–34. New York: Columbia University Press.

137. Ibid.

138. Gonzalez O'Brien (2018).

Chapter 3

139. Gallu, Joshua. (2019). "Trump Considers Sending Detained Migrants to Sanctuary Cities." *Fortune*, April 13. Available at http://fortune.com/2019/04/13/trump-sanctuary-cities.

140. National Immigration Forum. (2017). "Law Enforcement Leaders Condemn Sanctuary Cities Executive Order." Available at https://immigrationforum.org/article/law-enforcement-leaders-condemn-sanctuary-cities-executive-order.

141. Read more at https://www.brainyquote.com/quotes/joe_arpaio_476837.

142. See, for instance, National Immigration Law Center. (n.d.). Immigration Enforcement. Available at https://www.nilc.org/issues/immigration-enforcement.

143. Ibid.

144. Gallu (2019).

145. Ramey, Sara. (2018). "It's Not Local Law Enforcement's Responsibility to Do ICE's Job." *The Hill*, January 10. Available at https://thehill.com/opinion/immigration/368279-its-not-local-law-enforcements-responsibility-to-do-ices-job.

146. See, for instance, Ryan, Shane. (2019). "Report: Undocumented Immigrants Don't Commit More Crime, Violent or Otherwise." *Paste Magazine*, May 13. Available at https://www.pastemagazine.com/articles/2019/05/report-undocumented-immigrants-does-not-lead-to-mo.html.

147. Armenta, Amada. (2017). *Protect, Serve, and Deport: The Rise of Policing as Immigration Enforcement.* Oakland: University of California Press.

148. Police Foundation. (2009). *The Role of Local Police: Striking a Balance between Immigration Enforcement and Civil Liberties.* April. Available at https://www.policefoundation.org/publication/the-role-of-local-police-striking-a-balance-between-immigration-enforcement-and-civil-liberties.

149. Armenta (2017).

150. See Welch, Michael. (2002). *Detained: Immigration Laws and the Expanding INS Jail Complex.* Philadelphia: Temple University Press. See also Ewing, Walter, Daniel E. Martinez, and Rubén G. Rumbaut. (2015). *The Criminalization of Immigration in the United States.* Washington, DC: American Immigration Council.

151. Kang, S. Deborah. (2017). *The INS on the Line.* New York: Oxford University Press.

152. Ibid.

153. Ibid

154. Ibid.

155. Ibid.

156. Gomez, Alan. 2019. "Border Patrol Struggling to Hire, Keep Agents, but May Never Get 5,000 Trump Ordered." *USA Today*, March 29. Available at https://news.yahoo.com/border-patrol-struggling-hire-keep-095348531.html.

157. Ibid.

158. Ibid.

159. Ibid.

160. Ibid.

161. U.S. Immigration and Customs Enforcement. (2018). *Fact Sheet: Immigration and Customs Enforcement (ICE).* June 10. Available at https://immigrationforum.org/article/fact-sheet-immigration-and-customs-enforcement-ice.

162. Ibid.

163. Ibid.

164. Ibid.

165. WBUR. (2018). "Fifteen Years after Its Creation, Critics Want to Abolish ICE." June 25. Available at https://www.wbur.org/hereandnow/2018/06/25/immigration-abolish-ice.

166. Waxman, Olivia B. (2018). "The 'Abolish ICE' Movement Is Growing. Here's Why the U.S. Immigration and Customs Enforcement Agency Was Created." *Time*, June 29. http://time.com/5325492/abolish-ice-history.

167. Nixon, Ron, and Linda Qiu. (2018). "What Is ICE and Why Do Critics Want to Abolish It?" *New York Times*, June 3. Available at https://www.wbur.org /hereandnow/2018/06/25/immigration-abolish-ice.

168. Kang (2017).

169. WBUR (2018).

170. Ibid.

171. Kang (2017).

172. WBUR (2018).

173. Ibid.

174. Golash-Boza (2015).

175. U.S. Immigration and Customs Enforcement. (1996). "Delegation of Immigration Authority Section 287(g) Immigration and Nationality Act."

176. Cristina Rodriguez, Muzaffar Chishti, Randy Capps, and Laura St. John. (2010) "A Program in Flux: New Priorities and Implementation Challenge for 287(g)." Washington, DC: Migration Policy Institute. Available at http://www .migrationpolicy.org/research/program-flux-new-priorities-and-implementation -challenges-287g.

177. Kandel, William A. (2016). "Interior Immigration Enforcement: Criminal Alien Programs." Washington, DC: Congressional Research Service. Available at https://fas.org/sgp/crs/homesec/R44627.pdf.

178. Ibid.

179. Armenta (2017).

180. Starnes, Todd. (2019). "A List of Sanctuary Cities and States." April 15. Available at https://www.toddstarnes.com/show/a-list-of-sanctuary-cities-and -states.

181. See, for instance, U.S. Immigration and Customs Enforcement. (2018). "Secure Communities." March 20. Available at https://www.ice.gov/secure -communities; see also Law Enforcement Immigration Task Force. (2017). "A Path to Public Safety: The Legal Questions around Immigration Detainers." February 27. Available at https://leitf.org/wp-content/uploads/2018/01/The-Legal -Questions-Around-Immigration-Detainers.pdf.

182. Ibid.

183. Armenta, Amada. (2016). "Between Public Service and Social Control: Policing Dilemmas in the Era of Immigration Enforcement." *Social Problems* 63 (1): 191–210.

184. Ibid.

185. Armenta (2017).

186. Archibold, Randal. (2010). "Arizona Enacts Stringent Law on Immigration." *New York Times*, April 23.

187. Armenta (2017).

188. *Arizona v. United States*, 567 U.S. ____ (2012).

189. Armenta (2017).

190. Ibid.

191. Ibid.

192. Soloman, Danyelle, Tom Jawetz, and Malik Sanam. (2017). "The Negative Consequences of Entangling Local Policing and Immigration Enforcement." Center for American Progress, March 21. Available at https://www.ameri canprogress.org/issues/immigration/reports/2017/03/21/428776/negative-con sequences-entangling-local-policing-immigration-enforcement.

193. Mark, Michelle. (2017). "Trump's Immigration Crackdown Is Paving the Way for a 'Deportation Force.'" *Business Insider*, February 23. Available at http://www.businessinsider.com/trump-dhs-memos-pave-way-for-deportation-force -2017-2; LoBianco, Tom. (2015). "Donald Trump Promises 'Deportation Force' to Remove 11 Million." CNN Politics, November 12. Available at http://www.cnn .com/2015/11/11/politics/donald-trump-deportation-force-debate-immigration.

194. Ferrell, Craig E. (2006). "M.C.C. Immigration Committee Recommendations for Enforcement of Immigration Laws by Local Policy Agencies." Charlotte, NC: Major Cities Chiefs Association. Available at https://www.majorcitieschiefs .com/pdf/news/MCC_Position_Statement.pdf; see also Major Cities Chiefs. (2013). "Immigration Policy." Available at https://www.majorcitieschiefs.com /pdf/news/2013_immigration_policy.pdf.

195. Ibid.

196. Ramey (2018).

197. Ibid.

198. Ibid.

199. See, for instance, American Civil Liberties Union of Pennsylvania. (n.d.). "Galarza v. Szalczyk, et al." Available at https://www.aclupa.org/our-work/legal /legaldocket/galarzavszalczyketal; Edwards, Ashton. (2014). "Man Settles Immigration Lawsuit against Salt Lake County, Awarded $75,000." Fox 13 News, August 25. Available at http://fox13now.com/2014/08/25/man-settles-immi gration-lawsuit-against-salt-lake-county-awarded-75000; Mayes, Steve. (2015). "Woman at Center of Landmark Immigration Case Settles Suit That Changed Jail Holds in State, Nation." *The Oregonian*, May 18. Available at http://www.ore gonlive.com/clackamascounty/index.ssf/2015/05/woman_at_center_of_land-mark_im.html.

200. Armenta (2017).

201. Wilson, James Q., and George Kelling. (1982). "Broken Windows." *The Atlantic*, March. Available at https://www.theatlantic.com/magazine/archive /1982/03/broken-windows/304465.

202. Ibid.

203. Center for Evidence-Based Crime Policy. (n.d.). *Broken Windows Theory.* Available at https://cebcp.org/evidence-based-policing/what-works-in-policing /research-evidence-review/broken-windows-policing.

204. Ibid.

205. Kelling, George L., and Catherine M. Coles. (1996). *Fixing Broken Windows.* New York: The Free Press.

206. Center for Evidence-Based Crime Policy (n.d.).

207. Armenta (2017).

208. Ibid.
209. Ibid.
210. Ibid.
211. Ibid.
212. Ibid.
213. Ibid.
214. Ibid.

Chapter 4

215. Shoichet, Catherine. (2019). "The American Bar Association Says US Immigration Courts 'On the Brink of Collapse.' CNN, March 20. Available at https://www.cnn.com/2019/03/20/politics/american-bar-association-immigration-court/index.html.

216. Sessions, Jeff. (2017). "Attorney Jeff Sessions Delivers Remarks to the Executive Office of Immigration Review." October 12. Available at https://www.justice.gov/opa/speech/attorney-general-jeff-sessions-delivers-remarks-executive-office-immigration-review.

217. Torbati, Yeganeh. (2018). "Head of U.S. Immigration Judges' Union Denounces Trump's Quota Plan." Reuters, September 21. Available at https://www.reuters.com/article/us-usa-immigration-judges/head-of-u-s-immigration-judges-union-denounces-trump-quota-plan-idUSKCN1M12LZ.

218. U.S. Department of Justice, Office of EOIR. (2017). *Fact Sheet: Executive Office for Immigration Review: An Agency Guide.* Available at https://www.justice.gov/eoir/page/file/eoir_an_agency_guide/download.

219. Ibid.

220. Ibid.

221. Marouf, Fatima. (2018). "How Immigration Court Works." The Conversation, June 25. Available at https:/theconversation.com/how-immigration-court-works-98678.

222. National Immigration Forum. (2018). "Fact Sheet: Immigration Courts." August 7. Available at https://immigrationforum.org/article/fact-sheet-immigration-courts.

223. Ibid.

224. National Immigration Forum (2018).

225. U.S. Department of Justice, Office of EOIR (2017).

226. Ibid.

227. Ibid.

228. Ibid.

229. U.S. Department of Justice (2017).

230. Ibid.

231. Mossaad, Nadwa. (2019). *Annual Flow Report: Refugees and Asylees 2017.* Department of Homeland Security. Available at https://www.dhs.gov/sites/default/files/publications/Refugees_Asylees_2017.pdf.

232. Zong, Batalova, and Burrows (2019).

233. Ibid.

234. Marouf (2018).

235. National Immigration Forum (2018).

236. Eagly, Ingrid, and Steven Shafer. (2018). *Access to Counsel in Immigration Court*. Washington, DC: American Immigration Council.

237. Ibid.

238. Ibid.

239. Ibid.

240. Ibid.

241. Ibid.

242. Ibid.

243. Ibid.

244. Ibid.

245. Ibid.

246. O'Toole, Molly. (2019). "Trump Plan Fails to Cut Immigration Court Backlog, as Caseload Soars More Than 26%." *Los Angeles Times*, February 21. Available at https://www.latimes.com/politics/la-na-pol-immigration-court-back log-worsens-20190221-story.html.

247. Ibid.

248. Ibid.

249. Ibid.

250. National Immigration Forum (2018).

251. Shoichet (2019).

252. Ibid.

253. Zatz, Marjorie, and Nancy Rodriguez. (2015). *Dreams and Nightmares: Immigration Policy, Youth, and Families*. Oakland: University of California Press.

254. See, for instance, Wiseman, Andrew, and Michael Connelly. (2008). *Judicial Discretion and Sentencing Outcomes: Incorporating Data from the Courtroom*. Madison: Wisconsin Sentencing Commission; see also Rachlinkski, Jeffrey J. and Andrew J. Wistrich. (2017). "Judging the Judiciary by the Numbers: Empirical Research on Judges." 13 Annual Review of Law and Social Science; Tyler, Tom. (2016). "Police Discretion in the 21st Century Surveillance State." *University of Chicago Legal Forum*. Vol. 2016, Article 14. Available at http://chicago unbound.uchicago.edu/uclf/vol2016/iss1/14.

255. National Immigration Forum (2018).

256. Zatz and Rodriguez (2015).

257. Ibid.

258. Ibid.

259. Ibid.

260. American Immigration Council. (2018). "Fact Sheet: The End of Immigration Enforcement Priorities under the Trump Administration." March 7. Available at https://americanimmigrationcouncil.org/research/immigration-enforcement -priorities-under-trump-administration.

261. Ibid.
262. Ibid.
263. Ibid.
264. Ibid.
265. Ibid.
266. Ibid.
267. Ibid.
268. Ibid.
269. Kang (2017).
270. Ibid.
271. American Immigration Council (2018).
272. Ibid.
273. Lipsky, Michael. (1980). *Street Level Bureaucracy: Dilemmas of the Individual in Public Service.* New York: Russell Sage Foundation.
274. Nolo. (n.d.). "Prosecutorial Discretion All but Dead as Immigration Remedy Owing to Trump Order." Available at https://www.nolo.com/legal-en cyclopedia/prosecutorial-discretion-all-but-dead-as-immigration-remedy-owing -to-trump-order.html.
275. Ibid.
276. Ibid.
277. Marouf (2018).

Chapter 5

278. Bort, Ryan. (2018). "This Is the Prison-Like Border Facility Holding Migrant Children." *Rolling Stone*, June 14. Available at https://www.rollingstone .com/politics/politics-news/this-is-the-prison-like-border-facility-holding -migrant-children-628728.
279. Katz, Johnathan M. (2019). "Call Immigrant Detention Centers What They Are: Concentration Camps." *Los Angeles Times*, June 9. Available at https:// www.latimes.com/opinion/op-ed/la-oe-katz-immigrant-concentration-camps -20190609-story.html.
280. Bacon, John. (2018). "Detention Crisis: Trump Defends 'Zero Tolerance' Immigration." *USA Today*, June 18. Available at https://www.usatoday.com/story /news/nation/2018/06/18/detention-crisis-what-we-know-now/710718002.
281. Pfaff, John F. (2017). *Locked In: The True Causes of Mass Incarceration and How to Achieve Real Reform.* New York: Basic Books.
282. See McNamara, Robert, and Ronald Burns. (2017). *Multiculturalism, Crime, and Criminal Justice.* New York: Oxford University Press.
283. Alexander, Michelle. (2012). *The New Jim Crow: Mass Incarceration in the Age of Colorblindness.* New York: The New Press.
284. Ibid.
285. Ibid.
286. Ibid.

287. Latzler, Barry. (2018). "Why Michelle Alexander Is Wrong about Mass Incarceration." *National Review,* April 22. Available at https://www.nationalreview .com/magazine/2019/04/22/michelle-alexander-is-wrong-about-mass -incarceration.

288. Ibid.

289. Pfaff (2017).

290. Ibid.

291. Ibid.

292. Latzler, Barry. (2016). *The Rise and Fall of Violent Crime in America.* New York: Encounter Books.

293. Ibid.

294. Forman, James. (2017). *Locking Up Our Own: Crime and Punishment in Black America.* New York: Farrar, Straus, and Giroux.

295. Latzler (2018).

296. Ibid.

297. Ibid.

298. Pfaff (2017).

299. Ibid.

300. Macdonald, Heather. (2016). *The War on Cops.* New York: Endelmann.

301. Pfaff (2017).

302. Ibid.

303. Ibid.

304. Ibid.

305. Sawyer, Wendy, and Peter Wagner. (2019). "Mass Incarceration: The Whole Pie 2019." Prison Policy Initiative, March 29. Available at https://www .prisonpolicy.org/reports/pie2019.html.

306. Ibid.

307. Ibid.

308. Ibid.

309. Ibid.

310. Ibid.

311. Amada (2017).

312. Latzler (2018).

313. Pfaff (2017).

314. See Thompson, Christie, and Andrew R. Calderon. (2019). "More Immigrants Are Giving Up Court Fights and Leaving U.S." The Marshall Project, May 8. Available at https://www.themarshallproject.org/2019/05/08/more -detained-immigrants-are-giving-up-court-fights-and-leaving-the-u-s. See also Zatz and Rodriguez (2015).

315. Bains, Chiragg. (2017). "How Immigrants Make Communities Safer." The Marshall Project, February 28. Available at https://www.themarshallproject .org/2017/02/28/how-immigrants-make-communities-safer.

316. Johnson, Carla. (2019). "U.S. Birthrates Lowest in 3 Decades Despite Improving Economy." Associated Press, May 15. Available at https://news.yahoo

.com /fewer-babies-us-birth-rate-fails-rebound-economy-041958834 .html.

317. See, for instance, Knowles, David. (2019). "Immigrants and Crime: New Study Rebuts Trump Claims." Yahoo News, May 13. Available at https://news.yahoo .com/study-rebuts-trump-claims-linking-undocumented-immigrants-to-higher -crime-rates-181621537.html; Nowrasteh, Alex. (2018). "Criminal Immigrants in Texas: Illegal Immigrant Conviction and Arrest Rates for Homicide, Sex Crimes, Larceny and Other Crimes." Cato Institute, February 26. Available at https://www .cato.org/publications/immigration-research-policy-brief/criminal-immigrants -texas-illegal-immigrant; Light, Michael T. and Ty Miller. (2018). "Does Undocumented Immigration Increase Violent Crime?" *Criminology* 56 (2): 370–401.

318. Bains (2017).

319. Korte, Gregory, and Alan Gomez. (2018). "Trump Ramps Up Rhetoric on Undocumented Immigrants: 'These Aren't People. These Are Animals.'" *USA Today*, May 16. Available at https://www.usatoday.com/story/news/politics/2018 /05/16/trump-immigrants-animals-mexico-democrats-sanctuary-cities/61725 2002.

320. Ibid.

321. U.S. Immigration and Customs Enforcement. (2019). *Fiscal Year 2018 ICE Enforcement and Removal Operations Report*. Available at https://www.ice.gov /doclib/about/offices/ero/pdf/eroFY2018Report.pdf.

322. Gomez, Alan. (2019). "ICE Sets Record for Arrests of Undocumented Immigrants with No Criminal Record." *USA Today*, March 21. Available at https://www.usatoday.com/story/news/politics/2019/03/21/ice-sets-record -arrests-undocumented-immigrants-no-criminal-record/3232476002.

323. Ibid.

324. Ibid.

325. Ibid.

326. Wilson, William Julius. (1997). *When Work Disappears: The World of the New Urban Poor*. New York: Vintage.

327. Golash-Boza (2015).

328. Seville, Lisa Riordan, Hannah Rappleye, and Andrew W. Lehman. (2019). "22 Immigrants Die in ICE Detention Centers during Past Two Years." NBC News, January 6. Available at https://www.nbcnews.com/politics/immigration/22-immi grants-died-ice-detention-centers-during-past-2-years-n954781; see also Alverez, Priscilla. (2019). "Exclusive: DHS Watchdog Finds Expired Food, Dilapidated Bathrooms amid 'Egregious' Conditions at ICE Facilities in 2018." CNN, June 7. Available at https://www.cnn.com/2019/06/06/politics/ice-detention-center-ig -report/index.html.

329. Ibid.

330. Ibid.

331. Ibid.

332. Ibid.

333. Thompson and Calderon (2019).

334. Gotsch, Kara, and Vinay Basti. (2018). *Capitalizing on Mass Incarceration: U.S. Growth in Private Prisons.* Washington, DC: The Sentencing Project. Available at https://www.sentencingproject.org/publications/capitalizing-on-mass-incarceration-u-s-growth-in-private-prisons.

335. Ibid.

336. Ibid.

337. Ibid.

338. Ibid.

339. Ibid.

340. U.S. Department of Justice, Office of Inspector General. (2016). *Review of the Federal Bureau of Prisons Monitoring of Contract Prisons.* Available at https://oig.justice.gov/reports/2016/e1606.pdf.

341. Gotsch and Basti (2018).

342. Ibid.

343. Ibid.

344. Sawyer and Wagner (2019).

345. Erickson, Camille. (2019). "Detention Center Contractors Will Keep Reaping Profits Even after DHS Upheaval." Opensecrets.org, April 15. Available at https://www.opensecrets.org/news/2019/04/detention-center-contractors-keep-reaping-profit-after-dhs-upheaval.

346. Gomez, Alan. (2019). "Trump Administration to Relocate Some Migrants Caught along the Southern Border into South Florida." *USA Today,* May 16. Available at https://www.usatoday.com/story/news/politics/2019/05/16/trump-administration-release-hundreds-migrants-into-south-florida-southern-border-asylum-seekers/3697908002.

347. Ibid.

Chapter 6

348. Gomez, Alan. (2019). "Southern Border Crossings by Asylum-Seeking Migrants Kept Rising in April, Set New Record." *USA Today,* May 8. Available at https://www.usatoday.com/story/news/politics/2019/05/08/border-crossing-asylum-seeking-migrant-families-hit-record-april/1144303001.

349. Chapin, Angela. (2019). "Trump Administration to Deprive Migrant Kids in Shelters of English Lessons, Legal Aid." *HuffPost,* June 5. Available at https://www.huffpost.com/entry/migrant-children-shelters-english-lessons_n_5cf835cae4b0e3e3df14c99e.

350. Ibid.

351. Center for American Progress. (2017). *Keeping Families Together.* March 16. Available at https://www.americanprogress.org/issues/immigration/reports/2017/03/16/428335/keeping-families-together.

352. American Immigration Council. (2018). *U.S. Citizen Children Impacted by Immigration Enforcement.* Available at https://americanimmigrationcouncil.org/research/us-citizen-children-impacted-immigration-enforcement.

353. Ibid.

354. Ibid.

355. Zatz and Rodriguez (2015).

356. Ibid.

357. American Immigration Council (2018).

358. Ibid.

359. Ibid.

360. Transactional Records Access Clearinghouse. (2019). "Immigration and Customs Enforcement Detainees." Syracuse, NY: Syracuse University. Available at https://trac.syr.edu/phptools/immigration/detention/.

361. American Immigration Council (2018).

362. Ibid. See also U.S. Department of Justice, Executive Office of Immigration Services. (n.d.). "Workload and Adjustment Statistics, FY 2018." Available at https://www.justice.gov/eoir/workload-and-adjudication-statistics.

363. Ibid.

364. Tiano, Sara. (2018). "Report: Increased Deportation Could Put More Kids in Foster Care." Chronicle of Social Change, February 21. Available at https://chronicleofsocialchange.org/research-and-resources/report-increased -deportations-put-kids-foster-care/29875.

365. American Immigration Council (2018).

366. Ibid.

367. Ibid.

368. Ibid.

369. Ibid.

370. Buiano, Madeline. (2018). "ICE Data: Tens of Thousands of Deported Parents Have U.S. Citizen Kids." Center for Public Integrity, October 12. Available at https://publicintegrity.org/immigration/ice-data-tens-of-thousands-of-de ported-parents-have-u-s-citizen-kids.

371. Kandel, William. (2017). *Unaccompanied Alien Children: An Overview.* Congressional Research Service. Available at https://fas.org/sgp/crs/homesec /R43599.pdf.

372. Ibid.

373. Ibid.

374. Kandel (2018).

375. Chapin (2019).

376. Ibid.

377. Ibid.

378. Alvarez, Priscilla. (2019). "Roughly 8,700 Unaccompanied Children Turned Over to Refugee Office Last Month." CNN, May 3. Available at https:// www.cnn.com/2019/05/03/politics/unaccompanied-children-office-of-refugee -resettlement/index.html.

379. Kandel (2018).

380. Andrews (2019).

381. Ibid.

382. Ibid.

383. Kandel (2018).

384. Morales, Patty. (2018). "What Happens When a Child Arrives at the U.S. Border?" PBS, June 1. Available at https://www.pbs.org/newshour/politics/what-happens-when-a-child-arrives-at-the-u-s-border.

385. Andrews (2019).

386. Lind, Dara. (2019). "Hundreds of Families Still Being Separated at the Border." Vox, February 21. Available at https://www.vox.com/2019/2/21/18234767/parents-separated-children-families-border-trump-jails.

387. Ibid.

388. Ibid.

389. Cummings, William. (2019). "It May Take Two Years to Identify Thousands of Migrant Children Separated from Their Families." *USA Today*, April 7. Available at https://www.usatoday.com/story/news/politics/2019/04/07/immigration-family-separations-may-take-2-years-identify-children/3393536002.

390. Ibid.

391. Kandel (2018).

392. Gomez, Alan. (2019). "'Dangerous Overcrowding': 900 Migrants Cram into Border Patrol Center Designed for 125." *USA Today*, May 31. Available at https://www.usatoday.com/story/news/nation/2019/05/31/watchdog-finds-dangerous-overcrowding-el-paso-border-patrol-stations/1300906001.

393. Ibid.

394. Ibid.

395. Ibid.

396. Lind, Dara. (2019). "The Crisis of Children Dying in Custody at the Border, Explained." Vox, May 22. Available at https://www.vox.com/2019/5/22/18632936/child-died-border-toddler-patrol-three-five.

397. Alvarez (2019).

398. Jordan (2019).

399. Ibid.

400. Andrews (2019).

Chapter 7

401. Mascaro, Lisa. (2018). "Trump Complains about Allowing Immigrants from 'Shithole' Countries." *Los Angeles Times*, January 11. Available at https://www.latimes.com/politics/la-na-pol-trump-congress-dreamers-20180111-story.html.

402. McCarthy, Joe. (2017). "11 Quotes That Shows Angela Merkel Is a True Global Citizen." *Global Citizen*, July 17. Available at https://www.globalcitizen.org/en/content/11-quotes-that-show-angela-merkel-is-a-true-global.

403. San Martin, Ines. (2017). "Pope Says Immigrants Not a Threat but an Opportunity to Build Peace." Crux, November 24. Available at https://cruxnow.com/vatican/2017/11/24/pope-immigrants-not-threat-opportunity-build-peace.

404. See National Center on Homelessness and Poverty. (n.d.). "Criminalization Resources." Available at https://nlchp.org/criminalization.

405. Nevins, Joseph. (2018). "How U.S. Policy in Honduras Set the Stage for Today's Migration." The Conversation, October 25. Available at https://theconversation.com/how-us-policy-in-honduras-set-the-stage-for-todays-migration-65935.

406. Ibid.

407. Ibid.

408. Ibid.

409. Ibid.

410. Ibid.

411. Ibid.

412. Ibid.

413. Ibid.

414. Tseng-Putterman, Mark. (2018). "A Century of U.S. Intervention Created the Immigration Crisis." Medium, June 20. Available at https://medium.com/s/story/timeline-us-intervention-central-america-a9bea9ebc148.

415. Chen, Michelle. (2015). "How US Free Trade Policies Created the Central American Migration Crisis." *The Nation*, February 6. Available at https://thenation.com/article/how-us-free-trade-policies-created-central-american-migration-crisis.

416. Ibid.

417. Ibid.

418. Boner, Raymond. (2016). "Time for a U.S. Apology to El Salvador." *The Nation*, April 15. Available at https://thenation.com/article/time-for-a-us-apology-to-el-salvador.

419. Ibid.

420. Garcia, Maria Christina. (2006). *Seeking Refuge: Central American Migration to Mexico, the United States, and Canada.* Oakland: University of California Press.

421. Tseng-Putterman (2018).

422. Bonner, Raymond. (2018). "America's Role in El Salvador's Deterioration." *The Atlantic*, January 20. Available at http://theatlantic.com/international/archive/2018/01/trump-and-el-salvador/550955.

423. Lind, Dara. (2019). "MS-13, Explained." Vox, February 5. Available at https://www.vox.com/policy-and-politics/2018/2/26/16955936/ms-13-trump-immigrants-crime.

424. Ibid.

425. Ibid.

426. Arijeta, Lajka. (2019). "MS-13 and the Violence Driving Migration from Central America." CBS News, January 18. Available at https://www.cbsnews.com/news/ms-13-illegal-immigration-families-in-crisis-cbsn-originals.

427. Lind (2019).

428. Ibid.

429. Ibid.

430. Arijeta (2019).

431. Lind (2019).

432. Ibid.

433. Ibid.

434. Ibid.

435. Ibid.

436. Arijeta (2019).

437. Garcia (2006).

438. Ibid.

439. Ibid.

440. Ibid.

441. Tseng-Putterman (2018).

442. Ibid.

443. Ibid.

444. Garcia (2006).

445. Ibid.

446. Ibid.

447. Ibid.

448. Ibid.

449. Ibid.

450. Weaver, Fredrick Stirton. (1994). *Inside the Volcano: The History and Political Economy of Central America.* Boulder, CO: Westview Press.

451. Ibid.

452. Martinez, Oscar. (2017). *A History of Violence: Living and Dying in Central America.* New York: Verso Books.

453. Edwards, Adrian. (2018). Forced Displacements at Record 68.5 Million." UN High Commissioner on Refugees, June 19. Available at https://www.unhcr.org/en-us/news/stories/2018/6/5b222c494/forced-displacement-record-685-million.html.

454. Ibid.

455. Beauchamp, Zach. (2017). "9 Maps and Charts That Explain the Global Refugee Crisis." Vox, January 30. Available at https://www.vox.com/world/2017/1/30/14432500/refugee-crisis-trump-muslim-ban-maps-charts.

456. Wood, Johnny. (2019). "These Countries Are Home to the Highest Proportion of Refugees in the World." World Economic Forum, March 19. Available at https://www.weforum.org/agenda/2019/03/mena-countries-in-the-middle-east-have-the-highest-proportion-of-refugees-in-the-world.

457. BBC. (2019). "Why Is There a War in Syria?" February 25. Available at https://www.bbc.com/news/world-middle-east-35806229.

458. Ibid.

459. Ibid.

460. Ibid.

461. Ibid.

462. Ibid.

463. Ibid.

464. Ibid.

465. Beauchamp (2017).

466. Wood (2019).

467. Ibid.

468. UN High Commissioner on Refugees. (2019). "Syria Regional Refugee Response." June 3. Available at https://data2.unhcr.org/en/situations/syria.

469. Ibid.

470. Pierce, Sarah. (2019). *Changes in the First Two Years of Trump Administration*. Migration Policy Institute, May. Available at file:///C:/Users/mcnamararl/Downloads/ImmigrationChangesTrumpAdministration-FinalWEB.pdf.

471. Ibid.

472. King, Peter, and Tom Suozi. (2019). "A Grand Compromise on Immigration." *New York Times*, March 24. Available at https://www.nytimes.com/2019/03/24/opinion/a-grand-compromise-on-immigration.html.

473. Ibid.

474. Ibid.

475. Paletta, Damien, Nick Miroff, and Josh Dawsey. (2019). "Trump Says U.S. to Impose 5% Tariff on all Mexican Imports Beginning June 10 in Dramatic Escalation of Border Clash." *Texas Tribune*, May 30. Available at https://www.texastribune.org/2019/05/30/trump-threatens-mexico-tariffs-central-american-migrants-cross-border.

476. Reuters Graphics. (2019). "Trump Threatens to Shut U.S.-Mexico Border." March 29. Available at https://graphics.reuters.com/USA-IMMIGRATION-TRUMP/0100919N1TG/index.htm.

477. Fram, Alan. (2019). "House OKs Dems' Immigration Bill Despite Veto Threat." Associated Press, June 4. Available at https://news.yahoo.com/house-near-ok-dem-immigration-181256650.html.

478. Associated Press. (2019). "Trump: Migrants Can Opt 'Not to Come' If They Dislike Squalid Camps." Yahoo News, July 3. Available at https://www.yahoo.com/news/trump-migrants-opt-not-come-dislike-squalid-camps-210846109.html.

479. Blitzer, Jonathan. (2019). "How Trump's Safe-Third-Country Agreement with Guatemala Fell Apart." *The New Yorker*, July 15. Available at https://www.newyorker.com/news/news-desk/how-trumps-safe-third-country-agreement-with-guatemala-fell-apart.

480. Spagat, Elliot. (2019). 'Trump Expands Fast-Track Deportation Authority across U.S.' Associated Press, July 22. Available at https://news.yahoo.com/trump-expands-fast-track-deportation-164036724.html.

481. Glassner, Barry. (1999). *The Culture of Fear*. New York: Basic Books.

Epilogue

482. Associated Press. (2019). "Immigration Raids at Mississippi Food Plants Result in 680 Arrests." August 7. Available at https://wreg.com/2019/08/07/immigration-raids-underway-at-mississippi-food-plants.

483. Mansoor, Sanya. (2019). "Hundreds of Their Workers Were Arrested in Mississippi ICE Raids but No Employers Have Been Charged Yet." *Time*, August 9. Available at https://time.com/5649108/mississippi-ice-raids-no-employers-charged.

484. Ibid.

485. Associated Press (2019).

486. Jordan, Miriam. (2019). "The Flores Agreement Protected Migrant Children for Decades. New Regulations Aim to End It." *New York Times*, August 20. Available at https://www.nytimes.com/2019/08/20/us/flores-migrant-children -detention.html.

487. Ibid.

488. Ibid.

489. Ibid.

490. Ibid.

491. Ibid.

492. Ibid.

493. Shear, Michael, and Zolan Kenno-Youngs. (2019). "Migrant Families Would Face Indefinite Detention under New Trump Rule." *New York Times*, August 22. Available at https://www.nytimes.com/2019/08/21/us/politics/flores -migrant-family-detention.html.

494. Ibid.

495. Ibid.

496. Jansen, Bart. (2019). "19 States File Lawsuit Opposing Trump Administration Policy for Detaining Migrant Families." *USA Today*, August 26. Available at https://www.usatoday.com/story/news/politics/2019/08/26/migrant-families -19-states-sue-over-dhs-plan-indefinite-detention/2124483001.

497. O'Toole, Molly, and Eli Stokolis. (2019). "Trump Administration, Guatemala Sign Pact Barring Migrants from Claiming Asylum in U.S." *Los Angeles Times*, July 26. Available at https://www.latimes.com/politics/story/2019-07-26 /trump-agreement-guatemala-restrict-asylum-claims.

498. Ibid.

499. Dawsey, Josh, and Nick Miroff. (2019). "Mexico Border Wall: Trump Orders Aides to Seize Private Land and Disregard Environmental Rules." *The Independent*, August 28. Available at https://www.yahoo.com/news/mexico -border-wall-trump-orders-072616021.html.

500. Ibid.

501. Ibid.

502. Ibid.

503. Alvarez, Priscilla, Geneva Sands, and Tami Luhby. (2019). "Trump Administration Announces Rule That Could Limit Legal Immigration over Use of Public Benefits." CNN, August 13. Available at https://www.cnn.com/2019/08 /12/politics/legal-immigration-public-charge/index.html.

504. Ibid.

505. Ibid.

506. Madoni, Doha. (2019). "2 Mass Shootings in Less Than a Day Leave at Least 29 Dead and 53 Injured." NBC News, August 4. Available at https://www .nbcnews.com/news/us-news/2-mass-shootings-u-s-leave-least-29-dead-53 -n1039066.

507. Ibid.

508. Cole, Devan. (2019). "Trump Suggesting Tying Gun Measures to Immigration after Shooting That Targeted Immigrants." CNN, August 5. Available at https://www.cnn.com/2019/08/05/politics/donald-trump-gun-control -immigration-reform-mass-shootings/index.html.

509. Ibid.

510. Ibid.

511. Ibid.

512. Chappell, Bill, and Richard Gonzales. (2019). "'Do Something!': Calls for Action after Mass Shootings in El Paso and Dayton." NPR, August 5. Available at https://www.npr.org/2019/08/05/748239149/do-something-calls-ring-out-after -mass-shootings-in-el-paso-and-dayton.

513. Ibid.

514. Ibid.

Selected Bibliography

Alexander, Michelle. (2012). *The New Jim Crow: Mass Incarceration in the Age of Colorblindness.* New York: The New Press.

Alvarez, Priscilla. (2019). "Exclusive: DHS Watchdog Finds Expired Food, Dilapidated Bathrooms amid 'Egregious' Conditions at ICE Facilities in 2018." CNN, June 7. Available at https://www.cnn.com/2019/06/06/politics/ice-detention-center-ig-report/index.html.

Alvarez, Priscilla. (2019). "Roughly 8,700 Unaccompanied Children Turned Over to Refugee Office Last Month." CNN, May 3. Available at https://www.cnn.com/2019/05/03/politics/unaccompanied-children-office-of-refugee-resettlement/index.html.

American Immigration Council. (2016). "Public Education for Immigrant Students: Understanding Plyler v. Doe." October 24. Available at https://www.americanimmigrationcouncil.org/research/plyler-v-doe-public-education-immigrant-students.

American Immigration Council. (2018). *U.S. Citizen Children Impacted by Immigration Enforcement.* Available at https://americanimmigrationcouncil.org/research/us-citizen-children-impacted-immigration-enforcement.

Andrews, Arthur. (2019). "Unaccompanied Alien Children and the Crisis at the Border." Center for Immigration Studies, April 1. Available at https://cis.org/Report/Unaccompanied-Alien-Children-and-Crisis-Border.

Arizona v. United States, 567 U.S. _____ (2012).

Armenta, Amada. (2016). "Between Public Service and Social Control: Policing Dilemmas in the Era of Immigration Enforcement." *Social Problems* 63 (1): 191–210.

Armenta, Amada. (2017). *Protect, Serve, and Deport: The Rise of Policing as Immigration Enforcement.* Oakland: University of California Press.

Bains, Chiragg. (2017). "How Immigrants Make Communities Safer." The Marshall Project, February 28. Available at https://www.themarshallproject.org/2017/02/28/how-immigrants-make-communities-safer.

Baker, Peter. (2019). "Trump Declares a National Emergency and Creates a Constitutional Clash." *New York Times*, February 15. Available at https://www.nytimes.com/2019/02/15/us/politics/national-emergency-trump.html.

Beauchamp, Zach. (2017). "9 Maps and Charts That Explain the Global Refugee Crisis." Vox, January 30. Available at https://www.vox.com/world/2017/1/30/14432500/refugee-crisis-trump-muslim-ban-maps-charts.

Beech, Eric. (2019). "Trump Promises to Remove Millions of Illegal Aliens." Reuters, June 18. Available at https://www.yahoo.com/news/trump-says-u-agency-begin-013519516.html.

Blake, Aaron. (2019). "Trump Again Nods toward Violence by His Supporters—And Maybe Something Bigger." *Washington Post*, March 14. Available at https://www.washingtonpost.com/politics/2019/03/14/trump-again-nods-toward-violence-by-his-supporters-maybe-something-bigger.

Bonner, Raymond. (2016). "Time for a U.S. Apology to El Salvador." *The Nation*, April 15. Available at https://thenation.com/article/time-for-a-us-apology-to-el-salvador.

Bonner, Raymond. (2018). "America's Role in El Salvador's Deterioration." *The Atlantic*, January 20. Available at https://www.theatlantic.com/international/archive/2018/01/trump-and-el-salvador/550955.

Brotherton, David C., and Phillip Kretsedemas, eds. (2017). *Immigration Policy in the Age of Punishment*, 1–34. New York: Columbia University Press.

Buiano, Madeline. (2018). "ICE Data: Tens of Thousands of Deported Parents Have U.S. Citizen Kids." *Center for Public Integrity*, October 12. Available at https://publicintegrity.org/immigration/ice-data-tens-of-thousands-of-deported-parents-have-u-s-citizen-kids.

Calavita, Kitty. (2010). *Inside the State: The Bracero Program, Immigration, and the I.N.S.* London: Quo Pro Publishers.

Calfas, Jennifer. (2018). "They're Anxious: Separated Migrant Children in Foster Care Are Now in Limbo after Trump's Immigration Order." *Time*, June 22. Available at https://time.com/5317693/foster-care-family-separation-policy.

Center for American Progress. (2017). *Keeping Families Together*. March 16. Available at https://www.americanprogress.org/issues/immigration/reports/2017/03/16/428335/keeping-families-together.

Chapin, Angela. (2019). "Trump Administration to Deprive Migrant Kids in Shelters of English Lessons, Legal Aid." *HuffPost*, June 5. Available at https://www.huffpost.com/entry/migrant-children-shelters-english-lessons_n_5cf835cae4b0e3e3df14c99e.

Chen, Michelle. (2015). "How US Free Trade Policies Created the Central American Migration Crisis." *The Nation*, February 6. Available at https://thenation.com/article/how-us-free-trade-policies-created-central-american-migration-crisis.

Clemens, Michael. (2017). "What the Mariel Boatlift of Cuban Refugees Can Teach Us about the Economics of Immigration: An Explainer and a

Revelation." *Center for Global Development*, May 22. Available at https://
www.cgdev.org/blog/what-mariel-boatlift-cuban-refugees-can-teach-us
-about-economics-immigration.

Cohen, Stanley. (1972). *Folk Devils and Moral Panics*. New York: Routledge.

Craig E. Ferrell. (2006). *M.C.C. Immigration Committee Recommendations for
Enforcement of Immigration Laws by Local Policy Agencies*. Charlotte, NC:
Major Cities Chiefs Association. Available at https://www.majorcitieschiefs
.com/pdf/news/MCC_Position_Statement.pdf.

Cummings, William. (2019). "It May Take Two Years to Identify Thousands of
Migrant Children Separated from Their Families." *USA Today*, April 7.
Available at https://www.usatoday.com/story/news/politics/2019/04/07
/immigration-family-separations-may-take-2-years-identify-children
/3393536002.

Eagly, Ingrid, and Steven Shafer. (2018). *Access to Counsel in Immigration Court*.
Washington, DC: American Immigration Council.

Edwards, Adrian. (2018). Forced Displacement at Record 68.5 Million." UN
High Commissioner on Refugees, June 19. Available at https://www
.unhcr.org/en-us/news/stories/2018/6/5b222c494/forced-displacement
-record-685-million.html.

Erickson, Camille. (2019). "Detention Center Contractors will Keep Reaping
Profits Even after DHS Upheaval." Opensecrets.org, April 15. Available at
https://www.opensecrets.org/news/2019/04/detention-center
-contractors-keep-reaping-profit-after-dhs-upheaval.

Felter, Claire, and Danielle Renwick. (2018). "The U.S. Immigration Debate."
Council on Foreign Affairs, July 2. Available at https://www.cfr.org
/backgrounder/us-immigration-debate-0.

Forman, James. (2017). *Locking Up Our Own: Crime and Punishment in Black
America*. New York: Farrar, Straus, and Giroux.

Fram, Alan. (2019). "House OKs Dems' Immigration Bill Despite Veto Threat."
Associated Press. June 4. Available at https://news.yahoo.com/house-near
-ok-dem-immigration-181256650.html.

Garcia, Maria Christina. (2006). *Seeking Refuge: Central American Migration to
Mexico, the United States, and Canada*. Oakland: University of California
Press.

Golash-Boza, Tanya. (2015). *Deported: Immigrant Policing, Disposable Labor, and
Global Capitalism*. New York: NYU Press.

Gomez, Alan. (2019). "'Dangerous Overcrowding': 900 Migrants Cram into Border Patrol Center Designed for 125." *USA Today*, May 31. Available at
https://www.usatoday.com/story/news/nation/2019/05/31/watchdog
-finds-dangerous-overcrowding-el-paso-border-patrol-stations
/1300906001.

Gomez, Alan. (2019). "Southern Border Crossings by Asylum-Seeking Migrants
Kept Rising in April, Set New Record." *USA Today*, May 8. Available at
https://www.usatoday.com/story/news/politics/2019/05/08/border

-crossing-asylum-seeking-migrant-families-hit-record-april
/1144303001.

Gonzalez, Benjamin, Loren Collingwood, and Stephen Omar El-Khatib. (2017). "The Politics of Refuge: Sanctuary Cities, Crime, and Undocumented Immigration." *Urban Affairs Review*, May 7. Available at http://journals .sagepub.com/doi/abs/10.1177/1078087417704974.

Goode, Erich. (2009). *Moral Panics: The Social Construction of Deviance.* 2nd ed. New York: Wiley.

Gotsch, Kara, and Vinay Basti. (2018). *Capitalizing on Mass Incarceration: U.S. Growth in Private Prisons.* Washington, DC: The Sentencing Project. Available at https://www.sentencingproject.org/publications/capitalizing-on -mass-incarceration-u-s-growth-in-private-prisons.

Hall, Stuart. (1978). *Policing the Crisis: Mugging, the State, and Law and Order.* London: Macmillan.

Harvey, David. (2005). *A Brief History of Neoliberalism.* New York: Oxford University Press.

Heer, Jeet. (2016). "How the Southern Strategy Made Donald Trump Possible." *New Republic*, February 18. Available at https://newrepublic.com/article /130039/southern-strategy-made-donald-trump-possible.

Jacobsen, R. (2008). *The New Nativism: Proposition 187 and the Debate over Immigration.* Minneapolis: University of Minnesota Press.

Jordan, Miriam. (2019). "More Migrants Are Crossing the Border This Year: What's Changed?" *New York Times*, March 5. Available at https://www .nytimes.com/2019/03/05/us/crossing-the-border-statistics.html.

Kandel, William. (2017). *Unaccompanied Alien Children: An Overview.* Congressional Research Service. Available at https://fas.org/sgp/crs/homesec /R43599.pdf.

Kang, S. Deborah. (2017). *The INS on the Line.* New York: Oxford University Press.

King, Peter, and Tom Suozi. (2019). "A Grand Compromise on Immigration." *New York Times*, March 24. Available at https://www.nytimes.com/2019 /03/24/opinion/a-grand-compromise-on-immigration.html.

Klein, Rick. (2018). "Trump Said 'Blame on Both Sides' in Charlottesville, Now the Anniversary Puts Him on the Spot." ABC News, August 12. Available at https://abcnews.go.com/Politics/trump-blame-sides-charlottesville-now -anniversary-puts-spot/story?id=57141612.

Knowles, David. (2019). "Immigrants and Crime: New Study Rebuts Trump Claims. Yahoo News, May 13. Available at https://news.yahoo.com/study -rebuts-trump-claims-linking-undocumented-immigrants-to-higher -crime-rates-181621537.html.

Korte, Gregory, and Alan Gomez. (2018). "Trump Ramps Up Rhetoric on Undocumented Immigrants: 'These Aren't People. These Are Animals.'" *USA Today*, May 16. Available at https://www.usatoday.com/story/news /politics/2018/05/16/trump-immigrants-animals-mexico-democrats -sanctuary-cities/617252002.

Latzler, Barry. (2016). *The Rise and Fall of Violent Crime in America*. New York: Encounter Books.

Latzler, Barry. (2018). "Why Michelle Alexander Is Wrong about Mass Incarceration." *National Review*, April 22. Available at https://www.nationalreview.com/magazine/2019/04/22/michelle-alexander-is-wrong-about-mass-incarceration.

Law Enforcement Immigration Task Force. 2017. "A Path to Public Safety: The Legal Questions around Immigration Detainers." February 27. Available at https://leitf.org/wp-content/uploads/2018/01/The-Legal-Questions-Around-Immigration-Detainers.pdf.

Light, Michael T., and Ty Miller. (2018). "Does Undocumented Immigration Increase Violent Crime?" *Criminology* 56 (2): 370–401.

Lind, Dara. (2019). "The Crisis of Children Dying in Custody at the Border, Explained." Vox, May 22. Available at https://www.vox.com/2019/5/22/18632936/child-died-border-toddler-patrol-three-five.

Lind, Dara. (2019). "Hundreds of Families Still Being Separated at the Border." Vox, February 21. Available at https://www.vox.com/2019/2/21/18234767/parents-separated-children-families-border-trump-jails.

Lipsky, Michael. (1980). *Street Level Bureaucracy: Dilemmas of the Individual in Public Service*. New York: Russell Sage Foundation.

Long, Colleen, and Jill Colvin. (2019). "Trump: Not Looking to Reinstate Family Separation Policy." Associated Press, April 10. Available at https://news.yahoo.com/trump-says-not-looking-reinstate-family-separation-policy-164139863--politics.html.

Lopez, Gustavo, Kristen Bialik, and Jynnah Radford. (2018). "Key Facts about U.S. Immigration." Pew Research Center, November 30. Available at http://www.pewresearch.org/fact-tank/2018/11/30/key-findings-about-u-s-immigrants.

Lyons, C., M. Velez, and W. Santoro. (2013). "Neighborhood Immigration. Violence and City-Level Immigrant Political Opportunities." *American Sociological Review* 78 (4): 604–632.

Macdonald, Heather. (2016). *The War on Cops*. New York: Endelmann.

Martinez, Oscar. (2017). *A History of Violence: Living and Dying in Central America*. New York: Verso Books.

Martinez, R. J. Stowell, and M. Lee. (2010). "Immigration and Crime in an Era of Transformation: A Longitudinal Analysis of Homicides in San Diego Neighborhoods, 1980–2000." *Criminology* 48 (3): 797–829.

Mascaro, Lisa. (2018). "Trump Complains about Allowing Immigrants from 'Shithole' Countries." *Los Angeles Times*, January 11. Available at https://www.latimes.com/politics/la-na-pol-trump-congress-dreamers-20180111-story.html.

McCarthy, Justin. (2018). "Immigration Up Sharply as Most Important Problem." Gallup, November 20. Available at https://news.gallup.com/poll/244925/immigration-sharply-important-problem.aspx.

McNamara, Robert, and Ronald Burns. (2017). *Multiculturalism, Crime, and Criminal Justice*. New York: Oxford University Press.

Monterroso, Violeta. (2019). "Dividing Lines: The Human Face of Global Migration." *Time*, February 4–11: 22–46.

Montoya-Galvez, Camilo. (2019). "House Passes Latest DREAM Act, Hoping to Place Millions of Immigrants on Path to Citizenship." CBS News, June 5. Available at https://www.cbsnews.com/news/dream-and-promise-act-2019 -passes-house-approves-bill-that-would-place-millions-of-immigrants -on-path-to-citizenship.

Morales, Patty. (2018). "What Happens when a Child Arrives at the U.S. Border?" PBS, June 1. Available at https://www.pbs.org/newshour/politics/what -happens-when-a-child-arrives-at-the-u-s-border.

Nevins, Joseph. (2018). "How U.S. Policy in Honduras Set the Stage for Today's Migration." The Conversation, October 25. Available at https://theconversation .com/how-us-policy-in-honduras-set-the-stage-for-todays-migration-65935.

Ngai, M. (2004). *Impossible Subjects: Illegal Aliens and the Making of Modern America*. Princeton, NJ: Princeton University Press.

Nixon, Ron, and Linda Qiu. (2018). "What Is ICE and Why Do Critics Want to Abolish It?" *New York Times*, June 25. Available at https://www.wbur.org /hereandnow/2018/06/25/immigration-abolish-ice.

Nowrasteh, Alex. (2018). "Criminal Immigrants in Texas: Illegal Immigrant Conviction and Arrest Rates for Homicide, Sex Crimes, Larceny and Other Crimes." Cato Institute, February 26. Available at https://www .cato.org/publications/immigration-research-policy-brief/criminal -immigrants-texas-illegal-immigrant.

Paletta, Damien, Nick Miroff, and Josh Dawsey. (2019). "Trump Says U.S. to Impose 5% Tariff on All Mexican Imports Beginning June 10 in Dramatic Escalation of Border Clash." *Texas Tribune*, May 30. Available at https:// www.texastribune.org/2019/05/30/trump-threatens-mexico-tariffs -central-american-migrants-cross-border.

Pfaff, John F. (2017). *Locked In: The True Causes of Mass Incarceration and How to Achieve Real Reform*. New York: Basic Books.

Pierce, Sarah. (2019). *Immigration-related Policy Changes in the First Two Years of Trump Administration*. Migration Policy Institute, May. Available at https:// www.migrationpolicy.org/research/immigration-policy-changes-two -years-trump-administration.

Police Foundation. (2009). *The Role of Local Police: Striking a Balance between Immigration Enforcement and Civil Liberties*. April. Available at https://www .policefoundation.org/publication/the-role-of-local-police-striking-a -balance-between-immigration-enforcement-and-civil-liberties.

Powell, John A. (2017). "Us vs. Them: The Sinister Techniques of Othering and How to Avoid Them." *The Guardian*, November 8. Available at https:// www.theguardian.com/inequality/2017/nov/08/us-vs-them-the-sinister -techniques-of-othering-and-how-to-avoid-them.

Powell, John A., and Stephen Menendian. (2017). "The Problem of Othering: Towards Inclusiveness and Belonging." *Othering & Belonging*, June 29. Available at http://www.otheringandbelonging.org/the-problem-of-othering.

Radford, Jynnah. (2019). "Key Findings about U.S. Immigrants." Pew Research Center, June 17. Available at https://www.pewresearch.org/fact-tank/2019/06/17/key-findings-about-u-s-immigrants.

Rahim, Zamira. (2019). "Trump Told Border Agents to Break the Law but Bosses Told Them to Ignore Him, Report Claims." *The Independent*, April 9. Available at https://www.yahoo.com/news/trump-told-border-agents-break-084555838.html.

Ramey, Sara. (2018). "It's Not Local Law Enforcement's Responsibility to Do ICE's Job." *The Hill*, January 10. Available at https://thehill.com/opinion/immigration/368279-its-not-local-law-enforcements-responsibility-to-do-ices-job.

Rodriguez, Cristina, Muzaffar Chishti, Randy Capps, and Laura St. John. (2010). "A Program in Flux: New Priorities and Implementation Challenge for 287(g)." Washington, DC: Migration Policy Institute. Available at http://www.migrationpolicy.org/research/program-flux-new-priorities-and-implementation-challenges-287g.

Rumbaut, Ruben G. (2015). *The Criminalization of Immigration in the United States.* Washington, DC: American Immigration Council.

Ryan, Shane. (2019). "Report: Undocumented Immigrants Don't Commit More Crime, Violent or Otherwise." *Paste Magazine*, May 13. Available at https://www.pastemagazine.com/articles/2019/05/report-undocumented-immigrants-does-not-lead-to-mo.html.

Samuels, Brett. (2018). "Trump: You Know What I Am? I'm a Nationalist." *The Hill*, October 12. Available at https://thehill.com/homenews/administration/412649-trump-you-know-what-i-am-im-a-nationalist.

Sawyer, Wendy, and Peter Wagner. (2019). "Mass Incarceration: The Whole Pie 2019." Prison Policy Initiative, March 29. Available at https://www.prisonpolicy.org/reports/pie2019.html.

Singer, Audrey. (2012). *Investing in the Human Capital of Immigrants: Strengthening Regional Economies.* Washington, DC: Brookings Institute.

Soloman, Danyelle, Tom Jawetz, and Malik Sanam. (2017). "The Negative Consequences of Entangling Local Policing and Immigration Enforcement." Center for American Progress, March 21. Available at https://www.americanprogress.org/issues/immigration/reports/2017/03/21/428776/negative-consequences-entangling-local-policing-immigration-enforcement.

Srikantiah, Jayashri, and Sinnar Shirin. (2019). "White Nationalism as Immigration Policy." *Stanford Law Review*, March. Available at https://www.stanfordlawreview.org/online/white-nationalism-as-immigration-policy.

Sullivan, Katie, and Jeff Mason. (2019). "Immigration Detention in the United States—A Primer." Bipartisan Policy Center, April 24. Available at https://

bipartisanpolicy.org/blog/immigration-detention-in-the-united-states-a
-primer.

Taub, Amanda. (2016). "White Nationalism, Explained." *New York Times,*
November 21. Available at https://www.nytimes.com/2016/11/22/world
/americas/white-nationalism-explained.html.

Thompson, Christie, and Andrew R. Calderon. (2019). "More Immigrants Are
Giving Up Court Fights and Leaving U.S." The Marshall Project, May 8.
Available at https://www.themarshallproject.org/2019/05/08/more-detained
-immigrants-are-giving-up-court-fights-and-leaving-the-u-s.

Tiano, Sara. (2018). "Report: Increased Deportation Could Put More Kids in Foster Care." Chronicle of Social Change, February 21. Available at https://
chronicleofsocialchange.org/research-and-resources/report-increased
-deportations-put-kids-foster-care/29875.

Tichenor, D. (2002). *Dividing Lines: The Politics of Immigration in America.* Princeton, NJ: Princeton University Press.

Timm, Jane C. (2018). "Fact Check: Trump Says His Wall Is under Construction.
It Is Not." NBC News, July 3. Available at https://www.nbcnews.com
/politics/donald-trump/fact-check-trump-say-his-border-wall-under
-construction-it-n888371.

Torbati, Yeganeh. (2018). "Head of U.S. Immigration Judges' Union Denounces
Trump's Quota Plan." Reuters, September 21. Available at https://www
.reuters.com/article/us-usa-immigration-judges/head-of-u-s-immigration
-judges-union-denounces-trump-quota-plan-idUSKCN1M12LZ.

Tseng-Putterman, Mark. (2018). "A Century of U.S. Intervention Created
the Immigration Crisis." Medium.com, June 20. Available at https://
medium.com/s/story/timeline-us-intervention-central-america-a9bea
9ebc148.

UN High Commissioner on Refugees. (2019). "Syria Regional Refugee Response."
June 3. Available at https://data2.unhcr.org/en/situations/syria.

U.S. Border Patrol. (2019). *Southwest Border Apprehensions, FY 2019.* Available at
https://www.cbp.gov/newsroom/stats/sw-border-migration.

U.S. Department of Justice, Executive Office of Immigration Services. (n.d.).
"Workload and Adjustment Statistics, FY 2018." Available at https://www
.justice.gov/eoir/workload-and-adjudication-statistics.

U.S. Department of Justice, Office of EOIR. (2017). *Fact Sheet: Executive Office for
Immigration Review: An Agency Guide.* Available at https://www.justice.gov
/eoir/page/file/eoir_an_agency_guide/download.

U.S. Department of Justice, Office of Inspector General. (2016). *Review of the
Federal Bureau of Prisons Monitoring of Contract Prisons.* Available at https://
oig.justice.gov/reports/2016/e1606.pdf.

U.S. Immigration and Customs Enforcement. (2018). *Fact Sheet: Immigration and
Customs Enforcement (ICE).* June 10. Available at https://immigrationforum
.org/article/fact-sheet-immigration-and-customs-enforcement-ice.

U.S. Immigration and Customs Enforcement. (2018). "Secure Communities." March 20. Available at https://www.ice.gov/secure-communities.

U.S. Immigration and Customs Enforcement. (2019). *Fiscal Year 2018 ICE Enforcement and Removal Operations Report.* Available at https://www.ice.gov /doclib/about /offices/ero/pdf/eroFY2018Report.pdf.

Waxman, Olivia B. (2018). "The 'Abolish ICE' Movement Is Growing. Here's Why the U.S. Immigration and Customs Enforcement Agency Was Created." *Time,* June 29. http://time.com/5325492/abolish-ice-history.

WBUR. (2018). "Fifteen Years after Its Creation, Critics Want to Abolish ICE." June 25. Available at https://www.wbur.org/hereandnow/2018/06/25 /immigration-abolish-ice.

Welch, Michael. (2002). *Detained: Immigration Laws and the Expanding INS Jail Complex.* Philadelphia: Temple University Press.

Wilson, William Julius. (1997). *When Work Disappears: The World of the New Urban Poor.* New York: Vintage.

Wiseman, Andrew, and Michael Connelly. (2008). *Judicial Discretion and Sentencing Outcomes: Incorporating Data from the Courtroom.* Madison: Wisconsin Sentencing Commission.

Wood, Johnny. (2019). "These Countries Are Home to the Highest Proportion of Refugees in the World." World Economic Forum, March 19. Available at https://www.weforum.org/agenda/2019/03/mena-countries-in-the -middle-east-have-the-highest-proportion-of-refugees-in-the-world.

Yglesais, Matthew. (2007). "The Origins of the Southern Strategy." *The Atlantic,* November 20. Available at https://www.theatlantic.com/politics/archive /2007/11/origins-of-the-southern-strategy/47093.

Zatz, Marjorie, and Nancy Rodriguez. (2015). *Dreams and Nightmares: Immigration Policy, Youth, and Families.* Oakland: University of California Press.

Zeitz, Joshua. (2017). "The Real History of American Immigration." *Politico Magazine,* August 6. Available at https://www.politico.com/magazine/story /2017/08/06/trump-history-of-american-immigration-215464.

Zong, Jie, Jeanne Batalova, and Micayla Burrows. (2019). "Frequently Requested Statistics on Immigrants and Immigration in the United States." Migration Policy Institute, March 14. Available at https://www.migrationpolicy .org/article/frequently-requested-statistics-immigrants-and-immigration -united-states#Enforcement.

Index

About the Author

Robert Hartmann McNamara is currently a professor of criminal justice and director of the online program in criminal justice at The Citadel. He served as the associate provost and dean of the Graduate College and as the founding associate dean of evening undergraduate studies at The Citadel. He is the author of thirty books, including *Social Problems, Social Solutions*; *Juvenile Delinquency: Bridging Theory to Practice*; *Problem Children: Special Populations in Delinquency*; *Multiculturalism in the Criminal Justice System*; *Homelessness in America* (three volumes); *The Lost Population: Status Offenders in America*; *In My Father's Hands*; *Boundary Dwellers: Homeless Women in Transitional Housing*; *A New Look at American Society*; *Perspectives on Social Problems*; *Understanding Contemporary Social Problems*; *Crossing the Line: Interracial Couples in the South*; *Crime Displacement: The Other Side of Prevention*; *The Times Square Hustler: Male Prostitution in New York City*; *Sex, Scams, and Street Life: The Sociology of New York City's Times Square*; *Beating the Odds: Crime, Poverty, and Life in the Inner City*; *Police and Policing*; *The Urban Landscape: Selected*; and *Social Gerontology*.

McNamara has also served as a senior research fellow for the National Strategy Information Center; the Policy Lab; the Police Executive Research Forum in Washington, DC; and the Pacific Institute for Research and Evaluation in Baltimore, Maryland.

He has also authored numerous articles published on a variety of topics and has been a consultant for state, federal, and private agencies on topics that include AIDS, drug abuse, urban redevelopment, homelessness, policing, gangs, health care, and more. He also worked with the Regional Community Policing Institute at Eastern Kentucky University to study school safety in eight high schools across the state. He worked with the Mexican government and the National Strategy Information Center to develop an anticorruption curriculum in their public schools.

In 2015, McNamara was a fellow at the American Council on Education as part of the Emerging Leaders program. He has extensive leadership training and has worked with a number of institutions in higher education on a variety of issues. He holds a PhD in sociology from Yale University.